THEMATIC MAPS

Thematic Maps

THEIR DESIGN AND PRODUCTION

DAVID J. CUFF AND
MARK T. MATTSON

ROUTLEDGE
NEW YORK AND LONDON

First published in 1982 by Methuen, Inc.

Reprinted 1984
Reprinted in 1989 by
Routledge, an imprint of
Routledge, Chapman and Hall, Inc.
29 West 35 Street
New York, N.Y. 10001
and in Great Britain by
Routledge
11 New Fetter Lane
London, EC4P 4EE

Library of Congress Cataloging in Publication Data

Cuff, David J.
    Thematic maps.
    Bibliography: p.
    Includes index.
    1. Cartography.   I. Mattson, Mark T.   II. Title.
GA105.3.C88 1982   526   82–8216
ISBN 0-415-90158-8 (pbk.)

British Library Cataloguing in Publication Data

Cuff, David J.
    Thematic maps.
    1. Cartography
    I. Title   II. Mattson, Mark T.
    526   GA105.3
    ISBN 0-415-90158-8 (pbk.)
    (University paperback 774)

FOR BRIAN
and
FOR ERIN ANNE

Contents

Acknowledgements

The authors and the publishers wish to thank the individuals, companies and institutions who have granted permission to reproduce copyright material in the following figures:

2.22 Taken from Goode's Atlas, 15th edn. Copyright by Rand McNally & Company R. L. 81-S-124.

2.23 Reprinted from Waldo R. Tobler (1973) "Choropleth maps without class intervals?" *Geographical Analysis*, 5 (July), 262–5.

2.24 Reproduced from *Annals* of the Association of American Geographers (1963), 53, 19–21, by George F. Jenks.

3.3 Redrawn from Mark S. Monmonier (1967) "The ecology of sour cherry production in Adams County, Pennsylvania", *Proceedings*, Pennsylvanian Academy of Sciences, 41

3.4 Reproduced from *Annals* of the Association of American Geographers (1965), 55, 1–25, figs. 3, 4, and 5, by Peirce F. Lewis.

3.6 Taken from *The United States Energy Atlas* by David J. Cuff and William J. Young (Copyright 1980 by The Free Press, a division of Macmillan Publishing Company).

3.7 Taken from Goode's Atlas, 15th edn. Copyright by Rand McNally & Company R. L. 81-S-124.

3.9 Adapted from Rose (1936) *Geographical Review*, 26, by the courtesy of the American Geographical Society.

3.10 Reproduced from the *Annals* of the Association of American Geographers (1962), 52, 414–25, by Arthur H. Robinson.

3.11 Reproduced from the *Annals* of the Association of American Geographers (1957), 47, 379–91, by Arthur H. Robinson and Reid Bryson.

5.7, 5.8, Redrawn from Porter W. McDonnell and 5.9 (1979) *Introduction to Map Projections*, Marcel Dekker, Inc., New York.

5.13 Reproduced from G. R. P. Lawrence (1979) *Cartographic Methods*, 2nd edn, Methuen and Co. Ltd, London.

5.17 Reproduced from Alan Hodgkiss (1970) *Maps for Books and Theses*, David and Charles Ltd, Newton Abbot.

7.5 We acknowledge the permission granted by the International Paper Company to reproduce this illustration from the twelfth edition of its copyrighted publication, *Pocket Pal: A Graphic Arts Production Handbook.*

8.18 Reproduced from the *Annals* of the Association of American Geographers (1963), 53, 19–21, by George F. Jenks.

8.19 Taken from Waldo Tobler (1974) "A computer program to draw perspective views of geographical data", *The American Cartographer*, 1 (2) (October).

9.20 From Mark S. Monmonier, *Maps, Distortion and Meaning*, Resource Papers for College Geography, Association of American Geographers, Washington, DC, No. 75.4, figs. 12 and 13, pages 19 and 20.

Table 5.1 Adapted from J. A. Steers (1962), *An Introduction to the Study of Map Projections*, Hodder & Stoughton (formerly University of London Press), London.

Preface

The authors have been strongly influenced by the research, thought, and methods of numerous academic cartographers in the United States, Canada, and Great Britain, and also by the map designs of professional cartographers working in the journalistic realm. One Britisher, Alan Hodgkiss, deserves special mention — not so much because we have borrowed his ideas — but because of the example set by his book, *Maps for Books and Theses*, 1970. It is a brief and focused discussion by an experienced illustrator, and most suitable for classroom use. When it became unavailable in the United States, the need emerged for a textbook with similar goals.

The contribution of the present book may reside in its fresh organization of traditional concepts, and its highlighting of essentials that in other books have been submerged in more lengthy treatments or scattered through a number of chapters. Because of its organization and emphasis, our book is complementary to Monkhouse and Wilkinson, *Maps and Diagrams*, 1973, and Dickinson, *Statistical Mapping and the Presentation of Statistics*, 1973. The Monkhouse and Wilkinson book deals with mapping of different subjects such as population or landforms, and in so doing provides abundant examples of symbolization options. Our book shows fewer of the possible variations in symbols while focusing on the *types* of portrayals that apply to data of different types, such as quantitative data at points. The Dickinson book uses this latter kind of organization; and it treats the illustration of statistical data very thoroughly; but it does not emphasize verbal content, layout and design for publication, or production methods. We hope that both instructor and student will find the balance and the presentation of this new book useful, and we invite suggestions for improving the book and the accompanying Instructor's Manual.

Our book is intended as a text for an introductory course in thematic mapping, and necessarily omits a great deal that would be useful to the student of cartography in general. Map projections are discussed only briefly; the history of cartography is barely mentioned; and the subjects of airphotos and landform mapping are entirely excluded. For information on these and other cartographic subjects the student is directed to the books, articles, and monographs in the Additional Readings at the end of the book. For many of the topics, the books listed include Robinson, Sale, and Morrison, *Elements of Cartography* (4th edn), 1978, and Keates, *Cartographic Design and Production*, 1973, both of which are excellent references in the field.

Some of the items listed in the Additional Readings were gleaned from various editions of *Elements of Cartography*, and from the remarkable bibliography in Phillip Muehrcke's *Map Use: Reading, Analysis and Interpretation*, 1978. We thank John Pawling, our colleague at Temple, for sharing his expertise on materials in the field of remote sensing.

An early manuscript of the book was reviewed by Mark Monmonier and by George McCleary, whose suggestions have led to very substantial improvements. Of course, they cannot be held responsible for the book's organization, emphasis, or errors.

Our thanks to Paul Lee, formerly with Methuen, Inc., for his enthusiasm and ideas early in the project, and especially to Mary Ann Kernan, of Methuen & Co. Ltd, in London, who saw the project through to completion.

The transformation of rough notes into a clean and readable manuscript was accomplished with cheerful efficiency by Gloria Basmajian and her staff at Temple's Word Processing Center. Her contribution to this and other projects is very much appreciated. A number of the illustrations benefit from the thoughtful work of Joe Ochlak and Janet Kroupa. We wish them well in their cartographic careers.

Introduction

Maps and map making

Primitive man assembled maps from sticks or drew them on clay tablets for the same reasons modern man draws maps: to gain a perspective view of the important things in his world, and to create tools for navigation. The history of cartography (see especially Thrower, 1972) is a study of the evolution of man's ability to perceive and record the local and more distant parts of his earth. The maps of different societies in the past reveal how complete and how rational was their grasp of the world.

As geographers and surveyors explored and mapped, they dealt with questions that now have lost their urgency: "How large is the earth?," "How long is the Mediterranean Sea?," and "How can we determine the position of land just discovered?." Until the seventeenth century, virtually all mapping was concerned with the most literal aspects of the physical environment.

Special-subject, or thematic, mapping began in 1686 with Edmund Halley (the astronomer whose name is given to the comet). His maps, too, dealt with sailing and navigation, but were more specialized and went beyond the subject of coastlines and places. One of those early thematic maps showed trade winds of the world. A second Halley product, in 1701, was an isogonic map showing how magnetic north differs from true north in various parts of the Atlantic. This map was the first to use *isolines* to unite points assumed to have equal values or intensities. Geologic maps and shaded elevation maps were made in the early 1800s. A map showing northern hemisphere temperatures by isolines was made in 1817. By the middle of the nineteenth century, scaled circles had been used for city sizes, area shadings for population densities, and a dot map to show incidence of disease. Thematic mapping had been established.

Modern cartography involves a great variety of mapping activities which can be divided roughly into two groups.

The first group of activities carries on the early tradition of accurately measuring and charting earth features by making topographic and oceanographic maps, and aeronautical charts. Precise survey data and air photographs provide the information which is plotted with meticulous attention to the earth's shape and how best to represent the curved earth on a flat map. This field of mapping has benefited immensely from technological advances such as electronic survey methods, aircraft that made air photos practical, satellites that profoundly changed aerial photography, and computer-aided methods that have speeded production. Most of this sort of mapping is conducted by large national agencies in charge of surveying and mapping. In the United States, the US Geological Survey and the Defense Mapping Agency do a great deal of the work. In Canada, the dominant agency is the Department of Energy, Mines, and Resources. In Great Britain, topographic mapping is done by the Ordnance Survey.

The second group of mapping activities depends ultimately upon government work. Road maps, wall maps for classrooms, and thematic maps for atlases and textbooks fall into this group. The road maps, wall maps, and other large maps showing places and routes may be called *reference* maps. They deal with earth features and places, but are not made directly from primary work with air photos or survey. They are compiled instead from topographic and other maps made by the government agencies. *Thematic* maps also take their bases from existing maps (which may, in fact, be one of the reference maps) but they are distinguished further by the subject matter which usually is not the physical earth or locations upon it. The subject may be some distillation of physical phenomena, such as average annual temperature or precipitation values. Commonly, though, the subjects mapped are both abstract and non-physical, like crude birth rate per thousand persons. These maps depend on data gathered from a wide range of sources such as census tabulations, oil industry publications, or research that yields unique data never before mapped.[1]

The concern of thematic mapping rarely is the accurate location of features. More typically, the concern is for a sound presentation of the essence of some distribution. Preparing the best presentation requires a critical view of the data to be mapped, as well as the symbolization that may be used to portray it. It is not necessary to be a skilled artist to be a thematic cartographer because drafting can be done by the skilled, or in some cases by machine. What is essential for thematic cartographers is a firm knowledge of the principles that underlie the presentation of information and the design of an effective composition. A strong sense of *visual logic* is vital, and a knack for choosing the right words to accompany the graphics is equally important.

Thematic mapping and other activities in the second group are conducted by a variety of government, private, and college cartographers. The Central Intelligence Agency of the US Government produces thematic maps as well as general reference maps. Likewise, the US Geological Survey produces thematic atlases and land-use maps as well as topographic maps. A few well-known firms produce school atlases, wall maps, and road maps. Some private firms specialize in county road maps and city street maps, while others offer computer-mapping services to government and industry. Thematic maps and graphs to illustrate books are often designed and drawn by artists not trained in cartography because publishers are in the habit of seeking artists for illustration work. Many books, though, are illustrated by university cartographic laboratories or by moonlighting students and faculty.

The mapping in both broad groups, the more fundamental topographic work and the more derived mapping, can be done with the aid of computers. Government agencies, in particular, make use of the speed of production and ease of revision that are offered by computer-aided mapping. For this reason, base maps in computer-readable form have become very important. A rapidly growing facet of cartography now is the design and maintenance of such base maps (geographic base files) and the use of mapping systems that work with these bases and with data in machine-readable form.

Thematic mapping and cartographic communication

All maps are abstractions and simplifications of the real world. Certain real-world phenomena are selected by the cartographer, represented by symbols on the map, and presented to the map reader who interprets the map and learns something about the selected phenomena in their geographic setting (Fig. I). A willingness to accept and revel in this paper representation of the real world is what makes a mapophile love maps. This process may be viewed from the standpoint of general communication theory, which suggests there is a *signal* (the intended map message) which is to some extent garbled or distorted by *noise*, such as imperfect symbolization of the mapped data, or visual distractions that impede the reader in his efforts to read the map (see Guelke, 1977; Muehrcke, 1972; and Salichtchev, 1978). Map reading is complicated by the fact that the readership varies in age, educational level, experience, and attitude. If the readers are known to be young, the map information may be selected or symbolized with that in mind. It is more important, though, to recognize the perceptual limitations that are common to all map readers, and to design the map to accommodate those limitations.

SYMBOLIZATION ON REFERENCE MAPS AND THEMATIC MAPS

The idea that mapping may be described as symbolizing real-world features applies most clearly to reference maps (or to topographic maps) in which coastlines, roads, rivers, churches, and mines are frozen in symbol form and then rejuvenated by the imaginative reader. In thematic mapping the idea is most relevant to features of the *base maps*; but it applies differently to the *subject matter* which usually is much less tangible than black asphalt roads or tumbling streams. Subjects like average annual temperatures or population densities are abstract concepts not visible in the real world. Nevertheless, they must be captured cartographically and, again, brought to life with the collaboration of the map reader.

ORGANIZATION AND SCOPE OF THIS BOOK

The process of thematic map making involves three

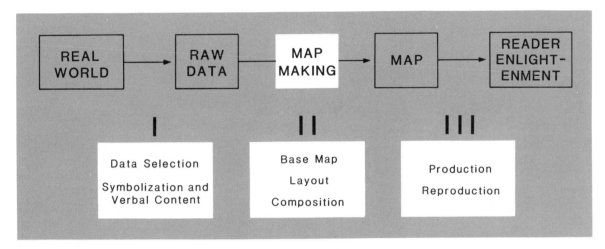

FIG. I Cartographic communication and thematic map making.

major operations (see Fig. I) which provide the rationale for the three parts of this book.

The phenomena selected for mapping are usually represented by data which the cartographer converts to map symbols, with due regard for two things: the spatial nature of the phenomenon being mapped *and* the nature of the data that represent that phenomenon. The symbolized information is explained and augmented by verbal material placed on the map or closely associated with it. Part One of the book is concerned with the selection of appropriate symbolization and verbal content.

Symbols and words do not make a map. A useful and attractive thematic map is one that successfully combines the mapped data with the more literal physical and political elements that constitute the *base map*. The process of choosing that base, sizing it, drawing its features, arranging the various map elements, and making visual distinctions between thematic information and base map features is the concern of Part Two.

Some thematic maps may be used as posters or similar displays. Most, however, are made to be reproduced and included in theses, journal articles, books, or atlases, making it necessary for the cartographer to be familiar with reproduction methods. Part Three deals with reproduction methods and how they relate to production work on the drafting table. Drafting tools and techniques needed in making maps suitable for reproduction are dealt with extensively in "Production hints," which is the last chapter in Part Three.

Note

1 A study of thematic mapping in Russia suggests a threefold division, with *special purpose* maps occupying a position intermediate between simple reference maps and true thematic maps (Castner, 1976). The more simple dichotomy between reference maps and thematic maps is asserted in a recent essay that points out the need to understand more fully thematic maps and their purposes (Petchenik, 1979).

References

Castner, Henry W. (1976) "Special purpose mapping in 18th century Russia: a search for the beginnings of thematic mapping," paper, Eighth International Conference, International Cartographic Association, Moscow.

Guelke, Leonard (ed.) (1977) *The Nature of Cartographic Communication*, Cartographica Monograph, 19, Toronto, Toronto University Press.

Hodgkiss, Alan G. (1970) *Maps for Books and Theses*, Newton Abbot, David & Charles.

Muehrcke, Phillip (1972) *Thematic Cartography*, Resource Paper, 19, Washington, DC, Association of American Cartographers.

Petchenik, Barbara Bartz (1979) "From place to space: the psychological achievement of thematic mapping," *The American Cartographer*, 6 (1), 5–12.

Robinson, Arthur H., Randall Sale, and Joel Morrison (1978) *Elements of Cartography* (4th edn), New York, Wiley.

Salichtchev, K. A. (1978) "Cartographic communication: its place in the theory of science," *The Canadian Cartographer*, 15 (2), 93–9.

Thrower, Norman J. W. (1972) *Maps and Man: An Examination of Cartography in Relation to Culture and Civilization*, Englewood Cliffs, NJ, Prentice-Hall.

PART ONE

The Graphic and Verbal Content

The cartographer must be expert in analyzing the data that need to be mapped. Those data may be gathered afresh in the field by the student or researcher; they may be taken from tabulations in some government document; or they may be presented to the cartographer by an author using them in a publication. In any case, the cartographer must decide upon the symbols, and hence the type of map, that will be used to portray that information. There is a logic that dictates what kinds of symbolization are appropriate, and the cartographer must be well versed in that. But he should also be aware of the latitude that exists within the boundaries established by logic, because some data can be portrayed by a variety of graphics, both conventional and unconventional.

The logic that guides the choice of symbols and map types is summarized in Figure II. Because of its 3 x 3 framework, that scheme resembles one used recently by other academic cartographers, but there is a substantial difference. The three columns of the scheme depend on spatial aspects of the data to be mapped – specifically, whether the data are gathered at points, from areas, or along lines.[1] When the spatial aspects of the data are combined with the three major levels of measurement (the three rows) the result is nine cells which house the appropriate *types of symbolization*. Toward the top of the scheme the types of symbolization dictated by data type and measurement level are quite simple and self-evident. Within the *quantitative* row, however, there are some important differences in phenomena and data which result in some cells being divided. The two dimensions of Figure II, locational aspects of the data and the measurement level, are elaborated below.

Locational aspects of data collection

Information is collected at (or belongs by nature to) either points, areas, or lines, and may be referred to as point data, area data, or line data. The actual *phenomenon* which is represented by the data also may "belong to" points, areas, or lines. Sometimes, however, the nature of the phenomenon and the form of the data *do not* coincide: in such cases the form of data is more important in the logic of cartographic presentation. As an example, some features of the physical environment, such as precipitation or atmospheric pressure, are extensive over large areas. The information that represents these phenomena, however, usually comes as point data, namely, a list of values associated with weather stations. This is the overriding consideration in how the data are mapped.

A problem of definition must be recognized here: "When is a point not a point?" Answer: "When it's an area." On a small-scale map, a city or town is only a point; but on a larger-scale map it appears as an area. There is no firm rule, and although the more logical choice will usually be evident, there will be ambiguous cases for which the data must be treated arbitrarily as belonging to either points or areas.

When dealing with quantitative point data, it will be seen later that the nature of the phenomenon being mapped must be recognized. The distinction between *continuous* and *discrete* phenomena will be crucial.

Measurement level

This universal trait describes the data, though it is intimately connected to the nature of the phenomenon

LOCATIONAL NATURE OF DATA

		Point	Area	Line
MEASUREMENT LEVEL OF DATA	Qualitative			
	Ranked			
	Quantitative			

Fig. II An overview of mappable data. The symbolizations and map types in the cells are the results of two universal traits of the data: locational nature and measurement level.

being mapped. Essentially, the measurement level recognizes that some information to be mapped is *qualitative* and deals only with differences in kind, whereas other information is *quantitative* and expressed by amounts or measures that are numerical. Intermediate between these two are data which order or rank some phenomena as larger and smaller, or major and minor.

A further distinction is between quantitative measures that are absolute amounts, such as numbers of persons, and those that are ratios such as persons per square mile. The distinction will be most important when symbolizing area data.

Figure II arranges the three data collection traits as columns and the three levels of measurement as rows. The resulting nine combinations and the symbolization options that apply to each are discussed in order in chapters 1 and 2. In that discussion, these aspects of Figure II will be clarified: first, four of those nine data

types are more often features of a base map than of the map theme itself; and second, certain of the quantitative data at points and for areas *share the same symbolization*.

Landform mapping

Portrayal of landforms falls into a category that is unique because it involves qualitative as well as quantitative (elevation) differences. Furthermore, the artistic techniques that capture the actual appearance of landforms are usually reserved for specialists. For these reasons, no effort is made to accommodate landform mapping in the overview of data possibilities, and no ideas on methods of presentation are offered in the book. Materials on the subject are listed in the Additional Readings.

The cartographer's choice: what to map

In course exercises the student may be handed some data and required to design and produce a map to convey that information. In practice, however, the cartographer very often has to decide what to map. He may use a simple list of numbers representing one variable; or instead, he may choose to map two variables on the same map to show a connection between them; or he may devise a ratio that expresses the relationship and map only that ratio. This choice will profoundly affect the complexity of the map and how challenging it is for the cartographer to design and produce.

Note

1 See Robinson, Sale, and Morrison (1978), p. 83, and Muehrcke (1979), p. 15. The columns in their schemes represent three different modes of symbolization. This leads to some organizational difficulties with quantitative data.

1 Symbolizing Qualitative and Ranked Data

Qualitative data

Information that is strictly qualitative distinguishes different *kinds* or *types* of phenomena, with no indication of quantities, intensities, or relative status.

AT POINTS

Here the phenomena in question may be settlements, mines, weather stations, or sample points of some kinds. Symbolization is a commonsense matter of selecting symbols that are distinctive, legible, and not inconsistent with established conventions. Figure 1.1 shows some of the symbols used on topographic maps by the US Geological Survey. Rarely would information of this type be the basis for a map theme: instead, it would be part of the base on which thematic information is imposed.

FIG. 1.1 Symbols for qualitative data at points.

FOR AREAS

Qualitative data for areas often will constitute the theme of a map. Land use, geologic formations, vegetation, climate types, and language families all are themes in which areas are distinguished from one another according to their "kind" or personality, with little or no use of numerical measures. Symbolization applied to the areas must be appropriate and distinctive, and must avoid the visual hazards so often present in making this kind of map.

A theoretical approach suggests that since quantities are *not* being symbolized the cartographer would not strive for differences in darkness. Darkness difference very strongly suggests differences in quantity. The logical variables to use undoubtedly are pattern and texture, because changes in these do suggest changes in kind. It is practically impossible, though, to hold darkness constant − especially if there are many area types to be symbolized.

Patterns for relatively small areas can be drawn by

School   Exposed Wreck   Windmill   Cemetery

hand; but for the sake of uniformity and ease of execution larger areas may be covered with ready-made commercially produced materials that offer a wide range of choices (Fig. 1.2). It is not advisable to mix hand-drawn and ready-made patterns within one series of patterns; but if there are two distinct series, or "families" on a map, e.g. one family to show crops and another for natural vegetation, then using hand-drawn for one and ready-made for the other would be useful (see below).

It is best to steer away from patterns that are coarse, i.e. having few lines or elements per inch. These are unsatisfactory for small areas which are virtually "missed" when a coarse pattern is applied. When two or more coarse patterns occur in juxtaposition, the effect can be disturbing (Fig. 1.3). When they are separated by a fine pattern, though, the trouble is averted. Certain area symbols, such as the one for swamplands, are well-established as conventions, and for that reason are desirable despite their coarse texture.

As a rule, dot patterns are preferable to line patterns, because they lack the strong directional character that

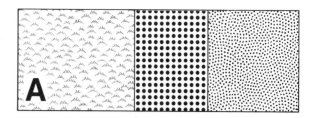

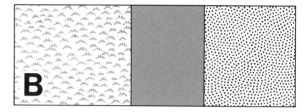

FIG. 1.3 A group of coarse patterns (A) may be disturbing visually; but such patterns may be used if separated by a neutral grey (B).

makes line patterns disturbing. The line patterns that are *cross-hatched* are very useful because they are easily distinguished from dot patterns, they are available in a range of densities, and they do not have the disturbing directional character of simple parallel lines (Fig. 1.4).

LOGICAL GROUPINGS WITHIN PATTERN SEQUENCES

When planning for a map that requires a large number of distinctive patterns, it is very productive to study the phenomenon being mapped and to choose patterns

FIG. 1.2 Ready-made artist's materials for showing qualitative differences.

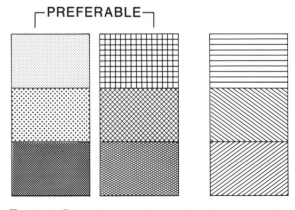

FIG. 1.4 Dot patterns and cross-hatching are preferable to simple parallel lines which tend to be dazzling.

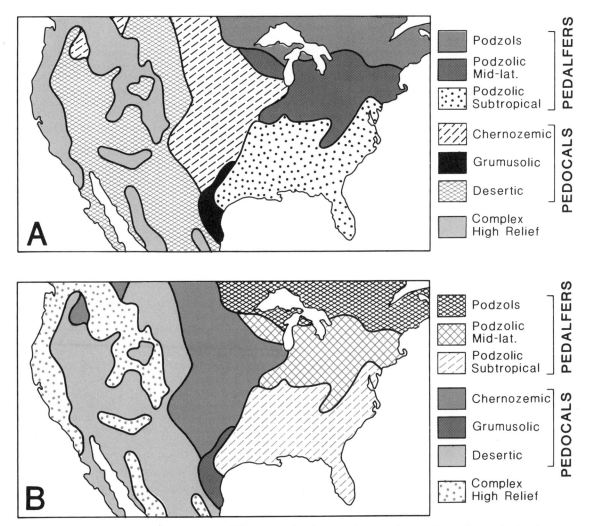

FIG. 1.5 Patterns for qualitative area differences should reveal natural groupings that exist in the mapped phenomena.

that recognize whatever natural groupings exist within the area types.

Mapping of soil types in North America provides an example (Fig. 1.5). Part A of the illustration shows a presentation that is acceptable, technically. Each soil type has been given a distinctive pattern which the reader can identify in the legend. Furthermore, the cartographer has followed the author's groupings which show *in the legend* that all the soils fall into two groups, pedocals and pedalfers. These all-important groups, however are *not evident on the map* because, as groups, they have no personality. In Part B, patterns of one kind have been assigned to the pedocals and a

different kind assigned to pedalfers. Differences among the members of each family still are clear; but, in addition, the map areas occupied by the two families are strikingly evident and point to the fact that pedocals are soils of the western dryland areas while pedalfers are associated with the more humid forest lands of the East.

A similar cartographic approach can illuminate other qualitative map subjects. The patterns used on a world map of languages should reveal broad groupings such as Indo-European versus Amerindian. Land-use maps should make all agricultural uses appear distinct from all other land-use types. Even the physiographic regions of a state can be given patterns that recognize natural groupings. For instance, two regions may owe their character to underlying sedimentary rock, and should be mapped with two patterns from the same family group, while two other physiographic regions may be generically related to igneous rocks and should be given a map character that reflects this difference.

In general, qualitative patterns should not be chosen arbitrarily. The most informative map will be produced if the information is interpreted before it is symbolized. In this regard, cartographers trained in geography, and familiar with both social sciences and earth sciences, can bring to the task an understanding that would not be expected of a commercial artist.

ON LINES

As with qualitative information at points, the symbols to represent lines of different sorts usually are part of the base map and are not thematic material. Nevertheless, roads, rivers, coastlines, and boundaries of differing status must be carefully distinguished or else they will tend to merge with each other and be incomprehensible.

Rivers can be made to look like rivers by using an old-fashioned nib rather than a technical pen. The nib makes a line that is irregular and can be gradually widened from headwater to downstream stretches. Boundaries and routes both can be drawn with a technical pen and distinguished from each other by different forms as shown on Figure 1.6.

The discussion here of purely qualitative differences among lines is somewhat artificial, because it usually is necessary when showing routes and boundaries to show differences of status or importance (these are discussed below).

Ranked data

In this category is information about the relative status of various phenomena; and, as such, the information is intermediate between qualitative and quantitative (numerical) data. It may be assumed here that the information to be mapped comes to the cartographer's desk as *ranked data only*. It will be apparent that more complete data that are truly quantitative may be, at the

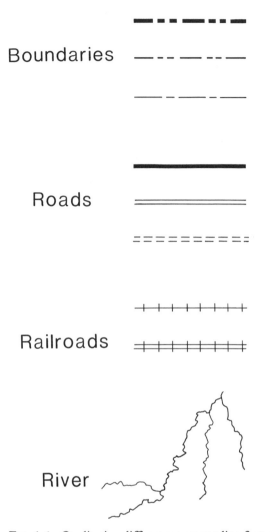

FIG. 1.6 Qualitative differences among line features.

cartographer's choice, *presented* as ranked. In reality this latter course is the more likely. This whole section, then, can be regarded as symbolization either for data of the ranked measurement level, or for quantitative data that are simplified for presentation.

AT POINTS

The same phenomena that may be shown by symbols of qualitative difference, e.g. settlements, mines, or churches, very often should be ordered or ranked to show differences that are useful to the reader. The

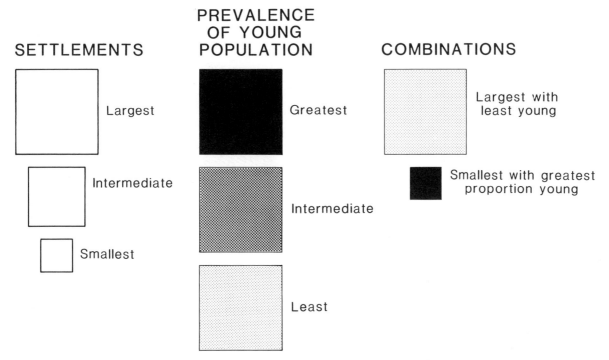

Fig. 1.7   Combination of symbol size and darkness of tone can show relative size of settlement and its ranking on some measure.

original data may reveal numerical differences that have to do with *size or quantity*, and other differences that are related to *intensity* of some characteristic. Differing size of settlement, or annual rates of production from a mine, are logically shown by varying the size of symbol. Differences in average level of income or proportion of Spanish-speakers would better be shown by different shading or tones imposed on the symbols. There is opportunity, therefore, to show variations in both kinds of characteristics at once (see Fig. 1.7). The shading is used here in the same way as for truly quantitative data: darker tones for greater intensity or higher levels.

FOR AREAS

The characteristic that distinguishes one area from another may entail a factor that is subtly quantitative, such as the difference between areas of intensive and less-intensive agricultural practice, or soils that are more and less suitable for a certain crop. On the other hand, the ranking may be quite explicit as in major

versus minor manufacturing areas. The cartographic treatment is the same for all such cases: areas should be assigned tones or patterns with variations in darkness that correspond to the variations of intensity of the phenomenon. If there happen to be two kinds of ranking on the same map or in the same map series, care should be taken that there are two qualitatively distinct series of patterns or tones each having its own progression of darkness (see Fig. 1.8).

ON LINES

Logical distinctions among routes of differing importance and among boundaries of differing status can be vital to a reader's comprehension of the study area's setting as well as the thematic message. Homogeneity of line symbols must be avoided if there are meaningful differences in the real world. Whether the cartographer is just symbolizing ranked differences that are provided him, or is himself classifying line phenomena on the basis of truly quantitative data, the approach is the same: creating differences in character

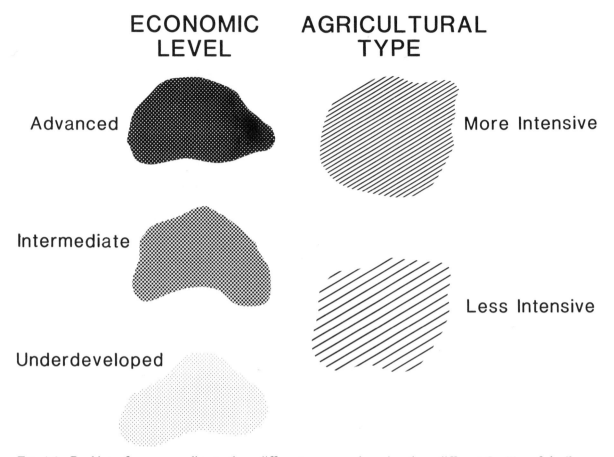

FIG. 1.8 Ranking of areas according to three different measures by using three different families of shading.

of routes, boundaries, or pipelines that will be recognizable on the final product. Logically, differences in *status* will be shown by differing line weights (width), while any *qualitative* distinctions are maintained by difference in the character of lines, such as solid versus dashed or dotted (Fig. 1.9). Since line width is vital to the symbolization, differences must be exaggerated enough so they will still be noticeable after photoreduction.

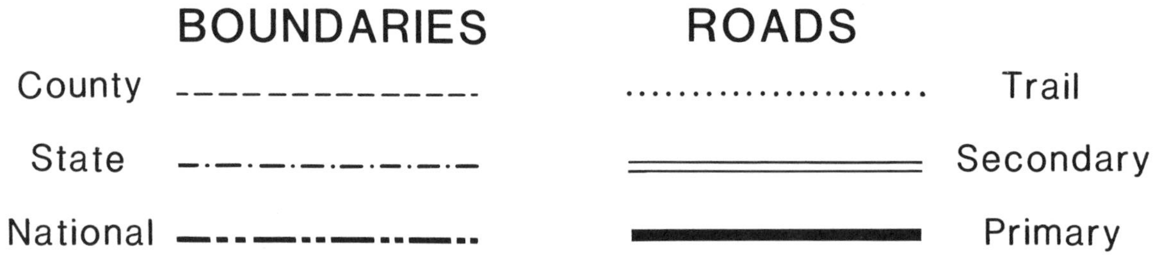

FIG. 1.9 Line symbols to show both qualitative and ranking differences.

2 Symbolizing Quantitative Data

Unlike qualitative and ranked data, quantitative information is expressed numerically.[1] This category is by far the most important of the three, because it includes a great range of popular map themes, from topographic and climatic subjects to statistical information about populations, their numbers, and their social and economic characteristics.

As with qualitative and ranked data, quantitative data occur in association with points, areas, and lines. Most of the mappable quantitative information, though, occurs at points or areas. It embraces a wide variety of measurements; and those measurements represent a wide variety of phenomena.

Quantitative data at points

The phenomena represented by quantitative data at points are of two different types. There are *continuous* phenomena, such as air temperature, which occur everywhere; and there are *discrete* phenomena, such as production from mines, whose amounts are tied to specific and separate locations.

FOR CONTINUOUS PHENOMENA: THE ISARITHMIC MAP

Since air temperature, or the concentration of pollutants in the air, or amounts of rainfall, occur in "blanket" fashion virtually everywhere, they are mapped as continuous despite the fact that information about them is available only at specific sample points. The goal of such thematic mapping is to construct a picture of the complete distribution, even though the information is fragmentary.

Actually, there are two kinds of point data for continuous phenomena, but they are mapped in the same way. The first is very concrete and immediate data, such as surface elevations, or the thickness of a sub-surface rock unit measured in a test hole, or the salinity of groundwater as measured in a specific well. Less concrete data would be (1) averages of weather phenomena, such as daily or January mean temperature, and (2) ratios or percentages, such as the proportion of precipitation that falls as snow. These averages or proportions cannot exist, of course, at any one time; nevertheless, they are firmly associated with the weather station or sample point whence they are derived.

If the phenomenon represented by the data is truly continuous, then it is reasonable to assume gradual change between sample points. If, for instance, the temperature is 70°F at one weather station and 50° at another nearby, then a temperature of 60° may be inferred midway between the two. This assumption of progressive change between sample points may sometimes be wrong, but it greatly eases the construction of a map to show trends in values and the rates at which they change from place to place.

The mapping device used for this purpose is based on elevation contours which have long been used on topographic maps to capture the form of the land as well as the specific elevations. Figure 2.1 shows how the arrangement and spacing of elevation contours reflect the shapes, and especially the slopes, of landforms. More crowded contours reveal steeper slopes; contours of low values that "invade" higher ground coincide with valleys; and contours of higher value that push into generally lower areas coincide with ridges. It is important to realize that greater and lesser crowding of contours is a valid indicator of slopes only when the contour interval remains constant throughout the map.

Maps of this style, when used for themes other than topography, are called *isarithmic* or isoline maps (from the Greek *iso*, meaning same). Contours for temperature are called isotherms; for atmospheric pressure

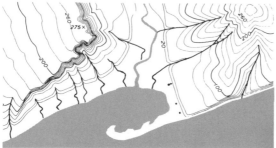

FIG. 2.1 Landforms represented by contour lines. These are a special case of isarithmic lines (isolines).

they are isobars; for rainfall amounts they are isohyets; and for many other phenomena, analogous terms have been developed.

DRAWING THE ISOLINES

Drawing such maps from data at points is a matter of *interpolation*, i.e. the process of deducing the values that occur between the points with definite values (Fig. 2.2).

Drawing the isolines is easier and more enjoyable when following a system. The mapper may begin with highest areas and define their extent, or start with the lowest areas and trace how the lows give way to the high areas. Whatever the system, it is imperative that the general directions toward high and low values be kept in mind; otherwise, isolines will be drawn on the wrong sides of sample points.

There are some rules and guidelines that must be followed (Fig. 2.3). First a contour or isoline never splits, or bifurcates (Part A). Second, extreme lows are never represented by a single isoline of the lowest value, even though it seems justified by the sample values. Instead, a *pair* of the lowest value isolines defines the low area or "trough." Similarly, a high area or ridge is defined by an isoline pair or loop which encloses the area deduced to be highest (Part B).

The finished ink drawing of isolines is not easy because smooth curves demand great skill with a pen. They *are* easily finished, though, by applying black tape which is ideal for the purpose (see chapter 9). The goal is to create bold isolines distinct from other lines such as boundaries and coasts. Isoline labels should be placed at rhythmic intervals, should break the lines, and should be aligned *with them*, not with the map frame or with parallels (see Fig. 2.3).

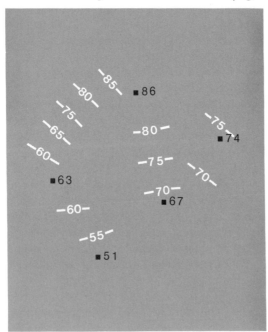

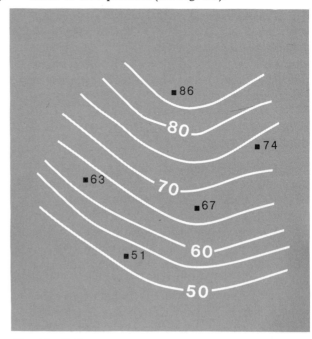

FIG. 2.2 The process of interpolation and drawing of isarithmic lines.

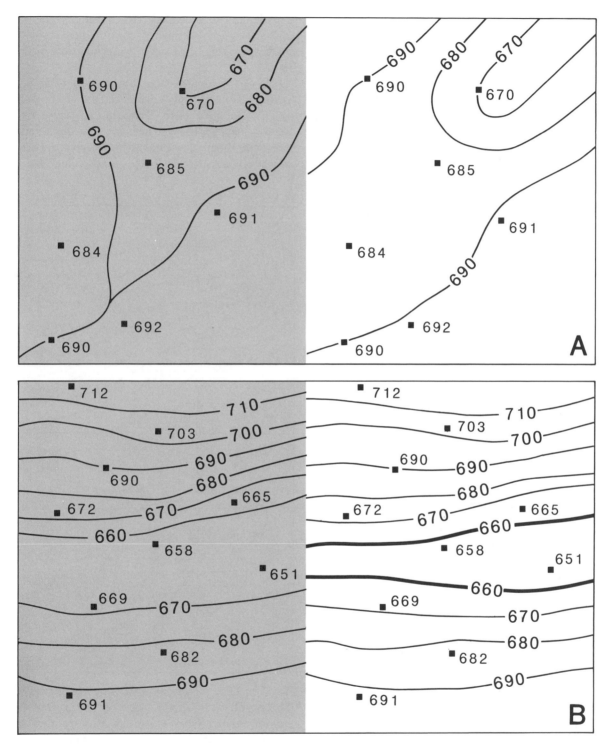

FIG. 2.3 Some conventions to be followed in drawing isolines. Shaded side shows incorrect method; unshaded side shows the preferred treatment.

The completed map always should include the stations or sample points, so the reader can appreciate to what extent the placement of isolines is controlled by densely spaced information, and where in the map the isoline pattern may be less reliable because of sparse information. Including the sample values on the map is desirable, but very often is not practical on maps of smaller scale.

THE ACCURACY OF ISOLINES

It is important to realize that information gathered at weather stations to represent the temperature or the rainfall of some region is a mere sample of the physical reality. Furthermore, the size (scale) of the map may not permit plotting all the weather stations that have information. The cartographer drawing those isolines, then, can never construct an accurate picture of the phenomenon because his information is incomplete. This can be quickly demonstrated by carefully drawing isolines on the basis of selected stations, then filling in the gaps with more stations from the listing. The values at those newly added stations are not likely to be consistent with the isoline pattern drawn. Similarly, drawing isolines to represent the elevation of some rock bed deep underground is an audacious attempt to construct the invisible form on the basis of a few drillholes. Additional drillholes often reveal a picture quite different from that portrayed by the isolines.[2]

For climatic data, two other facts render the work uncertain: first, the temperature, rainfall, or wind is likely to be expressed as a long-term average for each station − a quantity that really does not exist there; second, the reliability of that average depends heavily on the length of record which varies from station to station.

Variation in length of record can lead to variations in the average climatic values that are quite artificial. If, for instance, one weather station recorded rainfall only for the twenty years that happened to be rather dry, and a neighboring station recorded rainfall for eighty years, the values for the two stations will appear very different. Also, topographic factors can cause local variations in rainfall and temperature that are quite authentic, but nevertheless difficult to deal with on a small-scale map.

Whether the local variations are artificial or real,

they will lead to anomalous values that have to be *isolated* because isolines portraying the regional trends cannot reasonably be distorted to accommodate them (Fig. 2.4).[3]

Accuracy of isolines often can be improved by drawing them with knowledge of certain factors that can influence their form. Temperature values, for instance, tend to be lower in highland areas: isotherms drawn with a map of elevations in view (or under the work sheet) can be guided by the trend of a highland.

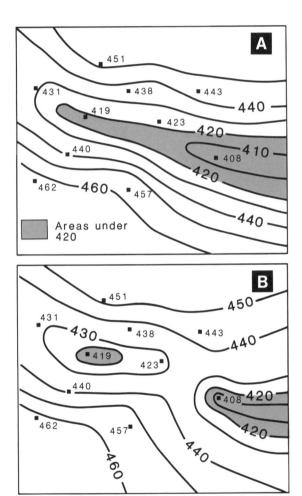

FIG. 2.4 Less conservative and more conservative treatment of an anomalously low value. Part A shows isolines drawn where not fully justified by station values because a valley or trough is assumed to be continuous. Part B shows a more conservative approach, isolating the 419 value.

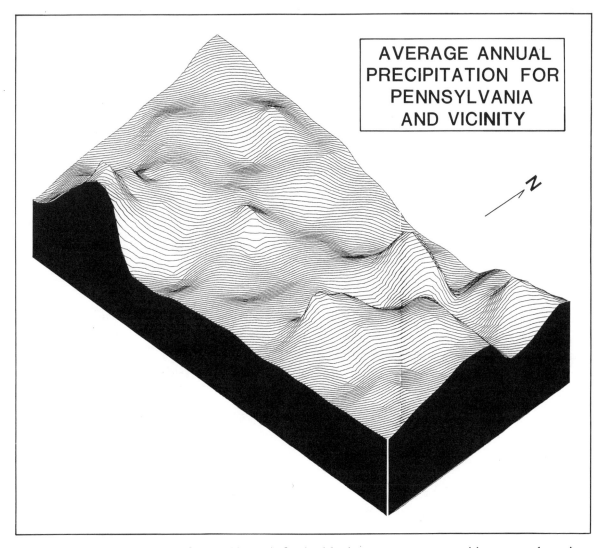

AVERAGE ANNUAL PRECIPITATION FOR PENNSYLVANIA AND VICINITY

FIG. 2.5 A smooth statistical surface used instead of an isarithmic map to portray quantities measured at points.

THE SMOOTH STATISTICAL SURFACE

The analogy between isarithms and elevation contours suggests that any continuous distribution may be portrayed by a surface which is the three-dimensional form represented by the isarithms (Fig. 2.5). The highs and lows of the distribution are shown as literal highs and lows, and the changes in values as slopes that are gentle or steep. As a substitute for isarithmic maps, surfaces are dramatic, and have been shown to convey information effectively, though they tend to emphasize foreground areas and hide any low features in the background. Drawing the smooth surface by hand is challenging; but the computer-driven plotter makes it easy. Programs for the purpose are referred to in chapter 8.

FOR DISCRETE PHENOMENA: THE USE OF SPOT SYMBOLS

Because discrete phenomena, such as production at a mine or population of a town, occur as separate entities at points, they are logically represented by symbols applied *at* those points, with no attempt to consider values that occur between or among them. The symbols are referred to here as *spot symbols*. The term, point symbols, may seem appropriate, but it is important to realize that the same symbols may also be applied to data from areas (see later section). As with ranked point data in chapter 1, the size of symbols is varied to show changes in absolute amounts, and the tone or pattern on a symbol may be varied to indicate different values on a scale of density or some other ratio. As well, patterns or tones can be added to a set of quantitative symbols to show qualitative differences. For instance, cities may be larger and smaller, and at the same time be either industrial type or non-industrial.

There are two very different approaches to the scaling of spot symbols to show quantities: one is to scale the symbols uniquely, in order to symbolize the actual amounts at each location; and the other is to use symbols to indicate only the group or category that applies to each location.

SCALING SPOT SYMBOLS FOR ACTUAL AMOUNTS

Size, or apparent size, of spot symbols may be varied according to three geometric systems: linear, areal, or volumetric. In addition, some special symbols can be created by the accumulation of items to build a stack or pile.

Linear scaling of spot symbols

A bar graph uses linear scaling if the length of bar is simply made proportional to the amount being shown. For example, on a linear scale 50 units would be shown by a bar twice that for 25 units (Fig. 2.6). As a cartographic symbol, bars (or columns) placed on a map have one compelling virtue: they are easily interpreted by map readers because lengths are so easy to compare. Their disadvantages for point data are the large amount of vertical space required, difficulty with neighboring points and overlapping symbols, and the unsuitability of linear scaling for values whose *range* is great.

A general principle will become evident when the traits of linear, areal, and volumetrically scaled symbols are reviewed. Those which are compact and space-conserving on a map lend themselves to data with great range between highest and lowest values, but they are not accurately interpreted by the reader; conversely, the

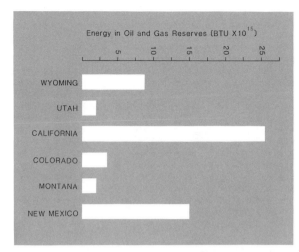

Fig. 2.6 A simple bar graph using linear scaling.

symbols that are more easily interpreted demand more space and are not so well suited to data of great range.

Scaling of linear symbols can be done by experimenting with different unit values, such as one-tenth of an inch to represent 100 of the quantity being symbolized. If the resulting bars do not satisfactorily serve both the largest and smallest values, then another unit value is tried. It is instructive, though, to see that a graphic scaling method can speed the experimentation in linear scaling and *also be a model for areal and volumetric scalings that ·follow.* In Figure 2.7 a horizontal line is scaled according to the values to be mapped. When a tentative largest bar is placed at the highest value, and a straight line drawn from its top to the zero point, the heights of bars for any values can immediately be seen. The bar to represent the smallest value may appear too short. If this is the case, a longer bar for greatest value may be tried, and a new hypotenuse line drawn. Ultimately the best "balance" will be realized without having to calculate bar lengths. In the legend there should be a bar or column as tall as the tallest symbol on the map if space will allow it (Fig. 2.8).

Areal scaling

Circles and squares are the familiar, and virtually the only, symbols whose *areas* are made proportional to

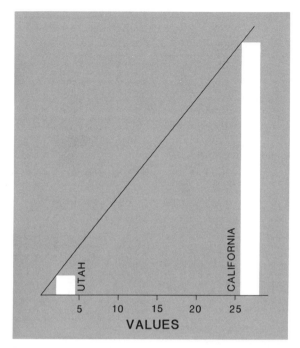

FIG. 2.7 Graphic scaling device applied to linear scaling of map symbols.

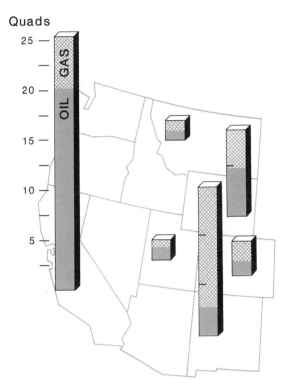

FIG. 2.8 Columns, instead of simple bars, as an effective way of symbolizing a small range of values.

values being mapped.[4] Circles and squares are popular – partly because they are easily drawn and easily overlapped in crowded portions of a map, but also because they can represent a large range of values more efficiently than symbols of the linear type. Their disadvantage is that readers do not perceive the symbols in the expected fashion, as will be explained below.

In scaling circles or squares, the practical need is to find a series of values of the *radius* (for circle) or values of the *side* (for squares) that will lead to symbols of convenient sizes. If the smallest values are to be visible, it may be necessary to allow overlap of symbols in the more crowded areas. This overlap should not be considered a flaw: it is a feature of the best-designed maps of this type and can be dealt with by methods outlined in chapter 9. Assuming that circles are the symbol being scaled, consider two data values, one twice the other. If the radius of one circle is made 1 unit and the other is 2 units, the area of the second circle will be not twice the first but 4 times as great because the area of a circle equals $\frac{22}{7}$ multiplied

by the radius *squared*. It is necessary, therefore, to scale the series of circle radii according to the *square root of the values* to be mapped, not the values themselves.

A listing of values and square roots of values may be made, and various unit values applied to the square roots in order to seek usable radii for map circles that will be appropriate for both largest and smallest values being mapped (Table 2.1). An attractive alternative is to use a graphic device like the one used for determining bar or column heights. On a simple horizontal scale of convenient length the *square roots* of the values to be symbolized are noted (Fig. 2.9). A large circle is placed experimentally at the highest square root value, a line drawn to zero, and the radius of the smallest circle deduced. No matter how the angle of the sloping line is varied when experimenting with different circle sizes, the indicated radii are proportional to distance along the horizontal: radii, therefore, are proportional to the square root of values. Radii for legend circles can be found quickly: for convenient values of 1000,

TABLE 2.1 For scaling of circles to symbolize actual amounts: listing of data values to be mapped, and application of a unit value to determine suitable radii for the series of circles

Values to be represented	Square root of values	Unit, or multiplier (inches)	Radius (inches)
1018	31.90	0.05	1.59
1002	31.65	0.05	1.58
927	30.44	0.05	1.52
779	27.91	0.05	1.39
613	24.75	0.05	1.24
445	21.19	0.05	1.05
296	17.20	0.05	0.86
212	14.56	0.05	0.73
206	14.35	0.05	0.72
167	12.92	0.05	0.64
133	11.53	0.05	0.58
119	10.90	0.05	0.55
76	8.72	0.05	0.44
59	7.68	0.05	0.38
57	7.55	0.05	0.38
41	6.40	0.05	0.32
28	5.29	0.05	0.26
23	4.79	0.05	0.24

Note: while the range of values is from 23 to 1018, the range of square roots is only from 4.79 to 31.90. Thus the "linear size" of circles (their radii) is made proportional to a list of numbers with short range and can fit onto a map. For the same data, linear-scaled symbols would occupy too much space.

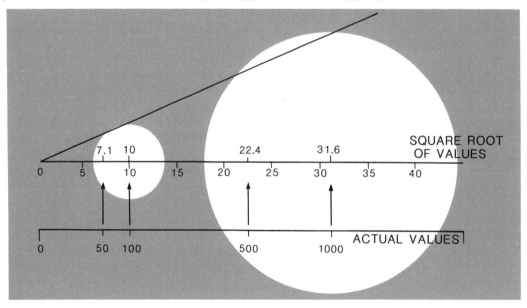

FIG. 2.9 Graphic scaling device applied to areal scaling of map symbols. The radii of circles are made proportional to square roots of values.

500, 100, and 50, the square roots are 31.6, 22.4, 10, and 7.1 respectively. Their positions on the horizontal scale indicate the four radii required. All this work of determining size of map circle and legend circles can be done without measurement, because compasses can be applied to the graphic device and set to the indicated radius for each circle. Comparable steps would be taken for scaling squares instead of circles.

Legend symbols may be arranged in two different ways (Fig. 2.10). Nested, the circles make for a very compact legend, a feature that is extremely desirable. Strung out as separate items, the legend circles are more easily used by the map reader, but demand a great deal of space and may be confusing because they seem like an extension of the map itself.

Scaling of circles to consider reader perception It has been found that map readers tend to underestimate the size of larger map circles, apparently being influenced by the linear dimension of the circles (the diameters) as well as by their areas. The cartographer who wishes a more accurate transmission of amounts by circle sizes may scale them according to the following scheme based on experiments by James Flannery (see Flannery, 1971).

Areas of larger circles must be systematically increased according to a factor indicated by reader testing. The procedure is best expressed as a modification of the square root calculation. If square roots of the values to be mapped were calculated by use of logarithms, the procedure would be to find the logarithm of the value, halve it, and then find (in an antilog table) the value of 10 raised to that power. For example, to find the square root of 100: the log (base 10) of 100 is 2. Half the log is 1, and 10^1 is 10. Flannery's testing showed that circle sizes will be adjusted properly if instead of halving the log of each value (multiplying it by 0.5) it is multiplied by 0.57. The altered square roots are used instead of normal square roots, in a listing such as Table 2.1, so that *circle radii are made proportional to these altered square roots*.

The cartographer has a choice, it seems, between a simple graphic scaling of radii in proportion to square roots and the calculation of altered square roots and use of a unit value. It is possible, however, to combine the Flannery adjustment with the convenience of the graphic scaling device – simply by plotting altered

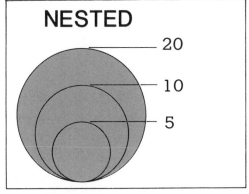

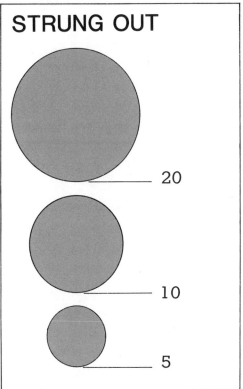

FIG. 2.10 Two styles of legend for circles that are scaled to actual (non-grouped) values.

roots on the horizontal as in Figure 2.11. Altered roots must still be calculated by the logarithm approach; but for values 0 to 999 they can be figured by applying the factors shown in the graph (Fig. 2.12). That plot shows, for instance, that if a value is 100, the altered

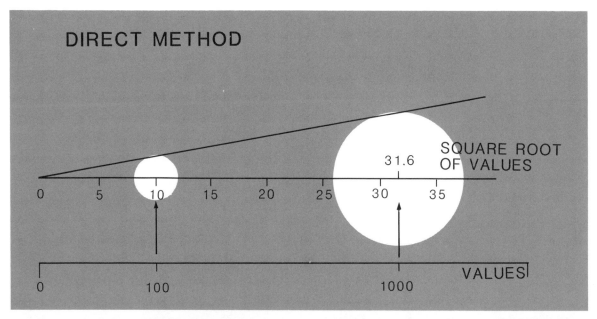

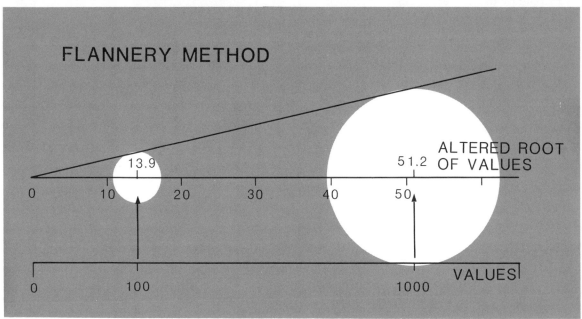

FIG. 2.11 Using altered square roots will noticeably enlarge the larger circles, and lead to more accurate reader estimates of the values symbolized.

square root is 1.39 times the simple square root. For a value of 200, the altered root is about 1.48 times the square root. For other values ranging up to 999 the multiplier can be read from the curve with sufficient accuracy.

It should be noted that the factors evident in Figure 2.12 apply *only to the values plotted*, from 0 to 999, and not to multiples of those numbers. For instance, altered root of 9000 will not be simply 1.63 times its square root. It can be calculated, though, by considering it to be 10 x 900, and multiplying the two factors

1.18 (for the 10) times 1.63 (for the 900). Thus the altered root of 9000 will be 1.92 times its normal square root.

Segmented circles and circle segments Circles are admirably suited for symbolizing an amount which has components to be shown: for instance, the tonnage of ore produced from a mine may be of various grades whose prevalence at different mines is a vital part of the production data. Circles are easily divided to show the component parts, and are easily interpreted because portions of a circle are readily estimated by map readers.[5] An example of such a map, Figure 2.13A, uses a divided bar as key to the tones or patterns and also to show the proportions that apply to the total production for the study area. Instead of the bar, another segmented circle may be drawn (Fig. 2.13B), but there are two arguments against it: the addition of yet another circle to the composition is undesirable; and the *size* of that circle, which represents the study area total, can never be made consistent

with the scaling system that governs all other circles presented.

If full circles would overlap unduly, then only portions of each scaled circle may be shown, appearing as segments or wedges narrowing to the data point (Fig. 2.14A). With this device, four separate scaled circle maps may be replaced by one, on which segments for one theme always are in the same quadrant (Fig. 2.14B). The resulting map is a compact graphic summary of the data but is so complex that it does not convey a clear picture of any one of the four distributions.

Volumetric scaling

For point data whose range of values is very great, linear symbols will be impossible to use; and even areally scaled symbols may be unable to symbolize both the low and the high end of the data list. For instance, if the lowest values are in the vicinity of 10

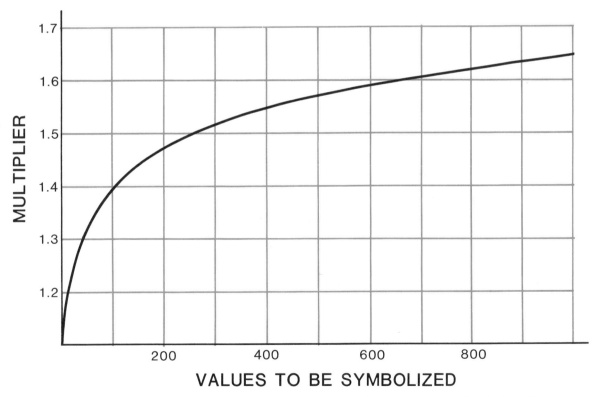

FIG. 2.12 Multipliers for converting square roots of values into altered square roots for circle scaling.

MOUNTAIN REGION ENERGY RESERVES, 1978

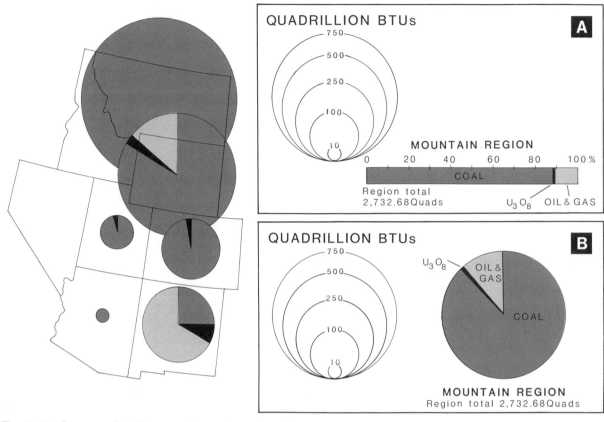

FIG. 2.13 Segmented circle map with two legend options.

FIG. 2.14 Using circle segments, rather than full circles, to conserve space.

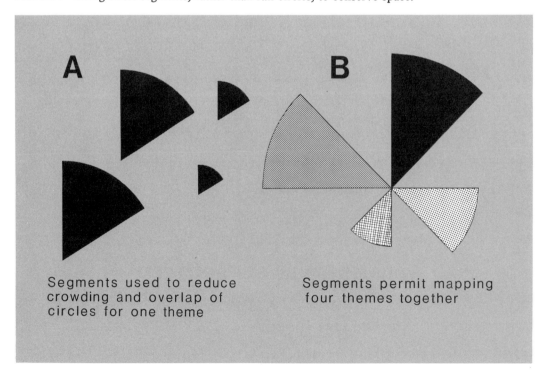

and the highest are of 10,000 magnitude, the square roots will be 3.16 and 100, respectively. Assuming a unit value of one-tenth of an inch, a circle with radius of 3.16 tenths (0.316″) will be suitable, but the large amount then is symbolized by a circle of 100 tenths, or 10 inches. In this circumstance the cartographer can resort to volumetric scaling which can better deal with an extreme range.

Spheres and cubes are scaled by making their radii proportional to the *cube root* of the data. As with circle scaling, the job can be done by listing cube roots and experimenting with unit values, or by the graphic device in which cube roots are plotted on a simple horizontal scale (Fig. 2.15). In either case, the cube roots must be calculated by taking one-third of the logarithm, or by using a calculator with an $x\sqrt{}$ key. As an alternative, trial and error with a calculator will yield approximate cube roots in a surprisingly short time.

Spheres or cubes will serve the cartographer by efficiently symbolizing data of great range, but research has shown that readers perceive the illusion of volume even less well than they perceive the areas of circles and squares; and no factor for adjusting volumetric symbols has been developed. These map symbols are used, then, with the knowledge that they convey only the *relative sizes* of mapped values and, at the same time, are interesting and dramatic (see Dickinson, 1973, pp. 108–16).

It is ironic that the geometric principle allowing spheres or cubes to symbolize data of wide-ranging values also stands in the way of their visual effectiveness. Not only is the volume illusion difficult to perceive accurately, but the cubes or spheres look too much alike: differences that are, in fact, quite significant are obscured by the translation of data values to their cube roots. For some data, scaling by cube root may be necessary. In other cases, it may be better to ask *whether the full range of values must be symbolized*. Presumably, the higher amounts are important; but some of the lower values may be considered trivial, and excluded from the symbolization.

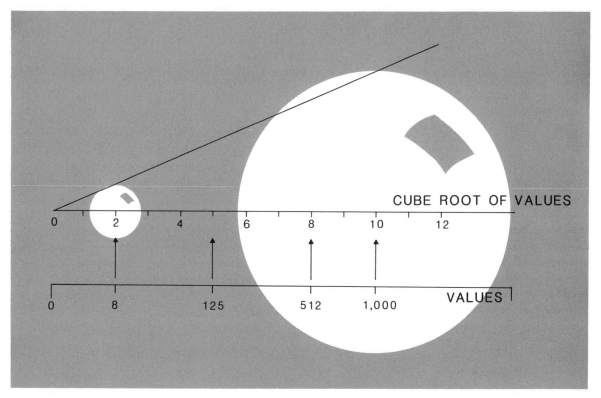

Fig. 2.15 Graphic scaling device for symbols whose apparent volumes are proportional to the values mapped. Here the radii of spheres are made proportional to cube roots of values.

TABLE 2.2 Bituminous coal production in Pennsylvania counties, 1979 (from Pennsylvania Department of Environmental Resources)

County	Tons	Square root of tonnage	Cube root of tonnage
Indiana	12,316,484	3509	231
Washington	11,345,774	3368	224
Clearfield	9,708,465	3116	214
Greene	8,815,129	2969	207
Cambria	7,871,528	2806	199
Somerset	6,988,157	2643	191
Armstrong	6,956,560	2638	190
Clarion	5,402,678	2324	176
Jefferson	3,365,698	1835	150
Allegheny	3,286,098	1813	148
Fayette	2,727,896	1652	139
Westmoreland	2,287,194	1512	132
Butler	2,267,859	1506	132
Centre	1,673,012	1293	119
Venango	949,301	974	98
Elk	669,495	818	87
Lawrence	614,419	784	85
Clinton	465,777	682	77
Tioga	406,163	637	74
Mercer	370,489	609	72
Lycoming	259,625	509	64
Beaver	170,099	412	56
Bedford	92,179	304	45
Huntingdon	63,374	252	40
Fulton	30,000	173	31

Coal production in Table 2.2 provides an example. Tonnages vary from 12.3 million to 30,000, a range that would be difficult to deal with by areal (square root) scaling, and impossible by linear scaling. The cube roots of the extreme numbers are 231 and 31, and can be used to proportion the sides of largest and smallest cubes without difficulty. Unfortunately, the cubes to represent 3.2 million and 2.2 million tons — to choose just one pair — will be very similar, because the cube roots are 148 and 132, respectively. In fact, the map will have numerous cubes with very subtle differences in size. The data range has evidently demanded volumetric scaling with a result that is less than ideal. It is not necessary, though, to let the data range dictate the symbolization. In this example, if the three counties with tonnages less than 100,000 are excluded from symbolization, then the square roots of the remaining values are in the proportions 3.5 to 0.4, and can be used for circle radii. If a more drastic shortening of the list is tolerable, then all tonnages less than 500,000 might be excluded, leaving actual values that range only from 12.3 to 0.6 million. These can easily be scaled in *linear* fashion to reveal production differences among the important counties. Counties excluded from symbolization would be given a shade or pattern which denotes "Counties with production less than 500,000 tons."

Accumulated symbols

An alternative to the conventional symbols scaled by length, area, or volume, is to use three-dimensional units that are accumulated to represent the desired quantities (Fig. 2.16). If the choice of unit value is

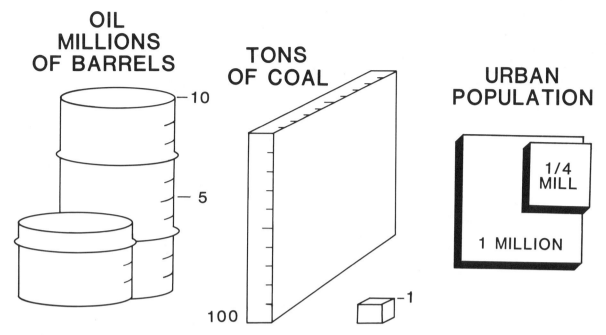

OIL
MILLIONS
OF BARRELS

TONS
OF COAL

URBAN
POPULATION

FIG. 2.16 Instead of geometrically scaled symbols, figures such as barrels, blockpiles, or tablets, can be drawn in accumulations to represent amounts for discrete phenomena at points. Barrels and blockpiles are more commonly used for absolute amounts for areas, not points.

carefully made, such accumulations of symbols will let the reader actually count units to gain an accurate estimate of the value symbolized. At the same time, the relative masses of two or more accumulations will convey the idea of relative magnitudes very effectively. Production of these symbols is discussed in chapter 9.

SPOT SYMBOLS FOR GROUPED DATA

It can well be argued that scaling spot symbols carefully to represent actual values is not wise, for two reasons.

First, because of perception limitations the reader does not receive all the information built into the symbols. This is most true of spheres and cubes and non-Flannery circles, and is least true for linear symbols.

Secondly, when a reader uses the map legend to estimate size of some particular map symbol, he is forced to interpolate between the symbols in the legend, and may learn only that the mapped value is greater than one legend value and smaller than the next one.

Because of these factors the cartographer may wish to abandon the literal scaling of symbols for each

unique data value and group the values as shown for circles in Figure 2.17. The map carries *only the circle sizes that are in the legend*; and they are made distinctive enough in size that the reader can readily connect any map circle to its mate in the legend (see Meihofer, 1973). The usual guideline for legend circles is to make their areas proportional to the square roots of middle values (the means) of each group. This approach, *range-graded* rather than *value-graded*, may logically be used also for spheres and cubes whose actual values are difficult for a reader to judge, but is not appropriate for symbols of linear type because their actual values can be easily judged by readers.[6]

The two approaches may be summed up this way. A map with range-graded symbols hides the contrasts between point values by grouping them; and it leads the reader very easily to legend information that is only approximate. On the other hand, symbols scaled to actual values reveal the contrasts between point values; and they offer a legend by which the skillful reader can estimate mapped values satisfactorily. For the cartographer, the range-graded approach requires more time and effort because a scheme of classification must be decided upon; furthermore, if there is a series

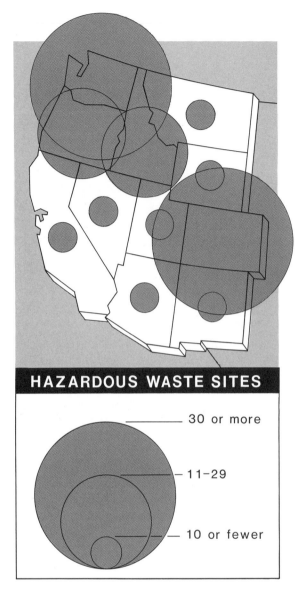

HAZARDOUS WASTE SITES

30 or more

11-29

10 or fewer

FIG. 2.17 Circles used for grouped values. Only the three circle sizes identified in the legend are used on the map.

of similar maps he must decide whether the classification scheme should be the same for all maps in the series or should be tailored to the data range of each map separately. For the sake of perspective, it should be realized that neither approach is ideal, and neither style of map should be expected to convey the amounts precisely. A realistic goal is for the map to convey the relative amounts at different points and to give the

reader a rough idea of amounts at the high and low end of the scale. The actual data, if essential, can be provided in a *tabulation*.

It is evident in Figure 2.18 that a map showing *range-graded* quantitative data is not far removed from a map that presents only *ranked data*. If the cartographer is able to state the numerical ranges of the data for each legend symbol, it is a quantitative presentation: if, however, the available information denotes only high, medium–high, medium, medium–low and low, then the presentation is ranked.

Quantitative data for areas

Many different kinds of information are gathered from areas such as census divisions, census tracts, townships, counties, provinces, states, or countries, which

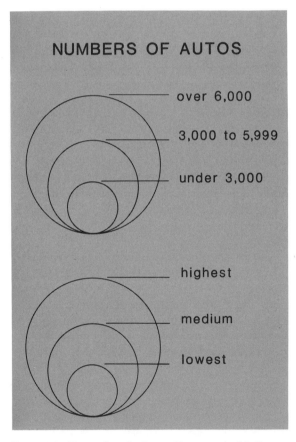

NUMBERS OF AUTOS

over 6,000

3,000 to 5,999

under 3,000

highest

medium

lowest

FIG. 2.18 Dropping the legend's numerical information changes a quantitative presentation of grouped values into a simple ranking.

may be referred to collectively as enumeration districts, or "data areas." For the sake of cartographic presentation it is most important to distinguish between *absolute quantities* that pertain to such areas and *density measures or other ratios.*

ABSOLUTE QUANTITIES GATHERED FOR AREAS

Instinctively, we may think of applying some pattern or tone *to the data areas* in order to symbolize amounts associated with the areas. Since the differences are quantitative, not qualitative, we would not vary texture or pattern (because this would suggest differences in kind) but would vary the darkness of the tone, or the darkness and the intensity if we had access to colored inks.

The effect of such shading is to create the impression of intensity or density which is ideal for a measure such as persons per square mile, and seems appropriate also for a number of ratios such as income per capita, or proportion of the population over age 65, or even proportion of housing units that are gas-heated. In all cases, these measures are averages that apply *across the whole of each data area*; and so it is appropriate to use an area symbol, i.e. a lighter or darker tone, that covers each area and suggests a status on the measure being mapped.

Absolute quantities, such as numbers of persons, numbers of foreign-born, numbers of housing units, or total income for the data unit, are different. First, they do not apply to the whole data area in the same sense that an average figure such as per capita income does. More important is the fact that the quantities may depend upon the size of data areas: for instance, a larger state or province *may* have a larger population, and a larger county may have a larger number of housing units. In such cases, symbolizing the quantities by area tones will give a false impression of density in a large data area. In many cases the impression will not be misleading; but the thoughtful reader will look at such a map and feel uncertain about its meaning. If all data units were identical in size, as with grid cells imposed on an area for sampling purposes, there would be no such uncertainty because density would automatically be implied by greater and smaller quantities occurring in data areas of equal area. The misleading effects that are assumed to follow from using area shadings to represent absolute quantities *have not*, in fact, been proven by testing. However, until research shows that such symbolization is safe it is best to adopt a conservative approach and avoid that application of shading.

USING SPOT SYMBOLS

To forestall any such difficulties it is best *not* to use area tones for absolute quantities. Instead, the spot symbols, reviewed in the previous section for symbolizing point data, are *applied to the areas.* All the variations used for data at points can be used when the data are gathered for areas: symbols scaled by linear, areal, or volumetric geometry; accumulated symbols; symbols for grouped or non-grouped data, and circles that are either simple or segmented. Because they are roughly centered in each data area there frequently is less crowding of these symbols than when they are applied to data points. Some examples of spot symbols applied to absolute quantitative data from areas are shown in Figure 2.19.

Because the same symbols and the same scaling procedures apply when spot symbols are used for area data and for point data, there is no need for further discussion of the symbolization. The brevity of this treatment, however, is not consistent with the importance of this use of the spot symbol. It is widely applied to population numbers, resource amounts, and other economic data gathered for countries, states, provinces, and counties. Incidentally, this use of spot symbols for two quite different forms of data is one of the key points in understanding all the quantitative data possibilities and how they may be mapped.

THE DOT MAP

The dot map is a very special thematic map. It uses a form of spot symbol to represent numbers of some phenomenon, and each dot is placed, necessarily, at a point. Nevertheless the original data is *for areas,* such as the numbers of persons or the numbers of livestock in a county. The cartographer is not content to symbolize the quantity by one symbol for each area, but seeks to show the actual pattern of distribution *within* each area. The dot map is unusual for another reason. It is one of the most down-to-earth and literal of thematic maps. The subject matter, typically, is

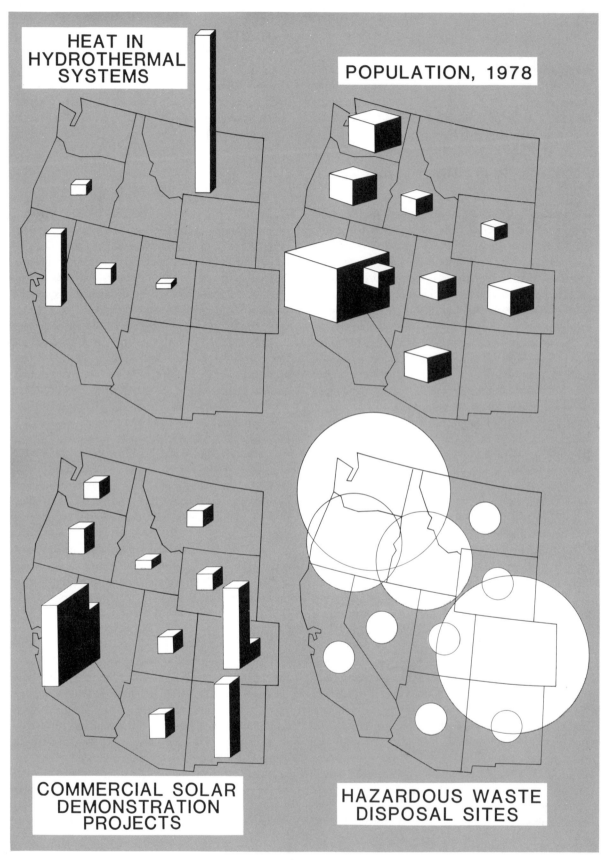

FIG. 2.19 Spot symbols applied to quantitative data for areas, when the data are of the absolute quantity type. This use of spot symbols applies to a great many map themes, and is just as important as the use of spot symbols for point data.

that of familiar visible items such as persons, tractors, or sheep; and the presentation strives to show those items as naturally as possible upon a realistic base map. A further distinction is that some relatively large-scale work is needed in the preparation of a dot map, whereas most thematic maps are strictly small-scale.

The map begins with investigation of those factors that actually control the distribution being mapped. An invaluable tool for this is a *land-use map* showing built-up areas, vacant land, land in crops, etc. In the absence of such explicit information, other sources can be used very effectively. In the example used here the distribution to be mapped is hogs in part of central Pennsylvania. The areas where those hogs will *not* occur can be mapped in a process of *progressive elimination* as shown on Figure 2.20. County boundaries, state forests, and state game lands were traced from an official state road map at scale of roughly 1 inch to 9 miles. The areal extent of cities and towns and also the areas of relatively steep slope were taken from US Geological Survey topographic maps at a scale of roughly 1 inch to 4 miles (1:250,000) with the aid of an optical reducing device. The remaining areas are assumed to be farmland where the hogs may occur. The map showing these areas is used as an underlay to guide placement of dots on the map itself.

Drawing the dot map requires a careful selection of *unit value* for the dot and *size of dot* (see Fig. 2.21). If each dot is assigned to a very large number of hogs, there will be too few dots to show the distribution adequately: if, on the other hand, the unit value of each dot is low, there will be too many dots to fit in the space. Dots that are large will give the map a very coarse appearance and overfill the spaces: dots that are too small will result in a map that looks too light and empty. The best procedure is to experiment with both unit values and dot sizes, testing them in data areas of both high and low density.

Ideally, the mapped information will be available for data areas smaller than those whose boundaries are drawn on the map. For example, the number of hogs would be gathered by township for a map showing county boundaries; or, in another case, number of hogs would be gathered by county for a map showing only state boundaries. Only with that kind of information will black clusters occur in certain parts of the map, because the cartographer must scatter the dots evenly throughout the areas that provide the information. In Figure 2.21, the placement of dots simulates the effect that might be obtained with numbers of hogs by township. The data actually came from counties.

THE CARTOGRAM

A very striking and communicative treatment of absolute quantities for areas is to distort the base map so that data areas are made proportional to the values being mapped. The townships, provinces, states, or counties for which the data are gathered are *used as the symbols* − and they are scaled areally to represent the mapped values (Fig. 2.22). The easier form to construct is the map in which each data area is independently sized. The areas are then arranged to correspond roughly to their real-world pattern (Part A of the illustration). In this presentation, the data areas may be recognizable, but the coherence of the larger political unit is lost. More interesting, and more difficult to construct, is the contiguous-area style of cartogram (Part B).

The cartogram tends to be most dramatic and interesting when distorted data areas are quite different in relative size from their normal areas. In these cases, the map offers a revealing new look at a familiar region or country. Sometimes, simply by accident, the relative magnitudes of the amounts being symbolized are roughly in proportion to the actual size of data areas. In this case the cartogram will be much less interesting, and may be abandoned in favor of more conventional symbolization.

Cartograms are used occasionally in books (see Woytinski and Woytinski, 1953, for extensive use) but are more often used in newspapers and magazines where creative cartography flourishes. They are not difficult to construct, especially now the procedure has been expressed in computer programs that make it possible to assemble the cartogram on a cathode ray tube (see Williams, 1978). Methods for construction without the aid of computers are provided in chapter 9.

FOR DENSITY MEASURES AND OTHER RATIOS

If the information gathered for areas is not absolute numbers or amounts, but ratios, then shading is applied to the data areas themselves.

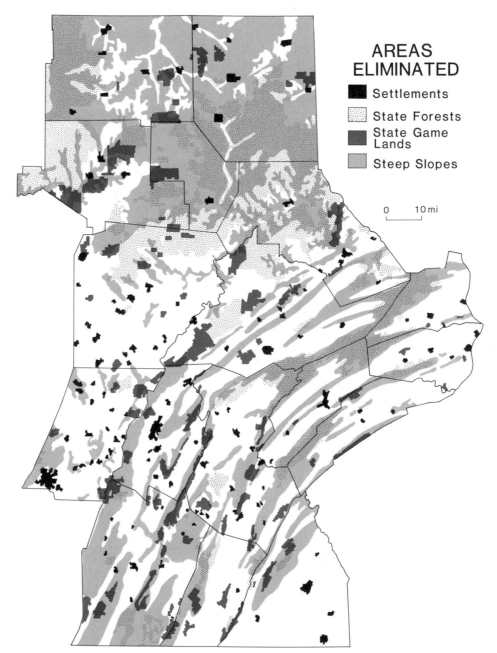

AREAS ELIMINATED

■ Settlements
▫ State Forests
▮ State Game Lands
▬ Steep Slopes

0   10 mi

FIG. 2.20 Progressive elimination of areas where a distribution (to be shown by dots) is *not* likely to occur.

FIG. 2.21 The effects of different dot sizes and unit values upon the patterns of a dot map: Part A, dot size too ▶ large; Part B, unit value too small; Part C, unit value too large; Part D, dot size and unit value both suitable. This illustration follows the example set by Robinson, Sale, and Morrison (1978), p. 204.

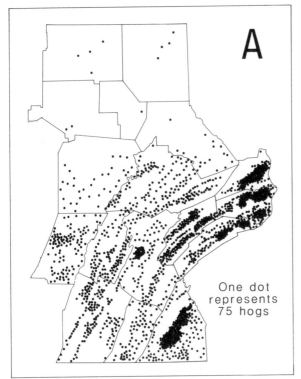

A

One dot
represents
75 hogs

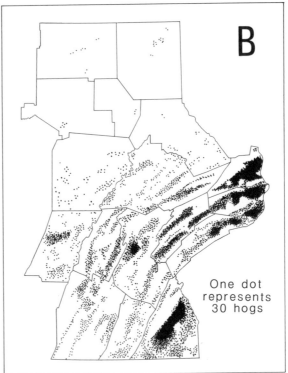

B

One dot
represents
30 hogs

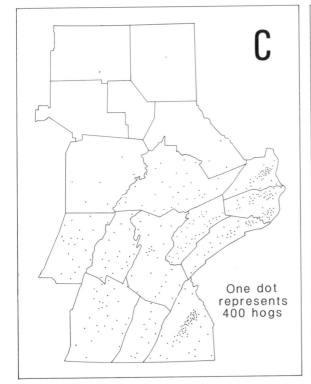

C

One dot
represents
400 hogs

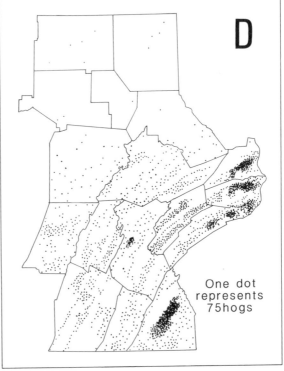

D

One dot
represents
75hogs

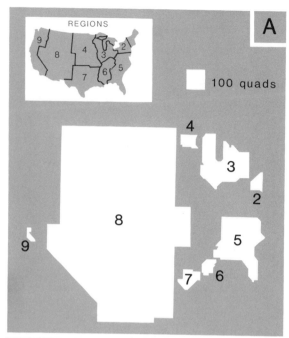

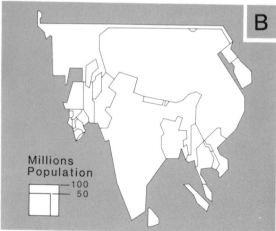

FIG. 2.22 Value-by-area cartograms: Part A, the non-contiguous-area type, showing energy resources in US economic regions; Part B, the contiguous-area type, showing world population numbers, taken from *Goode's World Atlas*, 15th edn.

THE CHOROPLETH MAP

This is the conventional treatment for density or ratio data, the map name being derived from the Greek *choros*, for place, and *plethos* for magnitude. The choropleth map always uses a sequence of shades or tones applied to the areas; and usually the shades are assigned to groups or classes of values.

The shading scheme

On maps with spot symbols, the size of symbols represents amounts. In choropleth maps, *darkness* is the analogue for position on a scale of density or some other ratio. One principle should be followed without question: areas of highest values or greatest densities should be assigned the darkest tones; areas of lowest values on the scale should be assigned the lightest tones; and areas of intermediate values should be intermediate in darkness.[7] Ideally, texture or pattern should be held constant. Experiments conducted with map readers show that such a scheme is very effective for a variety of map themes (Cuff, 1973). Choropleth maps (and shaded isarithmic maps as well) should all be treated the same – regardless of what a particular map theme may suggest. A theme such as proportion of the population that is literate, may suggest that dark, hence gloomy, shades be applied to areas that are *low* on the measure. If the map is made this way, the reader will have to deal with two conflicting messages: the greater darkness on such areas suggests "high" and "more"; but the legend says those areas are low on the measure. If the cartographer wishes to put gloomy shades on areas where few can read, then he should invert the measure and *map the proportion illiterate*. Other themes that carry the same hazard are level of income, and caloric intake by country. For both of these, darker tones on areas higher on the measures will effectively convey the quantitative message. The theme, as expressed by the cartographer in title or caption, is of critical importance. If the title is "Dietary deficiencies," and countries are grouped as most severe, intermediate, and no deficiency, then darkest shading on the disadvantaged countries is entirely appropriate; but that shading would be confusing if the title were "Caloric intake."

Classification or grouping

As with spot symbols, the scaling of darkness to represent ratio values may be approached two ways – scaling according to actual values, or scaling to represent grouped data. The conventional approach always has been to use grouping, partly because it has been difficult, if not impossible, to create shades of darkness that are consistent with each unique data value. Recently, however, the computer-driven plotter has been used to create line patterns whose percent black can be made proportional to any chosen mapped values (see Tobler, 1973; also Brassel and Utano, 1978), and a facsimile machine has been used to make solid grey tones with darkness proportional to mapped values (see Muller, 1978).

These experiments have shown that the unheard-of *classless choropleth map* is feasible (Fig. 2.23). Whether it is a sound way to present information is the subject of some dispute. Testing conducted with facsimile maps (Muller, 1979) and with plotter-drawn versions (Peterson, 1979) indicate that map readers *can* obtain useful information from maps of unclassed data; they can make surprisingly close estimates of the mapped values; and they can make useful comparisons between map pairs. Opposition to the classless choropleth map is based at least partly on the assumption that the cartographer should offer the reader an interpretation, hence a regionalizing of the data, by deciding which grouping offers the most useful simplification. It is further assumed that the reader should be able to identify quickly in the legend *every one of the shades* used on the map. The pros and cons of the unclassed choropleth map can be reviewed in the Muller and the Peterson articles cited above, and in a discussion that followed the Muller article (Commentary, 1980). The analogy with the question of

scaling spot symbols either literally or according to grouped (range-graded) values is very strong. Without grouping, the choropleth map offers the reader all the subtle differences that exist in density values, and makes the reader work to estimate those values. With grouping, the traditional choropleth map offers the reader only a few map shades which quickly lead him to a legend whose information is general.

No doubt, the process of grouping can distort the mapped information. There may be a considerable range of data values brought together in one group, all the members of which bear the same area shading. Conversely, there may be small differences between groups, but pronounced visual difference in order to make one shading distinctly different from the next. The cartographer is responsible for minimizing such faults by choosing a classification system that is best for the values being mapped. This custom-tailored approach may be abandoned, though, if a series of maps is made for a theme such as per capita income for a number of different states. For the sake of comparability of maps in the series it may be decided to use one classing system for all maps, though it is not ideal for any of them.

A number of different classification schemes for the same set of data is shown on Figure 2.24 which uses block diagrams to show the different *levels* that are implied by grouping data into classes for choropleth mapping (heights are proportional to the means of the classes represented). The block diagrams make it easier to see the following:

– there are pronounced "cliffs" at the edges of the data areas in any one class. These cliffs may either exaggerate or reduce the actual differences between members of adjacent classes, depending on the position of each member in its class
– a classification system with only two or three classes presents an extremely simple and easily interpreted picture of the distribution, masking many interesting differences, and creating very profound cliffs
– a larger number of classes leads to a more complex assemblage of levels and area patterns with much more subtle height differences between classes.

It is best, incidentally, to choose a classification scheme that is somewhat systematic, so the reader is not faced with a confusing progression of values in the

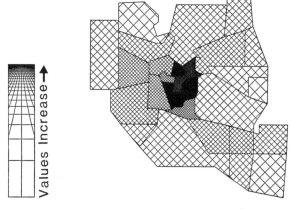

FIG. 2.23 The classless choropleth map. Areas are given darknesses proportional to actual (non-grouped) values. From Tobler (1973).

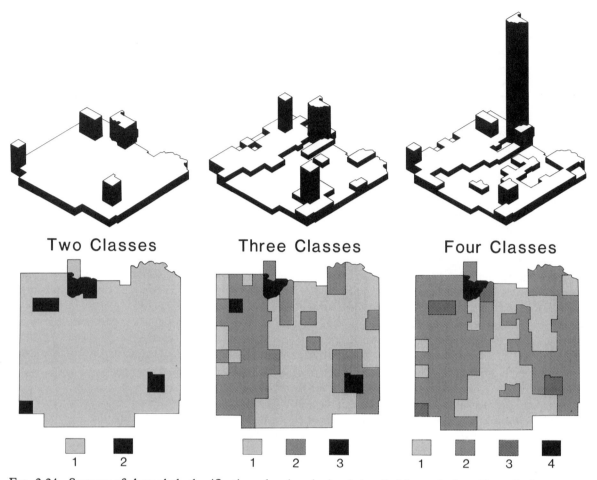

FIG. 2.24   Systems of choropleth classification, showing the levels implied by each class. From Jenks (1963).

map legend. For instance, one of the following systems may serve.

- five classes, of equal numerical range
- five classes in which the numerical range in each class increases geometrically toward the high end, i.e. the range of each higher class is double the range of the preceding class
- five classes, with an equal number of data areas in each, i.e. a quintile system.

Any such regular scheme may be modified to suit the peculiarities of the data set. To learn the nature of the data the first step is simply to arrange all the values (one for each data area) in a rank-order listing. Plotting the values this way on a linear scale will show the gaps and the clusters in the distribution of values and may be all that is needed to guide the choice of a suitable classification scheme. The goal always is to (1) recognize "natural breaks" in the distribution, (2) minimize differences within groups, and (3) maximize differences between groups.[8]

For the example shown (Fig. 2.25A) five classes equal in numerical range apparently are not suitable because all but four of the counties fall into the lowest density class so that the state appears to be virtually empty. Apparently, a false impression of any distribution can be conveyed to the map reader – either deliberately or accidentally – if the classification scheme is not suitable. The same information is mapped in Figure 2.25B with an equal number of counties in each class and a special category for Hudson County which is exceptional in density. The classification scheme is not ideal, but it does present a more informative picture of density variations.

When selecting class intervals, the cartographer

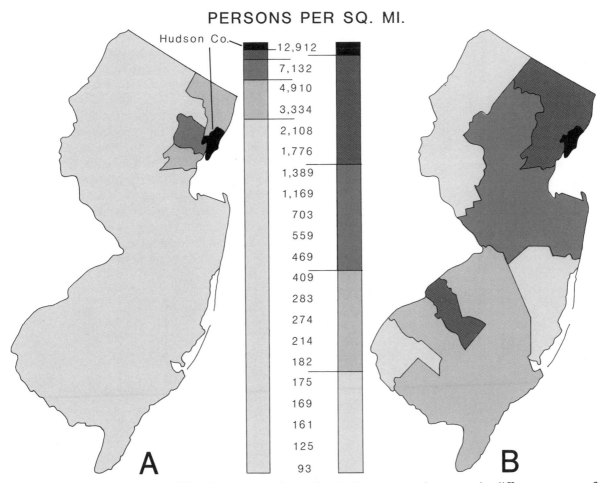

PERSONS PER SQ. MI.

Hudson Co.

12,912
7,132
4,910
3,334
2,108
1,776
1,389
1,169
703
559
469
409
283
274
214
182
175
169
161
125
93

A

B

FIG. 2.25 Choropleth maps of New Jersey's population density by county, using two quite different systems of classifying the same data.

always should consider a number of different classing systems while keeping in mind the salient features of the distribution. If some data area is truly exceptional, it should appear exceptional. The map reader will not study the classification system with great care, but instead will gain an immediate impression from the patterns of shaded data areas. That impression will be realistic only if the cartographer has studied the classification with care.

Execution of the choropleth map

The impression of darker and lighter tones on data areas can be created by hand-drawn effects or by applying ready-made artists' materials (Fig. 2.26). There are advantages and disadvantages either way.

Hand-drawn line or dot patterns require considerable skill with the pen if they are to be pleasing and uniform, and, because of their coarseness, they are rather difficult to look at. They can be produced economically, though, without dependence on an art supply store, and they will reproduce very well. Ready-made mechanical dot screens are relatively easy to apply, and create pleasing fine grey effects. They do involve expenditure, however, and they reproduce well only if both cartographer and photographer are careful. Suggestions in chapter 9 will help avoid the difficulties of ready-made choropleth symbols.

For data that include values above and below the mean value, net gain versus net loss, or other dichotomies, the symbolization required is a shading scheme that is bipolar − in effect, two shading schemes both

READY-MADE

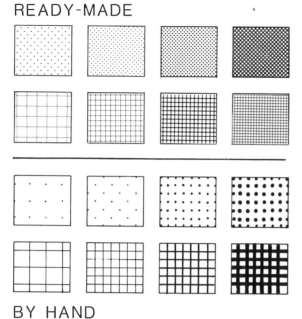

BY HAND

FIG. 2.26 Choropleth shading sequences produced by hand and by use of ready-made dot screens (graphic films).

progressing from a neutral middle value out to darkest extremes (Fig. 2.27).

ALTERNATIVES TO THE CHOROPLETH MAP

For the kind of data that lend themselves to choropleth mapping, that technique is the conventional presentation. Among the alternative presentations, one is a refinement of the choropleth, and two are rather bold departures.

The dasymetric map

In applying an area symbol to a county to show its level on some measure such as population density, the cartographer knows that the density reported for that county is only an average, and he realizes that in some parts the density will be higher than average and in some parts lower. The dasymetric map shows such differences, to the extent that they can be computed from information available.

The density for a certain county may be 250 persons per square mile (Fig. 2.28, Part A). Topographic maps show that half of the county is rugged mountain lands and virtually empty. The remaining parts of the

county must hold all the population, and the *density there* will average 500 per square mile (Part B).

That deduction is obvious because the mountainous area is assumed to be absolutely empty. If the occupied area is to be further divided into density zones, some simple arithmetic logic will need to be applied. For instance, assume that topographic maps show roughly 20 per cent of the occupied area is urban, while 80 per cent is rural. It is known from other precedents that urban areas often average 1200 persons per square mile, and it is reasonable to assume that urban density in this county. When this information is gathered in a small tabulation (Table 2.3) it becomes evident that the average density of 500 per square mile can be resolved into two density components *weighted* according to their respective areal

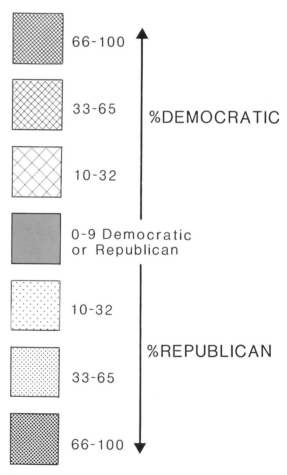

FIG. 2.27 Bipolar choropleth shading for a theme that demands two opposing sequences.

extents. Thus,

$$(0.20)(1200) + (0.80)(X) = 500$$
$$240 + 0.80 \, X = 500$$
$$0.80 \, X = 260$$
$$X = 325$$

Areas of the two density values, one assumed and the other calculated, can be mapped as in Part C. If information is available on the nature of the rural areas (true farmlands versus rural non-farm, for instance) this could be used to divide the area that averages 325 persons per square mile.

The stepped statistical surface

Stepped statistical surfaces were used earlier (in Fig. 2.24) to illustrate how data are assigned to different

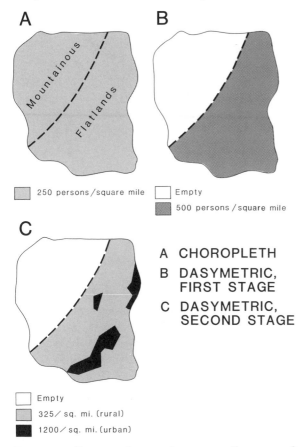

FIG. 2.28 Dasymetric mapping as a refinement of choropleth mapping. Areas of different densities are inferred from the density that applies to the entire data unit.

TABLE 2.3 Estimates used for deducing the rural population density within an area whose density averages 500 persons per square mile

	Estimated density	Estimated proportion of the area
Urban	1200	0.20
Rural	X	0.80

"levels" by choropleth mapping. The device, however, has much greater utility than is suggested by that application. For density or ratio data assigned to areas, the stepped surface may be used *instead of* a choropleth map. Because heights are far more easily interpreted than grey tones, there is no need to group the data. The stepped surface can present all the information, with *heights* of data areas made proportional to the actual values without grouping (Fig. 2.29). This, then, is the three-dimensional counterpart of the unclassed choropleth map but using linear scaling of heights rather than shades of darkness. Most important, a stepped surface does communicate effectively. Even when data areas are quite varied in size, and confront readers with some unintended variation in volumes under the raised data areas, most readers respond to just the heights (Cuff and Bieri, 1979). These surfaces are surprisingly easy to construct, using the method outlined in chapter 9.

The isopleth map, and smooth statistical surface

The qualities of an isoline map are very attractive. The map is easy to construct, and it very clearly shows the highs, the lows, and the rates of change in a distribution without the generalization that occurs when values are grouped and mapped choropleth-style. Cartographers have accepted the idea that these virtues justify assigning density values or other ratios to points at or near the centers of data areas, to make maps in the style of Figure 2.30, called *isopleth maps*. It could be argued that this should never be done because the original data are part of a distribution that by nature is stepped, not smooth. Density values surely are derived for the whole of data areas and change abruptly at their edges. But it could be argued with equal force that those sudden changes at the edges of data areas are themselves artificial and a feature of the data gathering, not the phenomenon.

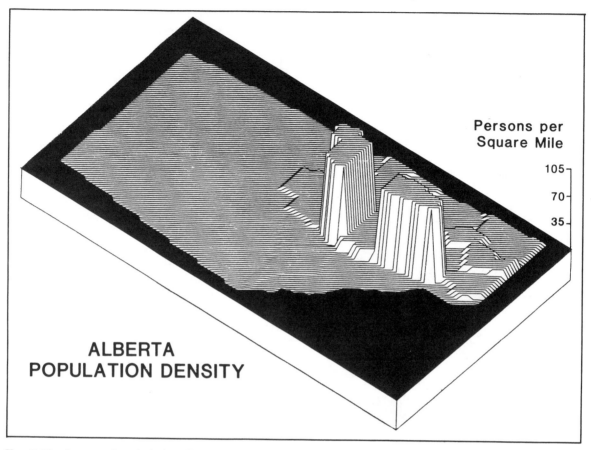

Persons per
Square Mile

105
70
35

ALBERTA
POPULATION DENSITY

FIG. 2.29   A stepped statistical surface as a substitute for a choropleth map. Non-grouped values are symbolized by heights of data areas.

Accuracy of isopleths   It was pointed out earlier that in drawing isometric lines the cartographer is always groping for a picture of some complete physical distribution (such as that of rainfall or temperatures) with the aid of limited sample points. His interpretation will inevitably deviate from the actual distribution. This is not the case in isopleth mapping, because a data point for every data area constitutes the entire "universe" of possible values for the distribution in question.

A serious flaw will exist if data areas are so large that interpolation places a number of isopleths *within* the data areas, thereby implying internal changes while in fact only one value applies to each area (Fig. 2.31). When data areas are small in relation to isopleth interval, then they more closely resemble points on the map, and as a result the unwarranted changes within data areas are minimized.

The completed map always should show outlines of data areas as well as their center points, so the structure of the mapped information is clear. It also is advisable to include, on the map or in the caption, a note such as "County averages assigned to county centers for mapping."

The smooth surface   As is the case for point data mapped conventionally by isoline technique, the pattern of an isopleth map can be transformed into a smooth statistical surface. Once the assignment of values from areas to center points has been accepted, there is no reason why the three-dimensional version of isarithmic mapping should not be used.

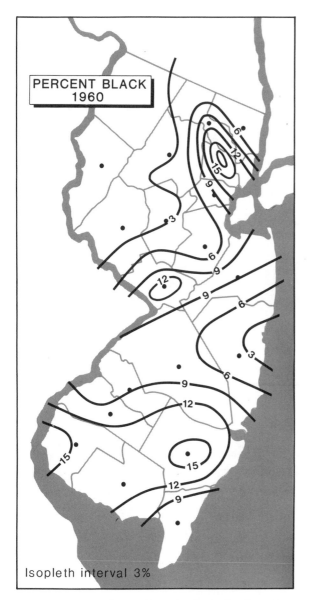

FIG. 2.30 Isopleth mapping. Ratio or density values for areas are assigned to points at area centers.

Quantitative data on lines

Not many types of quantitative data occur on lines: essentially every case is a flow of some kind. There are migrations of people, traffic flows, shipments of goods, or movements of materials such as crude oil (Fig. 2.32).

The mode of symbolization is to vary the width of

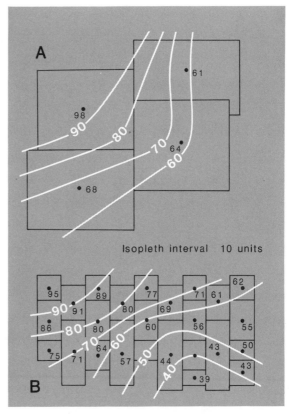

FIG. 2.31 Isopleths based on large data areas, as in Part A, will portray false value changes within the data areas. The problem is reduced when data areas (or the scale of mapping) are smaller, as in Part B.

line according to size of flow, and to vary the character of the line according to any qualitative differences that may be shown at the same time as flow magnitudes. Width of line is made in *linear proportion* to flow so that the reader may properly imagine that a given flow width, if prevailing for some specified time, would result in a certain volume of material transported. Since linear scaling does not effectively handle a large range of values, there may be difficulty with the smallest flows. Instead of scaling them in linear proportion to the largest on the map they may be assigned line symbols of a different character to show the shift in scaling. All flow lines, like spot symbols, can be scaled either literally or in range-graded fashion.

Solid black flow lines are adequate if the purpose is to show flow amounts and nothing else; but it may be desirable to show the roads, the rivers, or the pipelines

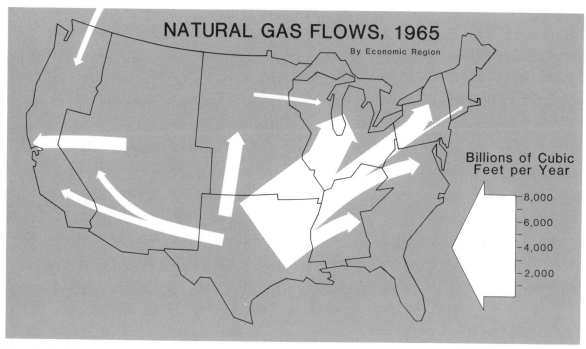

FIG. 2.32   Flow magnitudes as the best example of quantitative data along lines. From the *National Atlas of the United States of America* (1970).

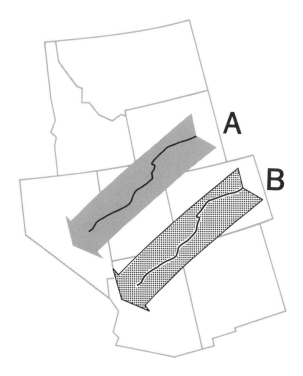

that carry the flows. For this purpose the routes of flow are superimposed onto the flow symbols (Fig. 2.33).

Summary of data possibilities and symbolization

The data types and how they can be symbolized and mapped are summarized by Figure 2.34. For the qualitative and ranked data at points, for areas, and on lines, some actual symbols are shown in the chart because for those six combinations of data location and measurement level there are not many options. Those symbols, therefore, can represent the logic of symbolization.

◀FIG. 2.33   Hypothetical routes of flow combined with arrow symbols that represent flow magnitudes: Part A, superposition; Part B, window sliced into graphic film (see chapter 9).

LOCATIONAL NATURE OF DATA

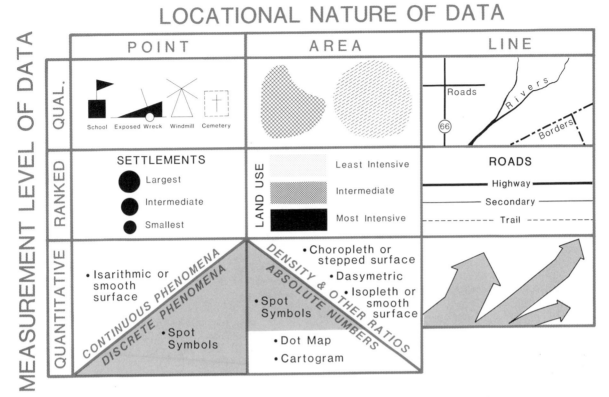

FIG. 2.34 Summary of data possibilities and the symbol and map types that are appropriate.

For quantitative data, and especially data for points and areas, there are a number of important distinctions to be made. For quantitative data at points, the major distinction is between data representing continuous phenomena and those representing discrete phenomena. In quantitative data for areas, the major distinction is between data that are density or other ratios and data that are absolute quantities. As shown in the chart, spot symbol maps can be used for some point data and some area data.

Notes

1 Most measurements are on a scale that has a meaningful and non-arbitrary zero point. Population numbers are an example. Other measurements, such as temperatures and historical dates, are made on scales with quite arbitrary zero points (see Muehrcke, 1972, pp. 14–16). The difference in scales has no direct influence in the cartographic symbolization and presentation, so it is not recognized in the main text.

2 This discrepancy between isolines and the real world is greatest for *isometric* lines, i.e. those drawn on the basis of measurements made at points where the physical world is sampled. For *isopleths* (see above, pp. 41–2) the validity of isolines is quite different.

3 The patchy appearance of the map can be avoided by *smoothing*. One smoothing method is simply to select an isoline interval that is broad or coarse enough to "miss" many small variations. The large local variations will still be there, however, and may be removed by formal smoothing procedures which average all the values that fall within a circle of certain radius, or within some rectangle defined by latitude and longitude lines. New values plotted at the centers of the circles or rectangles will indicate that conditions of that area will reflect to some extent the unusual values, yet will not be extreme.

4 A ten-sided form, or *decagraph*, may be substituted for the circle, especially when the symbol is divided in pie-chart fashion (see Balogun, 1978).

5 To facilitate the estimation of component parts, the cartographer may add ticks at ten or twenty per cent intervals on the inside of the circle circumference.

6 For circles, there are four possible ways to scale, since the data may be grouped or non-grouped, and the circles may

be scaled either by square roots or by the Flannery-adjusted square roots.

7 This assumes the use of only black ink. If colored inks or materials are used, then the intensity or richness of the color must be considered as well as darkness. The more intense or rich colors should be associated with greater densities or ratios.

8 More thorough approaches that seek ideal class intervals may be found in the following: Evans (1977); Jenks (1967), (1970), (1977); Jenks and Caspall (1971); Mackay (1955); Monmonier (1975).

References

Balogun, O. Y. (1978) "The decagraph: a substitute for the pie graph?," *The Cartographic Journal*, 15 (2), 78–85.

Brassel, Kurt E., and J. J. Utano (1978) "A computer program for quasi-continuous choropleth maps," *Proceedings*, American Congress on Surveying and Mapping, Annual Meeting, 3.

Commentary (1980) *Annals of the Association of American Geographers*, 70, 106–8.

Cuff, David J. (1973) "Shading on choropleth maps: some suspicions confirmed," *Proceedings*, Association of American Geographers, Annual Meeting, 50–4.

Cuff, David J., and Kenneth Bieri (1979) "Ratios and absolute values conveyed by a stepped statistical surface," *The American Cartographer*, 6 (2), 157–68.

Dickinson, G. C. (1973) *Statistical Mapping and the Presentation of Statistics* (2nd edn), London, Edward Arnold.

Evans, Ian S. (1977) "The selection of class intervals," *Transactions, Institute of British Geographers* (new series), 2 (1), 98–124.

Flannery, James J. (1971) "The relative effectiveness of some common graduated point symbols in the presentation of quantitative data," *The Canadian Cartographer*, 8 (2), 96–109.

Goode's World Atlas (1978) (15th edn, Edward Espenshade and Joel Morrison, eds), Chicago, Rand McNally.

Jenks, George F. (1963) "Generalization in statistical mapping," *Annals*, Association of American Geographers, 53 (1), 15–26.

Jenks, George F. (1967) "The data model concept in statistical mapping," *International Yearbook of Cartography*, 7, 186–90.

Jenks, George F. (1970) "Conceptual and perceptual error in thematic mapping," *Technical Papers*, American Congress on Surveying and Mapping, Annual Meeting, Washington, DC.

Jenks, George F. (1977) *Optimal Data Classification for Choropleth Maps*, Lawrence, Department of Geography, University of Kansas.

Jenks, George F., and Fred C. Caspall (1971) "Error on choropleth maps: definition, measurement, reduction," *Annals*, Association of American Geographers, 61, 217–44.

Mackay, J. R. (1955) "An analysis of isopleth and choropleth class intervals," *Economic Geography*, 31, 71–81.

Meihofer, Hans-Joachim (1973) "The visual perception of the circle in thematic maps: experimental results," *The Canadian Cartographer*, 10, 63–84.

Monmonier, Mark S. (1975) "Class intervals to enhance the visual correlation of choroplethic maps," *The Canadian Cartographer*, 12, 161–78.

Muehrcke, Phillip (1972) *Thematic Cartography*, Washington, DC, Association of American Geographers.

Muller, Jean-Claude (1978) "Choropleth map production by facsimile," *The Cartographic Journal*, 15 (1), 14–19.

Muller, Jean-Claude (1979) "Perception of continuously shaded maps," *Annals*, Association of American Geographers, 69 (2), 240–9.

Peterson, Michael P. (1979) "An evaluation of unclassed crossed-line choropleth mapping," *The American Cartographer*, 6, 21–37.

The National Atlas of the United States of America (1970) Washington, DC, US Geological Survey.

Tobler, Waldo R. (1973) "Choropleth maps without class intervals?," *Geographical Analysis*, 5, 262–5.

Williams, Anthony V. (1978) "Interactive cartogram production on a microprocessor graphics system," *Proceedings*, American Congress on Surveying and Mapping, Fall Technical Meeting, 426–31.

Woytinski, W. S., and S. S. Woytinski (1953) *World Population and Production: Trends and Outlook*, Baltimore, Lord Baltimore Press.

3 Combining Data to Show Relationships

The foregoing chapters were concerned with the most appropriate symbolization for specific kinds of data, and may have suggested that the cartographer is always occupied with a single data set. In fact, it often is more productive to consider more than one data set and to devise a map showing how those variables coincide (or fail to coincide) within the study area. A map can be more than an illustration; it can be a tool of analysis that helps the researcher and map reader to discover relationships. It is known, incidentally, that comparison of distributions on two separate maps is difficult for the map reader (McCarty and Salisbury, 1961). For this reason it is preferable to combine the

variables in some fashion. A distinction is made here between methods that combine the variables carto-graphically (visually) and those that make use of a statistical measure of correlation.

Cartographic correlation

Some correlations can be explored by superimposing a simple boundary upon an area of occurrence. Figure 3.1 shows a case in which the two variables are strictly qualitative in nature, areas irrigated from the Rio Grande in part of Texas, and the location of citrus

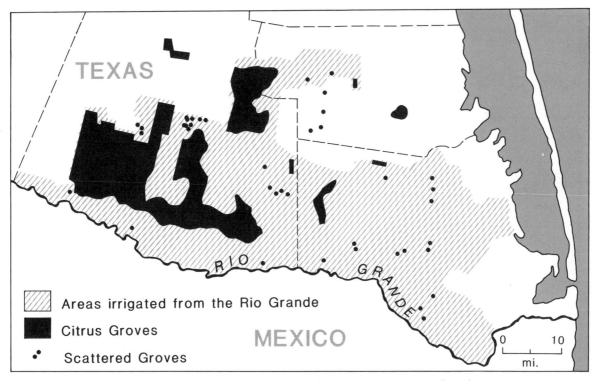

FIG. 3.1 Superposition of citrus-growing areas and areas irrigated from the Rio Grande.

orchards. Most orchards occur within the irrigated area; but there are some interesting anomalies which, on further investigation, prove to be orchards irrigated with ground water.

Often, a correlation can be shown by superimposing a distribution that is essentially qualitative onto a pattern or boundary that depends on some quantitative measure. Figure 3.2, for instance, explores the connection between citrus groves and slope as revealed by elevation contours. The correlation suggests that orchards are located on sloping land rather than on flat areas where cold air accumulates in times of frost.

In another ecological study, at a much smaller scale of mapping, the influence of slope upon orchard distribution is tested by combining a dot map of cherry trees with a county map of generalized physiography (Fig. 3.3). This procedure shows most trees to be in areas of moderate slope; but it also points out a few areas where, for some reason, cherry trees appear to be on flatlands and in steep mountain areas.

Some data may be converted to isarithmic form, and then combined with another distribution. An example from a study of voting behavior in Flint, Michigan

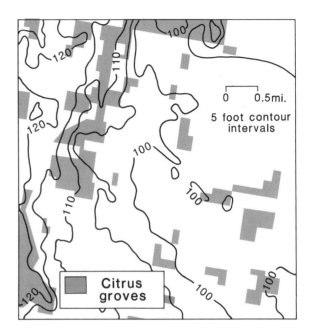

FIG. 3.2 Superposition of citrus groves and elevation contours (feet) in part of the Lower Rio Grande valley.

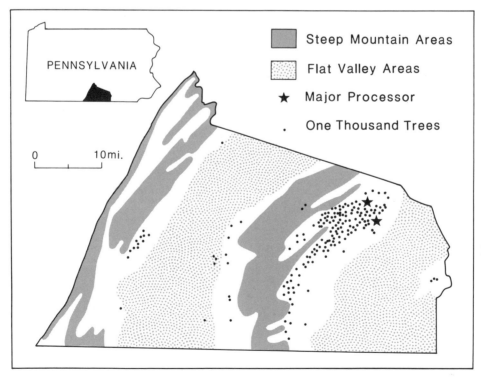

FIG. 3.3 Sour cherry occurrence and physiography in Adams County, Pennsylvania. From Monmonier (1967).

shows that areas of high income in Flint in 1950 appear to correspond, roughly, to areas of Republican strength (Fig. 3.4A and B). The correspondence is not convincing, however, because of the complexity of the choropleth map in Part B. When values from that map are assigned to precinct centers and given isopleth treatment (see chapter 2) the investigator can select an area bounded by a certain isopleth and impose it onto the areas of highest income, as in Part C of the illustration. The result is an explicit visual correlation. This technique was used successfully in a series of maps in the Flint study to show the relationships between Negro neighborhoods and Democratic strength through the period 1932–62 (Lewis, 1965).

Another possibility is to *combine two choropleth maps* in order to gain information that would not be evident through comparison of those two maps. The US Bureau of the Census has recently produced such maps in color (see Meyer, Broome, and Schweitzer, 1975) but they may also be rendered in black and white (see Smith, 1977). Figure 3.5 illustrates the principle by means of a four by four array that would constitute the *legend* for such a two-variable map. Variable X is represented by fine grey tones, the darkest being assigned to areas that are highest on the measure. Variable Y is represented by line patterns, the most dense being assigned to highest areas. Those areas that are empty are clearly low on both measures. Areas that are blackest are highest on both measures. Areas intermediate on both measures are much less distinctive, and must be identified by careful comparison of map areas with legend patterns. Such maps usually would be constructed expressly to identify the extreme areas, such as those high on both measures, so the difficulty with intermediate values may not be serious. Maps of this style could be used for pairs of variables such as the following:

– proportion non-white *and* average years of schooling completed (for census tracts)
– average size of farm *and* average value of farm products sold (for counties)
– gross national product per capita *and* energy used per capita (for world countries)

The two-variable choropleth map cannot be interpreted by a map reader without some practice. Despite that, the device is very appealing because it shows not only how frequent are the areas of coincidence but also their locations. Since the structure of the legend so

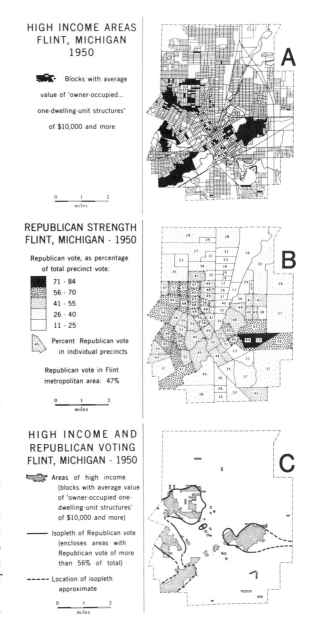

FIG. 3.4 Visual correlation of income and Republican strength in Flint, Michigan. Part A shows areas of selected income level; Part B is a choropleth map of percent Republican vote; in Part C, isopleths derived from B are imposed upon income areas from A. From Lewis (1965).

closely resembles the structure of a scatter diagram (see Fig. 3.8) the meaning of the visual correlation can be readily understood.

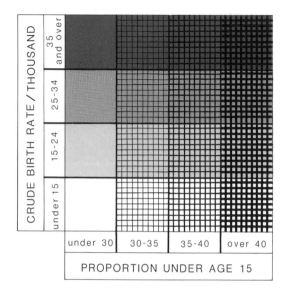

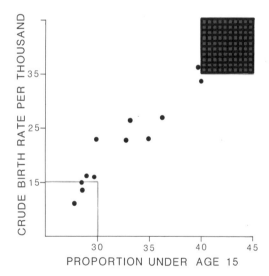

FIG. 3.5 The legend for a two-variable choropleth map.

COMBINING MORE THAN TWO VARIABLES

Figure 3.6 illustrates how a map can combine the areas of occurrence of four separate variables – in this case the areas are essentially qualitative, but owe their definition to some quantitative concept. Areas of high direct radiation, for instance, are defined as those where daily average *direct* radiation exceeds 8 KWhr per square meter. Areas of great *total* radiation are defined as those where average daily radiation exceeds 400 calories per square cm. Since there are four variables the theoretical combinations could be 24. In reality, only a few of the possible combinations occur, so the choice of patterns to represent those overlaps is feasible.

The presentation in Part A has the virtue of revealing the entire pattern for each distribution of interest, as well as showing the areas where two or more distributions coincide. If there are many areas of coincidence, a map of this kind may turn out to be extremely chaotic in its patterns. Equally important, it may be impossible for the cartographer to devise patterns to make all the superpositions clear. In such circumstances there are strong arguments for a different style of presentation. The map showing all superpositions can be used by the cartographer as a work map. From it he deduces the areas of coincidence and then makes a series of very simple maps (Part B). On the first map may be placed the areas where variable X coincides with variable Y. On the second map are areas where X coincides with Z. A third map shows areas where all three occur together. This certainly is the preferred style of presentation where there is some particular coincidence set that should be highlighted. It can be presented, of course, as a supplement to the superposition map which then serves as a record of all the distributions.

USE OF A CARTOGRAM AS A BASE MAP

As was pointed out in chapter 2, a cartogram is an interesting and dramatic substitute for a spot symbol map for the purpose of symbolizing absolute numbers of some phenomenon when that information is gathered for data areas such as census tracts, counties, states, or provinces. The cartogram can also be used *as a base* for choropleth mapping in order to add vital information that is missing from conventional choropleth maps – especially when they are used for ratios other than density per unit area. On a conventional choropleth map, average age of population or average income of population would be represented by darker to lighter tones applied to data areas that vary in size.

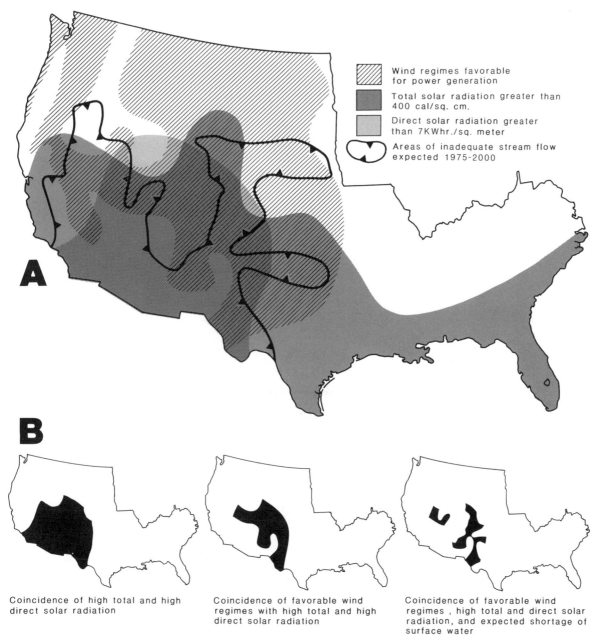

FIG. 3.6   Part A: cartographic superposition of resource areas; Part B: simple maps of selected areas of interest derived from the map of superposition. From Cuff and Young (1980).

These inequalities of data area lend greater visual impact to larger data areas than to smaller areas rendered in the same tone.[1] It can be argued that inequalities should be built into the map base deliberately, in order to emphasize those areas where greater numbers of the population reside.

If the map theme were average age of Hispanic population by state, then states of the USA would be made with areas proportional to numbers of Hispanics. For a map showing average age or average income for the general population, the data areas would be made proportional to the total population in each data area (Fig. 3.7).

One difficulty with the cartogram base is that the populous data areas may be extremely large and the less populous areas reduced to near-invisible proportions. It is best to accompany the cartogram–choropleth map with a conventional choropleth map, or at least an index map, to inform the reader of the actual data areas and their sizes.

Mapping statistical measures of correlation

Cartographic procedures for demonstrating correlations show the literal areas of coincidence and lack of coincidence − both of which may be of interest to the investigator. What cartographic correlation does *not* establish is the overall strength of a relationship within some study area or the extent to which some areas deviate from the general relationship that

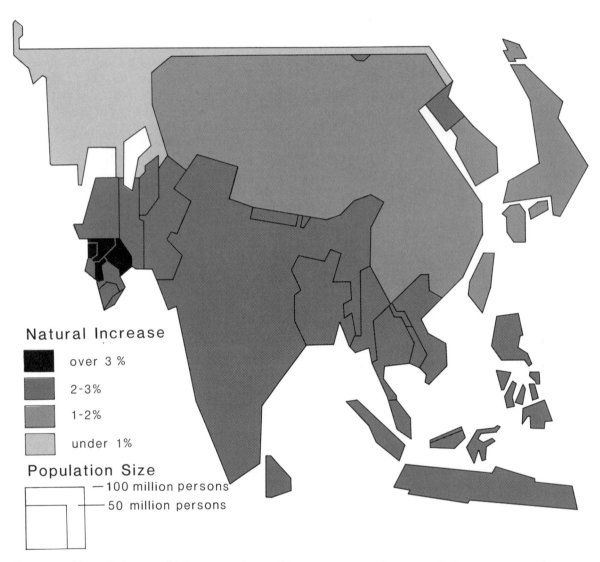

FIG. 3.7 Choropleth map of Asian rates of natural increase, 1980, using a population cartogram as base map. From *Goode's World Atlas*, 15th edn.

prevails. Mapping the results of statistical correlation can provide that kind of information and, by so doing, provide a fresh view of two distributions.

Statistical correlation makes use of *paired values*, one pair for each of the cases in a group. For instance, there may be 100 students (100 cases) in a small elementary school. For each student a record of *age* and *weight* provides the pair of values. The older students tend to be heavier, of course, so there is a positive correlation between the two variables.

A more geographic example involves nine hypothetical countries, each of which has information on *family income* and *proportion of the population that is urban*. The values listed in Table 3.1 suggest that the countries with higher average incomes also tend to be countries with greater proportion urban. Two choropleth maps (Fig. 3.8 A and B) also suggest that certain countries are high on both measures, while other counties are low on both measures – but the values are obscured by the grouping on those maps.

THE SCATTER DIAGRAM

The best graphic exploration is done with a scatter diagram (Fig. 3.8C). Each country is represented on the diagram by a dot whose position is dictated by the country's values on the two variables. The alignment and trend of the dots confirms that countries with higher incomes are generally more urban. This graphic expression of the relationship is gratifying;

but it leaves unanswered some questions that can be dealt with by calculating the *coefficient of correlation* and the formula for the *regression line*.

COEFFICIENT OF CORRELATION

The coefficient of correlation (or Pearson Product Moment Coefficient of Correlation) is an indication of the strength of the relationship between the two variables. If the dots on a scatter diagram were to align perfectly and slope upward to the right the coefficient would have a value of +1.00, indicating a perfect positive correlation. If the dots were to align perfectly but slope downward to the right, because lower numbers on one variable correspond to higher numbers on the other, then the value would be −1.00 and would indicate a perfect negative correlation. The actual coefficient can be calculated by a procedure found in most statistics textbooks and explained very well in the final chapter of Alexander and Gibson, 1979. Even without understanding the mathematics, anyone can obtain the coefficient by submitting the two variable lists to a computer program such as that in the Statistical Package for the Social Sciences (SPSS), or by using a calculator that has the procedure built in. For this hypothetical example, the coefficient is 0.76, which indicates a strong positive correlation.[2]

THE REGRESSION LINE

The regression line, or *line of best fit*, is the single straight line that best expresses the overall relationship, or dependence of one variable upon the other. As with the coefficient of correlation, procedures for defining the line may be studied in statistics text books or in the Alexander and Gibson book on economic geography referred to above. Essentially, the line is defined by calculating two characteristics:

1 Where the line intercepts an axis of the graph. This is given the term, *a*.
2 The slope of the line. This is given the term, *b*.

The regression line is defined by an equation in the form, $Y = a + bX$. In the present example, income is assumed to be the Y variable whose values depend on proportion urban, the X value. When the line is drawn onto the scatter diagram (Fig. 3.8C) it is clear that some of the plotted points fall above the line and some

Table 3.1 Per capita income and percent for urban for nine hypothetical countries		
Country number	*Per capita income*	*Urban population as proportion of total population*
	$	
1	5500	80
2	6000	75
3	4000	65
4	3500	60
5	5000	55
6	4500	60
7	2500	50
8	4000	45
9	3000	40

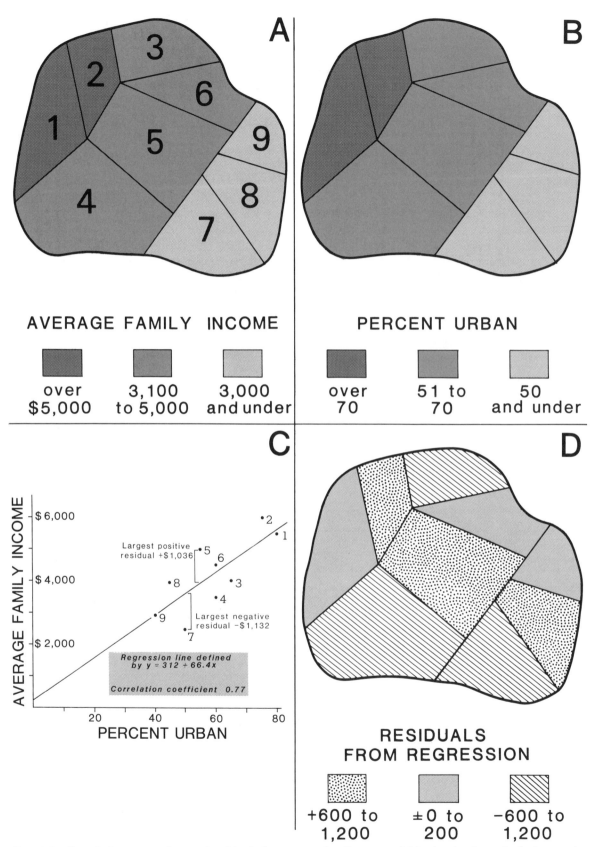

AVERAGE FAMILY INCOME

over $5,000 | 3,100 to 5,000 | 3,000 and under

PERCENT URBAN

over 70 | 51 to 70 | 50 and under

AVERAGE FAMILY INCOME

$6,000

Largest positive residual +$1,036

$4,000

Largest negative residual −$1,132

$2,000

Regression line defined by y = 312 + 66.4x

Correlation coefficient 0.77

20   40   60   80

PERCENT URBAN

RESIDUALS FROM REGRESSION

+600 to 1,200 | ±0 to 200 | −600 to 1,200

FIG. 3.8   Correlation, regression, and residuals from regression for two variables in nine hypothetical countries.

below it. Country #5, for instance, falls well above the line, and may be said to have a surprisingly high family income, considering its proportion urban. Countries like #3, #4, and #7 have incomes lower than the general relationship would predict.

RESIDUALS FROM REGRESSION

The income levels consistent with the general relationship can be calculated for *any* chosen value of proportion urban by using the equation that defines the regression line. In the case of country #5, the 55 per cent proportion urban suggests the family income should be $3964. The actual income is $5000, which is $1036 higher than predicted, and implies a positive residual value of $1036 for that country. Similar comparisons made for each of the countries (Table 3.2) show the magnitudes of the five positive and four negative residuals that are evident on the scatter diagram.

The residuals are mapped, choropleth-style, in Figure 3.8D. In real investigations this is the most exciting step of the analysis because it may point out

TABLE 3.2   Deriving residuals from regression for the relationship between income and proportion urban for nine hypothetical countries

Country	Actual per capita income	Income expected on basis of overall relationship	Difference between actual and expected
With positive residuals	$	$	$
2	6000	5292	788
5	5000	3964	1036
6	4500	4296	204
8	4000	3300	700
9	3000	2968	32
With negative residuals			
1	5500	5624	−124
3	4000	4628	−628
4	3500	4296	−796
7	2500	3632	−1132

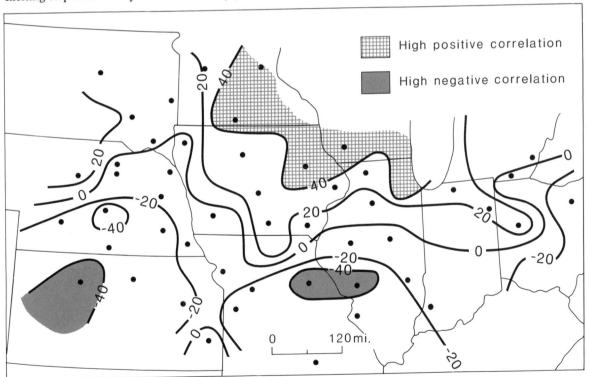

FIG. 3.9 Mapping of correlation coefficients based on data for a series of years. From Rose (1936).

cases that deviate drastically from the general relationship, and raises the question of why they should be so exceptional. It should be realized, incidentally, that the residuals and their magnitudes are only as significant as the relationship from which they are derived.

EXAMPLES FROM GEOGRAPHIC LITERATURE

Three studies of relationships are reviewed below in very brief accounts that emphasize the different methods by which paired values can be generated, and show how different kinds of results can be mapped. The studies referred to should be read in their entirety if their methodologies are to be fully appreciated.

A classic study of corn yields and climatic factors (Rose, 1935) mapped the simple correlation coefficients between corn yields and various climatic measures *through time* for 55 counties in the US Corn Belt. For each county, around 20 years of corn yields were collected and paired with climatic measures for those same years, resulting in roughly 20 pairs of

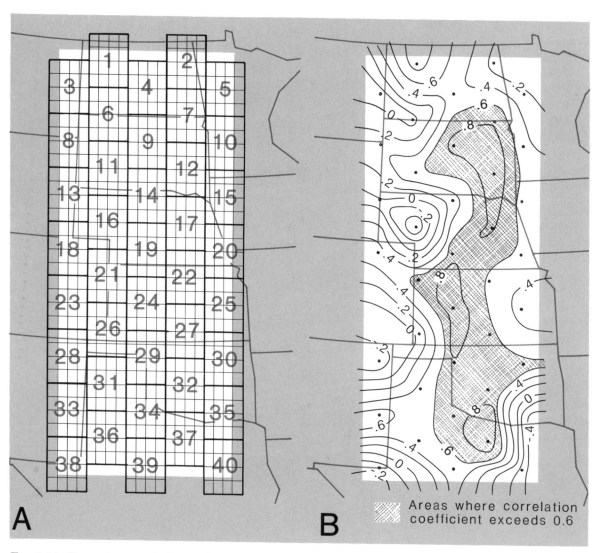

FIG. 3.10 Generating correlation coefficients for 40 areas by using paired values from 16 cells within each area. From Robinson (1962).

numbers to relate yields to temperature, and another 20 pairs to relate yields and annual rainfall. Correlation resulted in a single coefficient that was plotted at each county center (Fig. 3.9). Isolines reveal the trend of the coefficient values, while shading is used to emphasize areas of strong positive and strong negative correlation.

If two distributions are represented by existing isarithmic maps, they can be compared by the following method applied to population densities and precipitation in the Great Plains (Robinson, 1962). The grid shown in Figure 3.10A was applied first to an isarithmic map of population density, and then to a map of average annual precipitation in the preceding decade. Values were taken from the maps, so that within each of the 40 large rectangles 16 pairs of values were recorded – one pair at each of the 16 cells. These 16 paired values were subjected to correlation analysis which yielded a single coefficient that captured the degree of association for a rectangle. Forty of these were plotted at rectangle centers and mapped as in Figure 3.10B. This isarithmic map, derived from the two original isarithmic maps of population density and precipitation, expresses how those two variables correspond in different parts of the study area. This correspondence may be thought of as the varying degree of "fit" between two statistical surfaces which are superimposed.

A third example takes a different approach – seeking how local areas deviate from a general relationship that applies for a whole state (Robinson and Bryson, 1957; also see Thomas, 1960). The subject, again, is rural population density and average annual precipitation, both variables being represented on isarithmic maps (Fig. 3.11A and B). Those distributions are sampled at 26 regularly spaced sample points. The correspondence between the two variables, as derived from paired values at the 26 points, is shown by the scatter diagram and the regression line that expresses the overall relationship for the state of Nebraska (Fig. 3.11C). On the basis of those 26 points, the regression line "predicts" that for a given precipitation value a certain population density may be expected. The extent to which densities at actual locations deviate from the general relationship is evident in the positions of the dots above or below the regression line. Those deviations, i.e. residuals from regression, are mapped in Figure 3.11D.

The mapped residuals and their magnitudes are meaningful only to the extent that there is significance in the relationship between density and precipitation for the state as a whole. Unless the state's area is inherently significant with regard to population density or precipitation, or both, then the residuals are simply deviations from the relationship that applies to Nebraska as a whole. Results of a different meaning would be obtained if the method outlined here were applied to all US areas where grains are the dominant crop, or all areas where average annual precipitation ranges between 15 and 35 inches.

Notes

1 The effect probably is more serious when a choropleth map is used (wrongly) for absolute quantities.
2 The strength of a relationship is no assurance that the two variables are *causally* related. The investigator must judge whether the correlation is meaningful or accidental.

References

Alexander, John W., and L. J. Gibson (1979) *Economic Geography* (2nd edn), Englewood Cliffs, NJ, Prentice-Hall.

Cuff, David J., and William J. Young (1980) *The United States Energy Atlas*, New York, The Free Press.

Goode's World Atlas (1978) (15th edn, Edward Espenshade and Joel Morrison, eds), Chicago, Rand McNally.

Lewis, Peirce F. (1965) "Impact of Negro migration on the electoral geography of Flint, Michigan, 1932–1961: a cartographic analysis," *Annals*, Association of American Geographers, 55, 1–25.

McCarty, H. H., and Neil E. Salisbury (1961) *Visual Comparisons of Isopleth Maps as a Means of Determining Correlations Between Spatially-Distributed Phenomena*, Iowa City, State University of Iowa.

Meyer, Morton A., Frederick R. Broome, and Richard H. Schweitzer (1975) "Color statistical mapping by the US Bureau of the Census," *The American Cartographer*, 2, 100–17.

Monmonier, Mark S. (1967) "The ecology of commercial sour cherry production in Adams County, Pennsylvania," *Proceedings*, Pennsylvania Academy of Science, 41, 123–7.

Robinson, Arthur H. (1962) "Mapping the correspondence of isarithmic maps," *Annals*, Association of American Geographers, 52, 414–25.

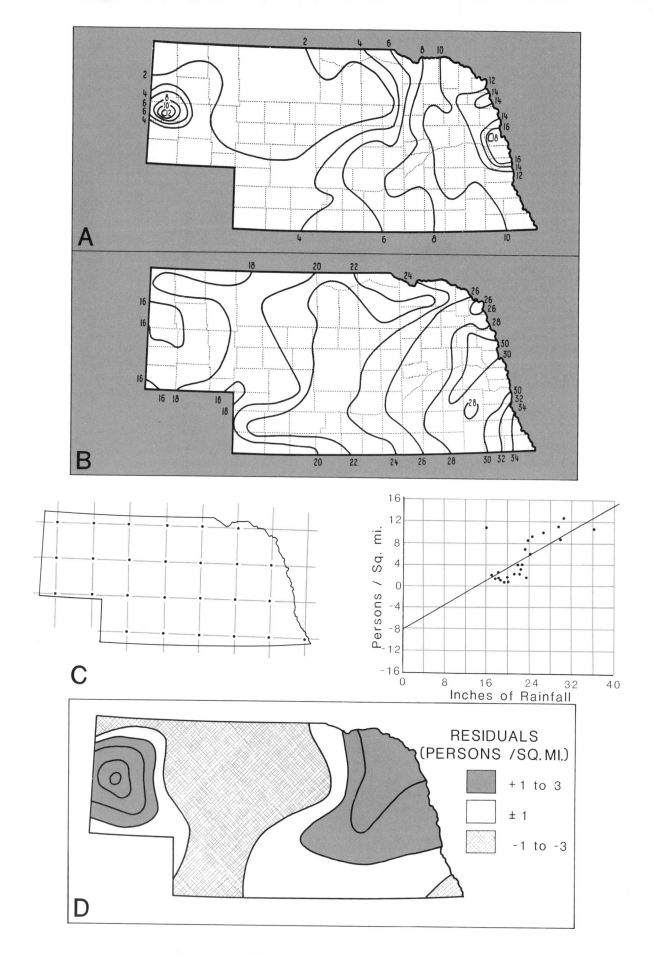

Robinson, A. H., and Reid A. Bryson (1957) "A method for describing the correspondence of geographical distributions," *Annals*, Association of American Geographers, 47, 379–91.

Rose, John K. (1936) "Corn yield and climate in the Corn Belt," *Geographical Review*, 26, 88–102.

Smith, Richard M. (1977) "The development of black and white two-variable maps: ongoing cartographic research," *Applications of Geographic Research*, Michigan State University.

Thomas, Edwin N. (1960) *Maps of Residuals from Regression: Their Characteristics and Uses in Geographic Research*, Iowa City, State University of Iowa.

◄FIG. 3.11   Population density and precipitation in Nebraska: Part A, rural farm population per square mile, 1950; Part B, average annual precipitation as of 1941; Part C, 26 sample points, and scattergram relating the two variables; Part D, deviations from the relationship that applies to Nebraska as a whole. From Robinson and Bryson (1957).

4 Verbal Content

The words and numerals placed on a map may be the most important items the cartographer selects. The words chosen will either clarify or obscure the message that has been symbolized; and furthermore, the style and placement of lettering can instantly brand the work as either amateurish or professional.

Choice of words

Careful choice of words is vital when dealing with the *title* (or caption) and the *legend heading*, because they tell the reader, respectively, what is being mapped, and how that is being accomplished.

TITLE VERSUS LEGEND HEADING

The title or caption has a purpose quite different from that of the legend heading. If the two purposes are confused there will be redundancy and confusion in the map.

First, it should be made clear that title and caption are interchangeable: a map has *either* a title or a caption that accomplishes essentially the same thing. A title is set in large lettering within the map frame. The caption, on the other hand, may be composed by the cartographer, but it is set in a few lines of type, by stenographer or publisher, under or over the map (Fig. 4.1). Since the caption will occupy page space, the ideal planning will allow for it and will shrink the map space accordingly (see chapter 5).

A caption may be preferable to a title, because it occupies less of the cartographer's time and none of the framed space. Furthermore, a caption can be expanded to include observations about features of the map, or the source of the data. Despite those advantages, it will be assumed here, for simplicity, that a title is being employed.

The title must be so worded that it captures the essence of the map theme and is consistent with the symbolization used; and, equally important, it must be complemented by the legend heading.

TITLE CONSISTENT WITH SYMBOLIZATION

In chapter 2 it was pointed out that symbolization and title must be logically related. A map of the theme "Caloric intake" should not apply darker tones to areas of low intake just because those areas are gloomy or disadvantaged. Here the other side of the coin is recognized: the title must be worded to reflect the mapped measure and how it is symbolized. If the measure mapped is an index of drought, the title "Moisture availability" is misleading.

Even more fundamental is the need to state what the mapped information portrays, and not to misrepresent it when composing a title. Inexperienced students may map the size of metropolitan populations, using scaled circles, and call the map "Population density" because that phrase is familiar. Such a map is no more (and no less) than "Metropolitan populations" or "Populations of Standard Metropolitan Statistical Areas," or perhaps, "Size of major cities." A map of density is quite a different thing. At the same time, there is no need for titles to be dull or unimaginative. The map of metropolitan populations could be titled, "Urban America" or, "Metropolitan America."

LEGEND HEADING COMPLEMENTARY TO TITLE

The legend heading must economically identify the mapped data and show how map symbols are to be interpreted. In doing so, it will claim certain key terms that should *not* be in the title. If the theme is, for instance, population density, the title will say that, while the legend heading will state the measure is "Persons per square mile" and will explain the use of darker and lighter tones for data groupings. In the legend heading, the term "Density per square mile" is

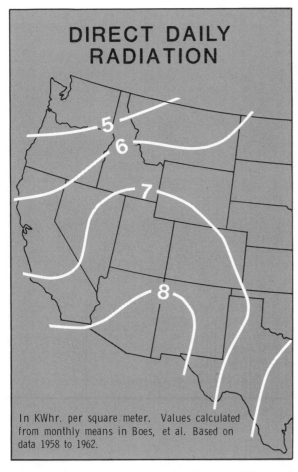

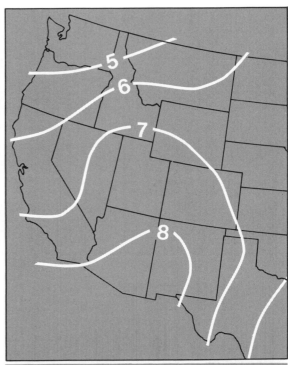

Fig. 1. Daily total of direct solar radiation normal to collecting surface. Annual mean values in KWhr. per square meter, calculated from monthly means in Boes, et al, based on data 1958 to 1962.

FIG. 4.1 A title or a caption may be used. The caption can include supplementary information and notes on sources.

redundant and inappropriate; and, at the same time, it is not ideal to use "Persons per square mile" as a title. If a map deals with amounts of some resource, then the title might be "Mineable amounts of bituminous coal." The symbolization would be spot symbols of some kind with scaling explained in the legend whose heading might be just "Tons." Incidentally, the inclusion of units in a legend heading can greatly reduce the efforts of both reader and cartographer: if "thousands of tons" is in the heading, it is not necessary to state those units repeatedly when showing values symbolized (Fig. 4.2).

The rule that usually serves to make title and legend heading complementary is this: the title identifies *the map theme*; while the legend heading (and the legend itself) deal with *the variable that has been mapped* and

the symbolization used to portray that variable. As a general rule, it is best to always provide a legend heading. In some cases, though, the title can serve a dual purpose: "Per capita income" may serve as a title and at the same time makes clear what variable the map symbols are showing. If the map is large and the legend rather far removed from the title, it would be preferable to use "Income levels" or "Wealth" as title and "Thousands of dollars per capita" for legend heading.

OMITTING THE WORDS "MAP" AND "LEGEND"

One touch that can instantly render a map less professional is to include the word "map" in the title, or to label the legend as "legend," or the scale as "scale."

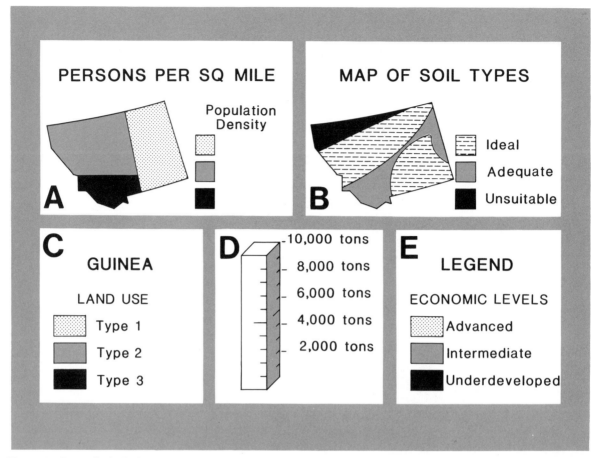

FIG. 4.2 Some faults in legends and titles: Part A, title and legend headings interchanged; Part B, the word *map* wrongly included in title; Part C, part of title wrongly included in legend; Part D, needless repetition of units in legend; Part E, the word *legend* wrongly included in legend heading.

It should be obvious that the map is a map; and, while that word does no harm it contributes nothing and should be discarded when composing a careful statement of the map theme. In geological publications authors frequently use maps and cross-sections: the cross-sections may be labelled "Section X–Y," or "Section A–B." Then, to be consistent, a map is entitled, "Map of surficial geology," when "Surficial geology" would be just as informative. In the same vein, the space available for legend heading is very precious and should be reserved for those key phrases that help the reader interpret the symbolization. He will find that information in the corner of the map just as quickly without the word "legend" to guide him there (Fig. 4.2). An exception to this would be in a series of maps with one legend to serve them all.

Then, an overall heading such as "Legend for Figures 8 through 12" would be justified.

EXPLANATORY NOTES

Many maps depend on information that needs to be explained or qualified, usually with regard to its date. As an example, demographic information is extremely changeable: any map that presents crude death rates, crude birth rates, or rates of natural increase without noting the *year* of the data is inadequate. Climatic information, such as long-term averages of temperature or precipitation, is heavily dependent upon the length of record at the weather stations used, because the longer records provide more reliable average values. Some statement about length of record, and whether it varies across the map should be included.

The cartographer should include the source of the information mapped. It is frustrating for a reader to encounter some interesting or surprising map pattern and have to ask "Who says so?" The map will gain authority and the cartographer or author will appear more thorough if the information source is stated. A note *on the map* or in the caption will make the map self-contained so the reader will not have to search for the source of information. Assuming there is a bibliography in the paper or book being illustrated, the map can bear a simple note such as "Jenkins, 1978, p. 46."

Lettering styles

Lettering styles, or *fonts*, are the distinctive letter forms, such as *Times Roman*, or *Grotesque*. Catalogues offer such a rich array of these that a choice can be extremely difficult without some guidelines. The fundamental advice is that no more than two styles are needed on most maps, and often one style will be enough (Hodgkiss, 1970, pp. 85–7). Since the styles may be grouped as either classic (with serif strokes) or sans serif (without serif strokes) the cartographer may choose one style from each of those two broad families (Fig. 4.3).

A style with serifs often is used for physical features, such as mountain ranges, oceans, rivers and lakes, while the sans-serif styles are used for cultural features

FIG. 4.3 Variations upon classic (with serifs) and sans-serif lettering styles, showing great variety available.

such as province and state names, cities, and towns. For oceans, rivers, and lakes the *italic* or slant form of serif lettering is usual: all capitals for oceans and lakes, capitals and lower case for rivers.

There are no hard rules for the use of different type styles; and to say that a certain practice is *conventional* is to ignore the variation that occurs among established cartographic houses. In this field, where the choices tend to be overwhelming, it may be advisable to choose a certain mapping agency (or firm) as a model and conform to its conventions. Some of the lettering practices seen on recent maps are summed up on Figure 4.4

There are so many *variations* of each type style – light, medium, bold, extended, compressed, and slanted – that, when combined with difference in *size*, these variations will accommodate any of the logical differences a cartographer needs to show, such as differences in size or type of settlement, or distinctions between country and township names. The variations and the size differences can be employed in an orderly way to make all the distinctions that will help the reader sort out different categories of information on the map. Legend heading and legend content should be in the same style and variation, but different in size. Explanatory notes might be in that same style and variation, but smallest in size. Visual logic suggests that settlements all of the same status should be in the same variation and size; but settlements whose difference is worthwhile should look different. *Difference in the variation* such as compressed or slanted would indicate qualitative difference; while *change in size* or boldness of lettering would indicate differing size or importance.

One of the most compelling needs is for a sense of the *hierarchy* that exists within the materials dealt with. On maps, and especially on illustrations such as bar graphs, the status of all the items labelled should be revealed to the reader by using diminished size or boldness of lettering for those items that are subordinate to others. Even the difference between ALL CAPITALS and Capitals and lower case can be enough to make a useful distinction in level.

Variety in lettering is a powerful tool, and should be used thoughtfully. It should also be used with restraint, so the reader is not faced with a dazzling variety of styles on a map. As suggested above, two *styles* will be enough for virtually any map. Many of

		NATIONAL GEO.		NATIONAL ATLASES		ATLASES		
		Ref.	Mag.	U.S.A.	Can.	CIA	Goode	Ox. World
WATER	Salt	*CAP*	*Cplc*	*CAP*	*CAP**	Cplc	*CAP**	*CAP**
WATER	Fresh	*Cplc*	*Cplc*	*Cplc*	*Cplc*	Cplc	*Cplc*	*CAP**
LAND FEATURES	Other	*CAP**	*Cplc*	CAP	—	CAP	CAP	CAP
LAND FEATURES	Peak	*CAP**	*Cplc*	Cplc	—	Cplc	Cplc	CAP
LAND FEATURES	Range	*CAP**	*Cplc*	CAP*	—	CAP	CAP	*CAP**
CULTURAL	City	Cplc	Cplc	CAP*	CAP*	CAP*	* * *	Cplc
CULTURAL	Park	*CAP*	*CAP*	*CAP*	—	—	CAP	*CAP*
CULTURAL	Polit.	**CAP**	**CAP**	**CAP**	**CAP**	**CAP***	CAP	CAP
THEMATIC	Notes	*Cplc*	Cplc	Cplc	Cplc	Cplc	Cplc	Cplc
THEMATIC	Lgnd item	**Cplc**	**Cplc**	Cplc	Cplc	Cplc	Cplc	Cplc
THEMATIC	Lgnd head	**Cplc**	**Cplc**	CAP	CAP	Cplc	Cplc	Cplc
THEMATIC	Title	**CAP**	* *	CAP	CAP	Cplc	CAP	Cplc

□ Sans Serif

* CAP or Cplc depending on map scale and status of feature

* * Lettering unique to map theme

* * * Cplc, CAP, or Cplc depending on status of feature

FIG. 4.4 Lettering conventions of some major map making establishments.

the styles available are quite unsuitable for cartographic work – partly because of their unconventional appearance, but also because they sacrifice readability for the sake of novelty (Fig. 4.5).

Size variety and limitations

When changing the size of a lettered map, the cartographer should keep in mind some limiting factors with regard to legibility and discernible differences. The largest lettering will be dictated by common sense

Data 70
DAVIDA
De Vinne
Dom Casual
Dynamo
Dynamo
Dynamo
Eckmann Schrift
Flash
Flash
Fraktur
GALLIA
Goudy Fancy
Hobo
Juliet
Kalligraphia
Lazybones
Le Griffe

FIG. 4.5 Available type styles not suited to cartographic work.

and space available within the frame. The smallest lettering must be handled with care to ensure that it is legible *on the finished product*.

The legibility limit is 3 to 5 point size, in which the "point" unit is equivalent to $\frac{1}{72}$ inch. Since most lettering is ordered according to point size, the actual dimension in inches or centimeters is usually not important. It is vital to realize, though, that any photoreduction will affect the lettering; so if art work is twice the product size, 10 point lettering is the smallest that can be used safely on the art.

Size is not the only factor to consider when choosing lettering for a map that will be substantially reduced. The style and the variation can both be important in this regard. A style or variant that uses thick (bold) strokes may look muddy when reduced by half because the subtle openings that define certain letters will close up. For instance, a 10 point Helvetica bold should not be reduced to 5 point size, whereas a 10 point Helvetica light will still be clear at that size.

The question of discernible differences can be important in the lettering of some maps. If size differences within one variant are used to reflect a hierarchy in settlement size, there should be no more than three levels. If more are needed, then a change in variant is advisable. The size difference should be *at least* 20 per cent: for lettering in the vicinity of 10 point size, this means a difference of 2 points; but for lettering near 20 point size the difference must be 4 points.[1]

Lettering placement

The placement of lettering may seem to be a mundane subject but, in fact, it is one of the main elements of *visual logic* in a map. The right placement of lettering can assist greatly in conveying information. The wrong placement can lead to both intellectual confusion and visual distraction.[2]

FOR MOST PLACE-NAMES

Names for cities, towns, states, and countries usually do not require any special alignment. They should be placed "squarely" on the map in a way that conforms to strong linear features of the base map. What features the lettering should conform to depends on the scale of the map, its orientation, the projection, and whether the meridians and parallels are shown.

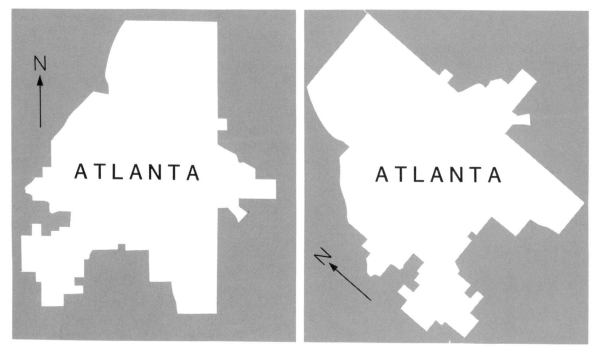

FIG. 4.6   Conventional alignment of lettering on large-scale maps.

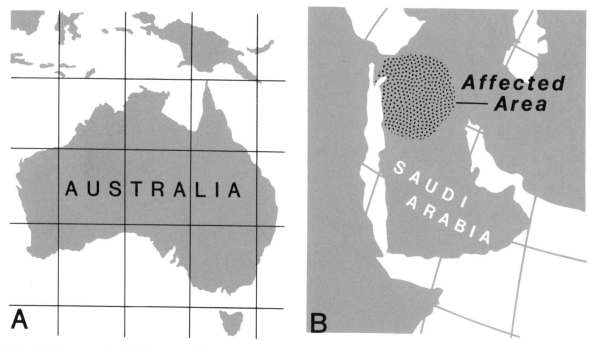

FIG. 4.7   Conventional alignment of lettering on small-scale maps.

The simplest case is that of the large-scale map in which north is at the top (Fig. 4.6). The graticule does not show on that illustration; but if it did, it would be square with the frame because the map covers such a small area. When north is not at the top, there still is no reason to skew the lettering, unless meridians and parallels are visible.

It is on small-scale maps that the graticule is most often visible, and frequently curved (Fig. 4.7). In the case of Australia, the graticule is visible, but parallels on the map projection chosen are square with the frame; consequently, horizontal lettering is the most pleasing (Part A). In the case of Saudi Arabia, the parallels are strongly curved, and demand that extensive lettering follow that curve (Part B). A guideline can be derived from this: if parallels are evident and bold, then lettering for the base map should conform to them. Otherwise, lettering of base features should be square with the map frame. Short thematic labels on a map such as the Saudi Arabian example can be aligned squarely with the frame to distinguish that information from features of the base map.

If lettering is to be squared with some dominant element such as the map frame, then *it must be squared*. Few faults are so glaring and so unnecessary as imperfectly aligned lettering (see chapter 9).

FOR LARGE AREAS, AND PHYSIOGRAPHIC FEATURES

Labels on certain map features must be placed in a way that gives the reader the maximum of information.

For a large area, such as the Arctic Ocean, a compact label placed on part of the ocean is misleading, and does not identify the feature as well as lettering *extended* to cover what the cartographer knows to be all Arctic Ocean (Fig. 4.8). Extensive land areas, such as the USSR should be given similar treatment.

Physical features, such as mountain ranges, should be labelled in a manner that suggests their extent and their trend. The elongation of such a feature will be recognized only if the lettering deviates from conventional alignment and follows the range (Fig. 4.9).

FOR LINEAR FEATURES

For the sake of convention, lettering for rivers should

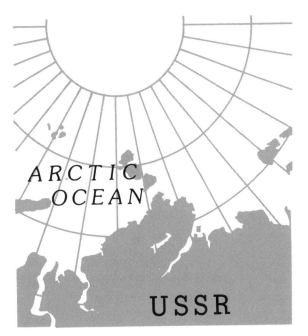

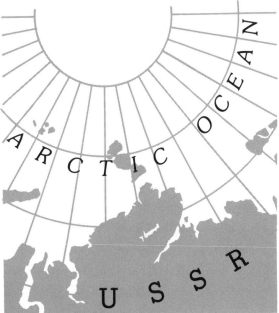

FIG. 4.8 Lettering should be extended if the feature is extensive.

be capitals and lower case in a slant or italic variation of the type style assigned to physical features. To associate the name unequivocally with the river, the

FIG. 4.9 For an elongated physical feature, the label should be elongated and conform to the extent of the feature.

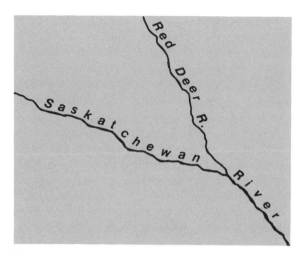

FIG. 4.10 River labels should be thoughtfully placed.

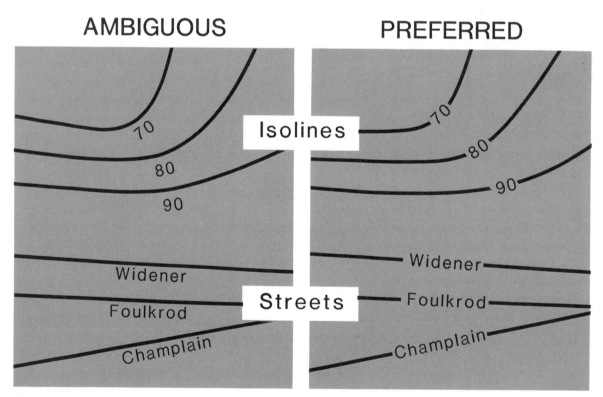

FIG. 4.11 Labels for isarithms or routes should break the lines, especially if the labels for routes are short and do not obscure too much of the routes.

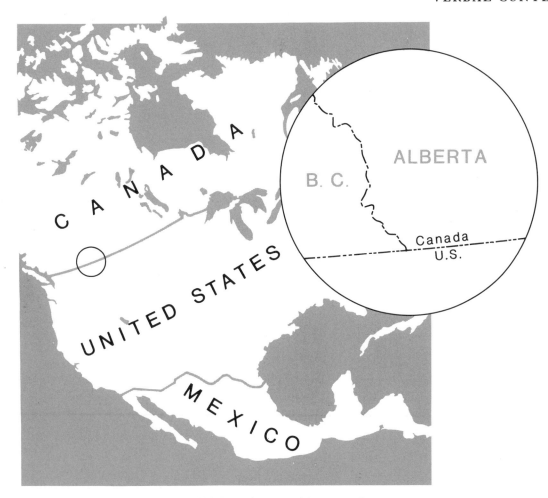

FIG. 4.12 Labelling of political divisions changes with map scale.

label should be contorted to follow its course – ideally in a section that is *not* straight. Thoughtful placement of the labels for main stream and tributary can clarify which of the two *is* the main stream, that is, the one that continues below the junction point (Fig. 4.10).

Certain linear features demand lettering that is placed *within*, rather than alongside the lines. Isolines are a clear case for this technique – as are streets and other routes. Very often, labels placed *along* the feature will appear clumsy and will be associated with the neighboring line rather than the right one.

When the scale of map permits it, a street label should break the street. The same applies to trails and roads; but often a long name will obscure too much of the route and should be replaced by a route symbol which is explained in the legend (Fig. 4.11).

POLITICAL DIVISIONS

When political divisions appear in their entirety their labels will usually be spread across their areas. But when only portions of the divisions appear, the best procedure is to place a label along the boundary to explain its function or status (Fig. 4.12).

LEGENDS

Legends frequently include either a string of symbols to be identified or a series of patches to represent area shadings on the map. With a little care, the items and their labels can be placed so the reader gains information without effort. Without care, the cartographer may present the reader with ambiguity (Fig. 4.13).

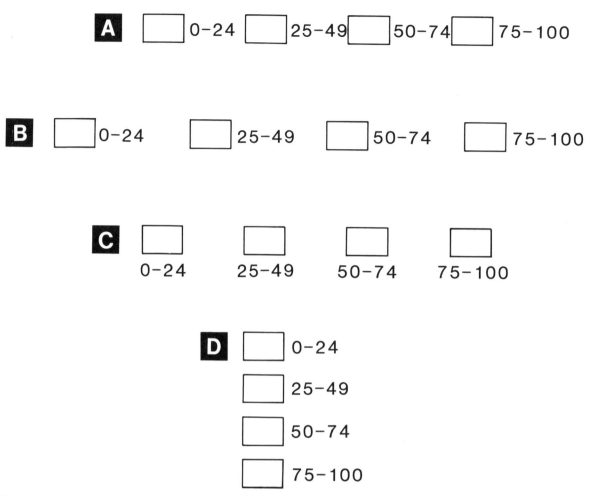

FIG. 4.13 Labels for legend boxes, or any series of items, must be clearly associated with their respective items: Part A, confusing; Part B, improved, but extravagant of space; Part C, improved, and more compact; Part D, best solution, if space permits.

The illustration shows only one case, that of boxes in a legend. The cartographer, however, is continually faced with analogous situations in which map features or legend items need to be identified. The application of *visual logic* will always lead to the best solution within the constraints of the particular map or graph.

Notes

1 These guidelines are taken from Robinson, Sale, and Morrison (1978), p. 328, and are essentially confirmed by testing that shows the minimum difference should be 22 per cent (Shortridge, 1979). Published materials on the subject of lettering legibility have been summarized by Bartz (1970).

2 An exhaustive treatment of lettering placement, with many illustrations of deficient and preferred treatments is provided by Imhof (1974).

References

Bartz, Barbara S. (1970) "An analysis of the typographic legibility literature," *The Cartographic Journal*, 7, 10–16.

Hodgkiss, Alan G. (1970) *Maps for Books and Theses*, Newton Abbot, David & Charles.

Imhof, Eduard (1974) "Positioning names on maps," *The American Cartographer*, 2 (2), 128–44.

Robinson, Arthur H., Randall D. Sale, and Joel L. Morrison (1978) *Elements of Cartography* (4th edn), New York, Wiley.

Shortridge, Barbara G. (1979) "Map reader discrimination of lettering size," *The American Cartographer*, 6 (1), 13–20.

PART TWO
Presentation of the Map

No matter how appropriate the symbolization of data, and how carefully words are chosen and applied, the map will be unsuccessful if its features are too small because of failure to make full use of the space available. At the same time, an illogical arrangement of map elements can detract from the presentation. Both these aspects are dealt with in chapter 5. Although it is discussed here in Part Two, the effective use of space must be planned in the earliest stage of making maps for book or journal illustration – even before the outline of the study area is drawn. For instructional purposes, the matters of symbolization and verbal content *can* be practiced in exercises that do not include careful sizing of the drawing; but it must be recognized that a vital step has been omitted.

A map may be ineffective because it is visually confusing to the reader. There are different reasons for what may be called confusion or clutter in a map, and a great deal can be gained by identifying what causes this lack of clarity. Two major dimensions of the problem are dealt with in chapter 6. Orientation is concerned with making the map understandable as a map – with recognizable places in a recognizable setting. Composition is concerned with avoiding homogeneity (or clutter) and ensuring the all-important *contrasts* that lend clarity as well as beauty to a cartographic work.

5 Use of Space, Layout, and Compilation

Planning for effective use of space

A successful map begins with *layout*, which considers the space in the publication the map is planned for, and also considers effective use of space within the map frame. The two matters are related, but should be dealt with separately.

SPACE AVAILABLE ON THE PUBLICATION PAGE

Whether the map is intended for a graduate thesis, a journal article, or an expensive atlas printed in four colors, the first step is the same – to learn the size of page and the space available on it.

The space available is the space occupied by a block of text that fills a page completely (Fig. 5.1). In fact,

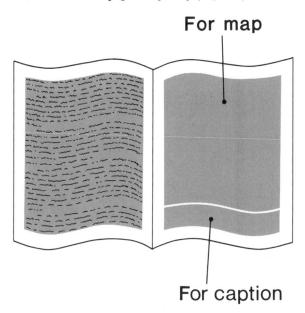

For map

For caption

FIG. 5.1 Maximum space available in the target publication.

what the printer calls the *image area* may be larger than this; but it is best to be conservative. The measurement of space available is important because it reveals the *proportion of length to width* as well as the actual size of the space.

SIZING AND PROPORTIONING THE ART WORK

It is usual to scale-up the art work to a size that is $1\frac{1}{2}$ or 2 times the finished product.[1] There are two distinct reasons for this:
- fine work cannot be drawn easily at the finished size
- the process of reduction to finished size improves the product by reducing small irregularities.

If the map is being planned to fill an entire page, then the first step is to draw a pencilled frame that is roughly $1\frac{1}{2}$ times the dimensions of the available publication space. Note that if a caption is used, rather than a title, space must be reserved for it and the map space diminished accordingly (Fig. 5.1). It is not important that the map frame be scaled-up by some precise ratio. It *is* important that the *proportions* of the frame coincide with the proportions of the available space. Thus, if the available space were 6″ x 9″, the map frame could be 9″ x $13\frac{1}{2}$″ (up to $1\frac{1}{2}$ times) or $10\frac{1}{2}$″ x $15\frac{3}{4}$″ (up $1\frac{3}{4}$ times) or 12″ x 18″ (up 2 times). It is not wise, incidentally, to use art work that is more than 2 times the final product, because it is difficult to forsee the final product; and furthermore, certain lines and patterns may suffer on reduction. Figure 5.2 shows two versions of a scaled-up map frame. In Part A, the frame is proportioned to the available space, and when reduced fits the space perfectly. In Part B, the frame is of the wrong shape, and when reduced does not fill the space effectively. In the second case the map and other elements within the frame probably are more crowded than they need to be.

When the map is to be upright and filling only part

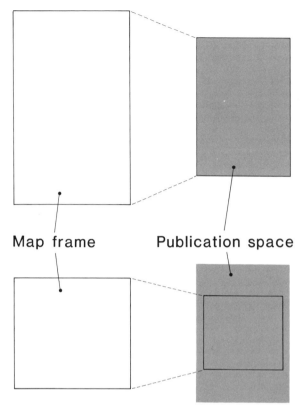

FIG. 5.2 A map frame correctly proportioned for publication space, and one that is not correctly proportioned.

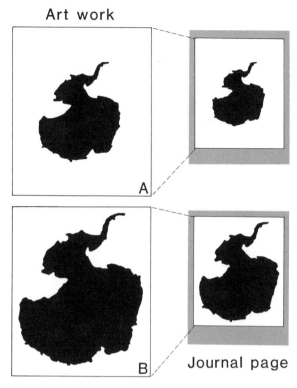

FIG. 5.3 The frame should be filled, as in Part B, to ensure that the map itself is as large as possible.

of the page, then the planning is different, since only one dimension is constrained. It should be decided whether the graphic is simple enough to be shown in only one column or whether it needs two columns or perhaps the whole width of the page. Whatever the final width, the width of art work will be roughly $1\frac{1}{2}$ times that dimension.

Many simple maps, incidentally, can be drawn *at the finished size* – especially if the drawing work is so clean it does not need to be enhanced by reduction. The benefit of working at the finished size is that the product is completely predictable, with no unforseen effects due to reduction.

LAYOUT TO FILL THE MAP FRAME

Sizing and proportioning the map frame must be

followed by planning an economical arrangement of map and other elements within that frame (Fig. 5.3). Part A of the illustration shows a study area that does not fill the frame. If the frame is inked and permanent, the photographer or printer must reduce the art work image *until the frame fits the specified dimensions.* When it does, the map itself is far smaller than necessary.

In Part B, the study area fills the frame more fully and is a generous size when the frame has been reduced. A useful guideline is: "Minimize white space on the art work." Another way to express the same idea is to say the layout should be *compact*. A more compact arrangement can be made to fit the publication space *with less photo-reduction* than an arrangement that is sprawling. This is an important principle that often is overlooked.

Not all maps and graphs must be enclosed within an

inked frame. While a pencilled frame with proportions the same as the available space is recommended for planning the most effective layout, the frame may be omitted from the finished map in order to make a less formal presentation. If the frame is inked, it should be in a simple fine line that does not attract attention.

During the planning, space must be provided for map elements other than the study area. A legend with heading usually is needed, as is a note on the source and date of the mapped data. A graphic scale can be fitted into some small space. If the map is for a slide or overhead projectual, then a title will be essential; but for a published map a caption instead of a title should be considered – especially if there is no natural space in the layout to accommodate a title.

The following points should be considered when working toward a satisfactory layout (see Fig. 5.4):
– make a number of rough layout sketches. Do not be satisfied with the first attempt

– avoid top-heavy or side-heavy arrangements. Strive for a roughly balanced composition (Part A)
– treat the study area itself as an element that can be positioned or skewed so as to make the best use of space (Part B). Skewing the area will frequently allow it to be larger than if a conventional orientation were used
– place the scale in a recessive location
– do not always shrink the study area to create free space at its edges (Part C). Instead, the map may be drawn larger and still offer non-vital areas where title, legend, and other elements can be placed.

Because of the study area's shape, it may be impossible to completely fill the scaled-up rectangle that represents space available in the publication. This rectangle, enclosed by a (pencilled) tentative frame on the work map, will be truncated on the finished drawing so the inked frame does not enclose any obviously non-functional white space.

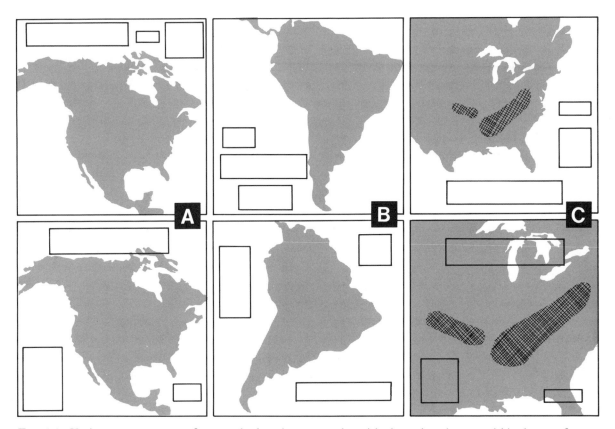

FIG. 5.4   Various arrangements of map and other elements such as title, legend, and notes, within the map frame.

Goodkin

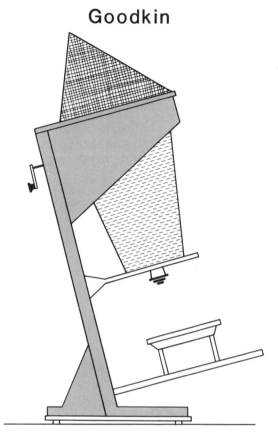

Map-O-Graph

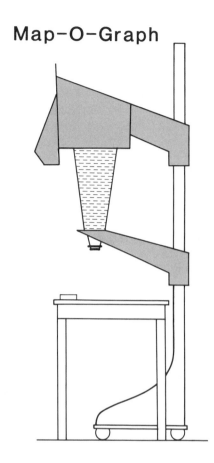

FIG. 5.5 Optical devices for reducing and enlarging.

MAKING THE STUDY AREA FIT THE SPACE

It is conceivable that the study area can be traced from a source map whose dimensions are just right to fill a map frame scaled-up $1\frac{1}{2}$ or 2 times from the finished product. More likely, the source map (see below) must be altered in size until it and other elements will fill the frame. In doing this, it is better to begin with a source map larger than needed and reduce it, rather than enlarging a smaller map.

An optical reducing device of the projector type (Fig. 5.5) is very useful because it throws the map image onto a piece of tracing paper (with tentative map frame) and makes it easy to experiment with map sizes and different arrangements of map, legend, title, and any other elements. As an alternative, a photostat (see chapter 7) can be used to reduce all or part of a source map; but this method lacks the flexibility of working with a projected image. Finally, map features can be transferred from one size to another with the aid of *similar squares* (Fig. 5.6). This method may seem crude, but it can serve well, especially if the source map is very detailed and needs to be simplified.

Base map sources

Those who make topographic maps must carefully compile the images from air photos and fit them to some selected system of parallels and meridians in order to make a map that accurately locates earth features. The thematic cartographer, on the other hand, can select some existing reference map and adapt it to serve as the base for his presentation.

Many base maps can be derived from atlases in the reference section of any college library. World and national atlases are especially valuable, as are atlases

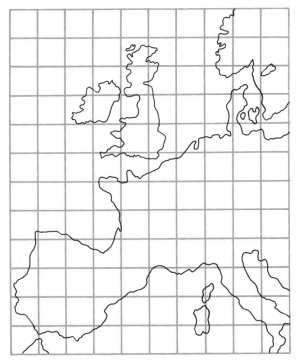

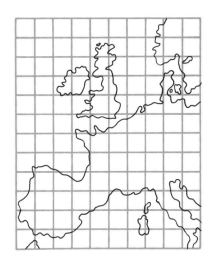

FIG. 5.6 Changing map scale by using similar squares.

devoted to states and provinces. Single maps published by the National Geographic Society, by the American Geographical Society, and by John Bartholomew & Son are excellent for base maps of continents, regions, and countries. Some of the most useful published maps of individual countries are the General Reference Maps drawn by the Central Intelligence Agency and distributed through the US Government Printing Office.

Federal governments are among the best sources of base map materials. The US Government Printing Office sells outline maps showing all the counties (and states) of the United States, and also a set of 50 state outline maps showing counties. Census Canada sells maps of the country and individual provinces, showing census subdivisions. Of course, for large-scale detailed maps of parts of the USA, the US Geological Survey topographic maps are invaluable. Comparable maps for Canada are published by the Department of Energy, Mines and Resources; and in Great Britain topographic maps at various scales are produced by the Ordnance Survey.[2]

In the United States, certain public and university libraries have been selected as federal depositories, and receive at no cost one copy of each of the maps produced by federal agencies. Such libraries are, of course, exceptional sources of maps.

Base maps for large-scale mapping projects can be obtained from county, regional, and city planning commissions, along with thematic maps showing such information as land use. County road maps and county soil maps are often excellent as large-scale bases. City planning commissions can provide base maps that show the Census tract and Census blocks that are essential for mapping the most recent demographic and socio-economic information.

THE MATTER OF COPYRIGHT

Because the thematic cartographer frequently does not create his base map "from scratch" but instead makes use of an existing map, the question of copyright is most relevant. In general, a map – like a musical composition or a book – is protected by copyright to discourage others from copying and benefiting unfairly from the creative work of the author without his permission. The unfair benefit might be realized by copying and publishing a map either for financial gain or for enhanced professional reputation. In the case of maps there are three separate aspects of the problem to be understood.

First is the content to be borrowed. The boundaries and coastlines of a country as they would appear upon a certain projection are "universal" and not subject to copyright. However, a cartographer's rendering of a coastline requires his decisions about generalizing coastal features and is technically his creative effort. If the coastline is drawn in a uniquely stylized fashion that is easily recognized it should certainly not be copied without permission. Similarly, the thematic symbolization a cartographer has devised is a creative effort analogous to a musical composition and is definitely in the sensitive realm.

Second, is the manner in which the original cartographic materials are used. Photographic copying and reproduction of a map is the most blatant violation of copyright. *Redrawing*, especially those parts like coastlines and boundaries, will alter them and is generally acceptable. Redrawing of thematic information such as areas of occurrence or simple symbolization can alter those features enough so that proof of copyright violation may be difficult: there is no need, however, to risk offense and lawsuit in such cases. If it is necessary to redraw map features that represent original creative work, then written permission should be requested. Usually, permission will be granted on the basis of due acknowledgement of the source because publicity is gained for the original work. A fee may be charged, however.

Third, and most important, is the author or publisher of the original map. Maps printed by commercial publishing houses will be copyrighted in the name of the author or the publisher. Maps produced by a United States government agency are *not* copyrighted and are considered to be *in the public domain*. Their base features as well as their symbolization may be redrawn or even photocopied without hesitation for publication anywhere in the world. This is not true for maps produced by other nations, for instance the Ordnance Survey in Great Britain, and so caution is advised.

The choice of map projection

For maps that cover a continent or larger areas of the world, the cartographer must choose a base map that is drawn on an appropriate projection. If the mapped area is small, such as a metropolitan area, or a small state, the choice of projection is of lesser importance.

Fundamentally, map projections are ways of transforming all or parts of the earth's curved surface to the flat surface of a paper map. Practically, they may be regarded as different ways of drawing the earth's graticule of parallels and meridians onto which continent and country outlines are plotted. Because this transformation and plotting has been done for the map reader in countless atlas and textbook maps, it is easy to overlook the significance of this process.

First, the familiar flat map of the world is an extremely useful device. It is not the most faithful representation of the world: that would be a globe. But a globe cannot be carried easily; and it presents only half the earth's surface to view. A world map can show the whole surface at a glance; and it can be large enough to include details and still be quite convenient.

Second, it should be realized that making a map of the whole earth or large parts of it is a rather presumptuous undertaking because the surface of a sphere cannot be flattened without distorting it considerably. Different projections for world maps are attempts to accomplish this feat with minimal distortion and with distortions that are clearly defined. Since earth curvature is at the root of all projection distortion, it can be seen readily that maps of small areas such as cities do not require careful choice of projection because they cover so little of the earth's curved surface. Furthermore, the cartographer seeking base maps for such small areas will not be faced with numerous projections to choose from. It is for world and continental maps that the selection of map projection is important. Coincidentally, the base maps available are on a great number of different projections; so the choice of map projections is a real, not hypothetical problem.

The choice of projection must be made with due regard for two considerations:
– the map theme may demand that the base map have certain characteristics. This is the more important of the two
– the ease of drawing the map projection. It is

assumed here that thematic cartographers need not develop and draw the map projection from a knowledge of earth geometry. Nevertheless, the graticule lines usually appear on maps of world or continental scale and must, therefore, be drawn. On some projections the graticule has shapes that can be drawn with compass and straight edge. On others the forms are more complex, and require the use of special curves.

BASE MAP CHARACTERISTICS

The characteristics that may be desired in a base map are essentially four. These are reviewed below, and also appear in a later tabulation of map projections.

EQUIDISTANCE

This implies uniformity of map scale (see later section for more information on map scales). No projection of a large area is without some scale change because flattening of earth curvature will cause more stretching of the surface in some areas than in others. Nevertheless, some projections have uniform scales *in certain directions*. On some, for instance, the map scale may be constant along selected parallels of latitude. On others the scale may be constant along all meridians, that is, scale in the north–south direction is the same everywhere on the map. This latter characteristic is desirable on climatic maps to show readily that certain locations are farther poleward while others are more equatorial. On maps for air routes or seismological studies it is desirable to show true distances *in all directions* from a given point. A projection exists for that purpose, as well.

PRESERVATION OF BEARINGS, OR AZIMUTHS

For maps used in airport operations or radio broadcasting it is best if compass directions (azimuths) are correct from a certain point. Ideally, scale would also be constant in any direction from that central point. The projections called *azimuthal* do provide correct bearings from a point; and a specific version of the azimuthal will also provide for constant scale in any direction. If the purpose of the map is navigation on a world scale, then it would be useful for the map to show true compass bearings anywhere on the map.

PRESERVATION OF AREAS

Despite the inevitable distortions that occur in transforming the earth's surface to a flat page, it is possible to maintain the relative areas of earth features. Base maps with this *equal-area* property are desirable for many map themes and are essential for a dot-distribution map. Fortunately, a number of equal-area projections do exist for continental and world-scale maps. These projections maintain area relationships at the cost of some distortion of shapes. A circle on the globe would appear as an ellipse on an equal-area map, with its axes in such proportions that the circle's area is maintained (Fig. 5.7).

PRESERVATION OF SHAPE, IN CONFORMAL PROJECTIONS

If the shapes of all global features were preserved on a map, then the map would not distort the earth at all; and that of course is impossible. What is possible is the preservation of shapes of very small areas. Projections that accomplish this have no *angular* deformation, and are said to be *conformal*. As an illustration of the property, a small circle on the globe would appear as a circle on the conformal map. Another way of defining conformality is to state that map scale is uniform in all directions around any given point. It is because of this

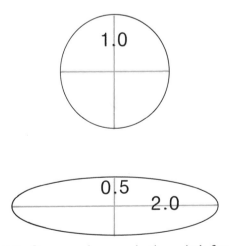

FIG. 5.7   On an equal-area projection a circle from the globe becomes an ellipse on the map with its axes so proportioned that the area of ellipse equals that of the global circle. From McDonnell (1979).

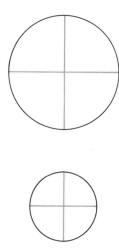

FIG. 5.8 On a conformal projection, a small circle from the globe is shown as a circle on the map. In most parts of the map the size of circle will be different from that on the globe. From McDonnell (1979).

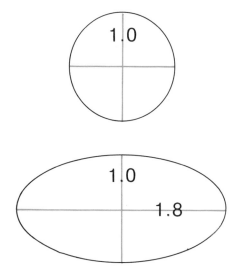

FIG. 5.9 On a projection that is neither equal-area nor conformal, a circle from the globe will become a non-circular ellipse of different area. From McDonnell (1979).

that the shape of a very small area escapes distortion (Fig. 5.8).

This characteristic of conformality is needed in maps used as the basis for plane coordinate systems used in surveying because observations measured at various angles from any point can be plotted accurately. For navigation maps, such as aeronautical charts, conformality is needed so that course directions can be plotted accurately. In one special case of conformal projection, the one called Mercator's, any straight line drawn on the map to join two points will indicate the true compass bearing of the route between those points. Thus, because of the conformality characteristic this map has correct bearings not only from a central point (as in the azimuthals) but between any two points on the map.

Conformality is accomplished at the cost of *distorting areas*. Because of this it is not true to say that a conformal map preserves shapes, because this does not apply to large areas. The conformal map may alter the area more in one part of a continent than in another, thus distorting the shape of the continent. This sacrifice of the equal-area characteristic for the sake of conformality is the counterpart of distorting shapes for the sake of equality of areas. It is impossible on any one projection to preserve both conformality and area

relationships, though some projections that are neither equal-area nor conformal have only moderate distortions of areas and shapes (Fig. 5.9).

THE GRATICULE AS AN INDICATION OF PROJECTION CHARACTER

A carefully constructed globe may be considered the ideal scaled-down representation of the earth and its features. Only the scale of the real world has been altered. Map projection may be regarded as the next step in which the scaled-down global surface is transformed to a flat surface. The graticule, or reference system of parallels and meridians, is drawn on the map, and the outlines of continents and countries are fitted to that graticule. Comparing the map's graticule with that of the globe can be a very useful way of understanding the characteristics of any projection used for world or continental maps.

The global graticule has the following features (see Fig. 5.10):

- parallels are not only parallel, but they also define the east–west direction on the globe
- parallels are equally spaced along any meridian[3]
- the length, or circumference, of parallel circles is greatest at the equator and diminishes to zero at

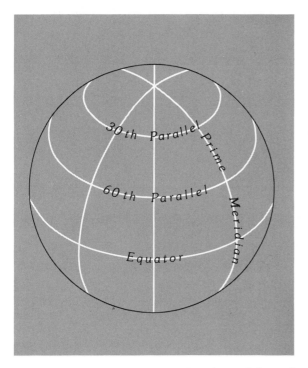

FIG. 5.10 The global graticule of parallels and meridians.

either pole. The parallel whose length is half that of the equator is the 60th, not the 45th

- meridians run due north–south, are most widely spaced at the equator, and converge to meet at either pole
- parallels and meridians intersect at right angles, if the earth's curvature at intersection points is ignored.

These characteristics, so commonplace on the global graticule, cannot all be present in any map of the world or large portions of it. Two very different projections illustrate the point (Fig. 5.11). In Part A, the projection is Mercator's, often used for plotting wind directions. On the map, the parallels and meridians meet at right angles so that the compass directions of wind arrows appear on the map as they would on the globe. Those right-angle intersections, however, are possible only because the meridians fail to converge. That introduces, of course, a pronounced east–west stretching of land masses which in the real world exist on meridians that do converge. The

east–west stretching is deliberately offset by progressively greater spacing of parallels in higher latitudes in order to preserve shapes. Altogether there is great enlargement of high latitude areas, both land and water, making this projection most unsuitable for any map in which relative areas of countries is important.

In Part B of Figure 5.11 is a world projection of the Mollweide type. On it, parallels are parallel, but meridians and parallels do not meet at right angles. The reader will correctly infer this map is not conformal since right-angle intersections are essential for that property. It is, in fact, an equal-area projection in which conformality is deliberately sacrificed.

Figure 5.12 shows the relevance of projection choice in thematic mapping. In Part A, two countries are drawn as they appear on Mercator's projection. The population in Scandinavia appears very sparse when compared to that of Borneo. In Part B the two countries are as they appear on an equal-area Homolosine projection; and in that case the density of population seems roughly the same in the two countries.

DIFFERENT CLASSES OF MAP PROJECTION

The classic approach to map projections is to assume the optical projection of the global graticule onto some convenient surface. This projection can be done literally, by the use of a light source and a transparent globe whose graticule shadows are cast onto a sheet of paper. Or, the projection can be just imagined with the aid of sketches (Fig. 5.13).

ZENITHAL, OR AZIMUTHAL, PROJECTIONS

These assume the graticule is projected onto a plane surface which touches the globe at one point. As the name suggests, all projections in this class preserve correct bearings or azimuths from the central point. The most familiar zenithal projections are those centered on the North or South Pole. These projections, though, may be centered on any point for themes such as air routes or broadcasting.

If the light source is imagined to be at certain points within or beyond the globe, then certain specific characteristics can be attained in the map. This idea is applied in the stereographic, the orthographic, and the gnomonic types of azimuthals, all of which are referred to as *perspective* types because they depend on

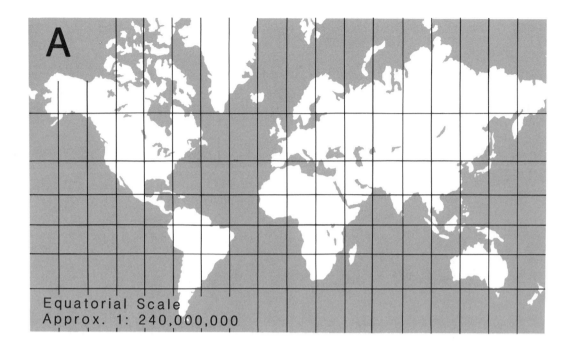

Equatorial Scale
Approx. 1: 240,000,000

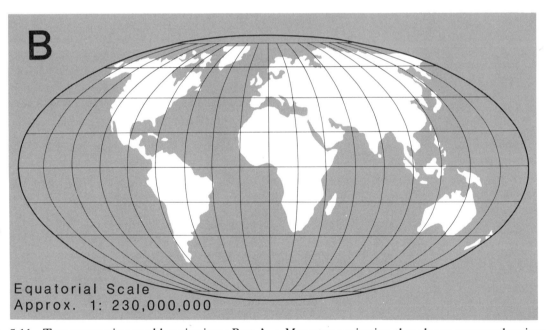

Equatorial Scale
Approx. 1: 230,000,000

FIG. 5.11 Two contrasting world projections: Part A, a Mercator projection that shows compass bearings as straight lines; Part B, a Mollweide projection which has the equal-area property, but distorts shapes and compass bearings.

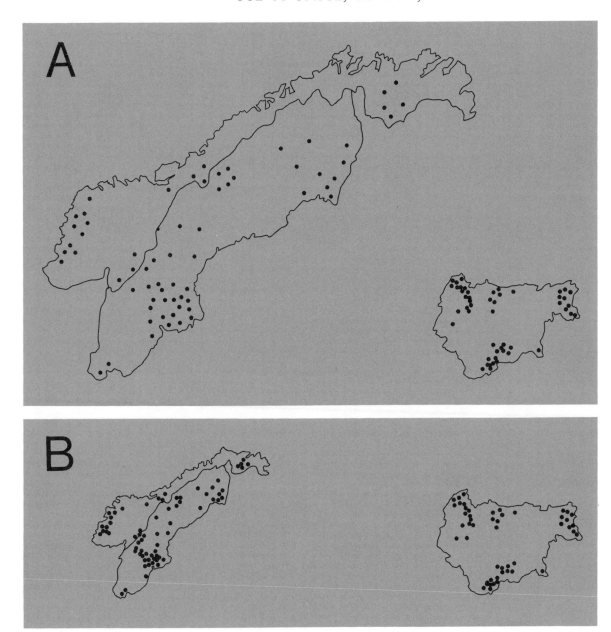

FIG. 5.12 Hypothetical dot-distribution maps on two projections: Part A, because of enlargement of high-latitude areas, the density appears low in Scandinavian countries; Part B, when an equal-area projection is used, the density appears the same in Scandinavia and Borneo.

an imaginary light source at some specified position. Equally important are the non-perspective azimuthals in which the map graticule is adjusted to make the projection equidistant along meridians or to make it an equal-area projection.

CONIC PROJECTIONS

These assume the graticule is projected onto a conical sheet of paper which either rests on the globe, touching it at one parallel, or slices through the globe and

ZENITHAL

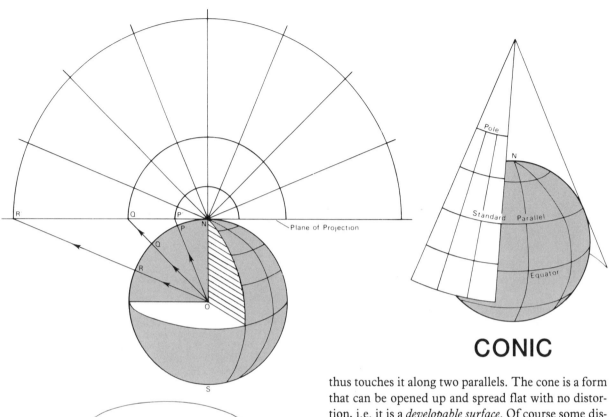

CONIC

CYLINDRICAL

FIG. 5.13 The origins of azimuthal, cylindrical, and conic classes of projection. From Lawrence (1979).

thus touches it along two parallels. The cone is a form that can be opened up and spread flat with no distortion, i.e. it is a *developable surface*. Of course some distortion occurs in the process of transferring the graticule to the sheet of paper. Because the cone is imagined to touch the globe at one or more *standard parallels*, the scale along those parallels is constant and is true to the global scale.

A number of conic-style projections can be drawn by modifications that stray from the strictly perspective derivation. There are, for instance, Alber's equal-area conical, and the Lambert conformal conic – each devised for the special purpose revealed in its name. As well, there are some pseudo-conical projections such as the Polyconic, Bonne's, and the Sinusoidal – all of which are drawn to maintain or to approximate the equal-area characteristic.

CYLINDRICAL PROJECTIONS

These are based on the idea that the graticule is projected onto a cylindrical sheet of paper that encloses the globe and touches it along some line such as the

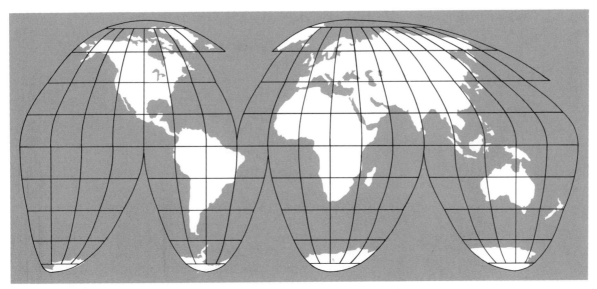

FIG. 5.14   The interrupted Homolosine projection. Coherence of the map is sacrificed for the sake of reduced
distortion in continental areas.

equator. In fact, many projections of the cylindrical style do not depend on any specific process of projecting the graticule but are drawn according to mathematical logic in order to preserve some desirable map characteristic. For instance, an equal-area cylindrical can be made; and the famous Mercator's projection is drawn to be conformal by adjusting the graticule with that purpose in mind.

OTHER PROJECTIONS

A number of projections devised to represent the whole world do not follow the models of either azimuthal, conical, or cylindrical. These are sometimes called *conventional* projections (Steers, 1962, p. 159). Among these are Hammer's equal-area, the Mollweide equal-area, and Eckert's projection.

An interesting group of projections is the interrupted type (Fig. 5.14) in which the quest for a coherent flat map of the earth's curved surface has been abandoned in favor of maps that represent a torn surface. Sacrificing ocean areas this way allows continental areas to be drawn with reduced distortion.

A GUIDE TO THE BETTER-KNOWN PROJECTIONS

The cartographer who wishes to select a projection for a certain continent and for a particular purpose needs a listing that anticipates those needs. The following tabulation (Table 5.1) is based on two most useful books on the subject (Steers, 1962, p. 225; and McDonnell, 1979, pp. 21–77). On the other hand, the cartographer may encounter a named projection in some book or atlas and need some assurance that it has the appropriate characteristics for the thematic map he has in mind. The projection and its characteristics can both be found by scanning the tabulation.

Compiling and generalization

After a source map of suitable area coverage and suitable projection has been found, map features must be selected by the cartographer and drawn in a manner that suits the purpose of his thematic map.

FEATURES OF THE BASE MAP

Selection of base features is important. The goal must be to include all features that are relevant to the theme and to exclude those features that are not. If the map theme deals with fur trade and explorers' routes, then drainage features are vital – and indeed would be unavoidable. But, if the theme is the size of religious congregations or the diffusion and spread of hot tubs, then river systems should not be drawn – even though

TABLE 5.1 Selected map projections arranged according to application and characteristics

A. *According to application* (taken largely from Steers, 1962, pp. 222–5)

Application	Characteristics	Suitable projections
Maps of the world in single sheet	Equal-area Conformal Generally useful	Sinusoidal, Mollweide, Hammer, Eumorphic Mercator's Gall's Stereographic, Van der Grinten's, Winkel's, and Eckert's
Maps of the world in hemispheres	Equal-area Conformal Generally useful	Azimuthal equal-area (Lambert's), Mollweide Azimuthal stereographic Azimuthal equidistant
Continental maps		
1. Asia and North America	Equal-area Generally useful	Azimuthal equal-area (Lambert's), Bonne Azimuthal equidistant
2. Europe or Australia	Equal-area Generally useful	Azimuthal equal-area (Lambert's), Bonne, Alber's conic equal-area with two standard parallels Simple conic with two standard parallels
3. Africa or South America or countries near the equator	Equal-area Generally useful	Azimuthal equal-area (Lambert's), Sinusoidal, Mollweide, Hammer Azimuthal equidistant, Mercator's (equatorial case)
4. Many continents	Conformal	Transverse Mercator
Polar regions	Equal-area Equidistant	Azimuthal equal-area (Lambert's) Azimuthal equidistant
Large countries in middle latitudes such as USA, USSR, China	Equal-area Generally useful	Azimuthal equal-area, Conic equal-area, Alber's conic equal-area with two standard parallels, Bonne Simple conic with two standard parallels, conical conformal with one or two standard parallels
Small countries in middle latitudes	Equal-area Generally useful	Conic equal-area with one standard parallel, Alber's, Bonne Simple conic with one or two standard parallels
For world and hemispheric navigation		Mercator's (compass bearings indicated by straight lines drawn on map), Azimuthal Gnomonic (shows great circle routes as straight lines)

B. *According to characteristics* (taken from McDonnell, 1979, pp. 21–117)

Characteristics	Projections and applications
Equidistant projections with one standard parallel. These all have constant scale in north–south direction because parallels are equally spaced as on the globe. Scale in the east–west direction is constant along only the standard parallel	*Cylindrical equidistant, Conic equidistant, Azimuthal equidistant*
Equidistant projections with two standard parallels	*Cylindrical equidistant with two standard parallels, Conic equidistant with two standard parallels*
Equal-area projections with straight meridians (easy to draw)	*Cylindrical equal-area* *Alber's projection.* Used throughout the *National Atlas of the United States.* Is not far from being conformal within the boundaries of the country *Azimuthal equal-area* (polar case)
Projections with all parallels standard. Scale is uniform along parallels	*Sinusoidal.* For whole-world equal-area maps or for regions extending on both sides of the equator *Bonne.* For equal-area maps of regions that are roughly square and well-removed from the equator (such as France). The *Times Atlas of the World* uses Bonne for Australia and New Zealand and for Europe *Polyconic.* Used for many years for the 1:24,000 scale topographic maps of the US Geological Survey. While it is neither equal-area nor conformal, it is, in its central portions, virtually equal-area in character. It is used by the National Geographic Society for the British Isles and for Japan. Rand-McNally & Co. use it for India, Indonesia and the Philippines, China, and Alaska *Azimuthal orthographic.* These have a globe-like appearance, especially in the oblique views (not polar or equatorial) that suggest an astronaut's view of earth
Conformal projections with straight meridians (easy to draw)	*Mercator's* *Conic conformal* (Lambert's). Used widely for atlas maps, for aeronautical charts, and for plane coordinate systems in surveying *Azimuthal sterographic, polar case*

they are on the source map that came to hand. For many themes it is important to include enough cities, towns, and political boundaries so the reader can relate the map's thematic material to the real world. For a theme such as resource amounts by state for the whole USA, a base map showing only state boundaries is appropriate. But if the theme is flow of migrants from region to region, then major cities in the destination areas become relevant and helpful.

Related to the selection of base features is the need to provide a recognizable "setting" for the study area. This important matter is discussed separately in chapter 6.

APPROPRIATE DETAIL IN BASE MAP FEATURES

The source map should always be larger than the base being compiled and should be reduced to fit the framed space. If, instead, a small map is enlarged, its features − which are necessarily very general − appear as coarse thick lines. Careful tracing along the edge of such thick lines with a fine pen will make a map that looks accurate but depends upon inaccurate features (Fig. 5.15).

When following the preferred procedure of tracing features from a reduced source map, some care must be taken not to introduce false details, and at the same time, not to preserve *all* the subtle features. Because the cartographer's art work will itself be reduced, the work must not be too fine and detailed. Carefully drawn inlets on a complex coastline can merge on the reduced map product to give an odd effect dismaying to the reader and to the person who drew so meticulously (Fig. 5.16). The solution is to *generalize* complex map features to an extent that is consistent with the map's purpose. If the full details of some portion of a coastline are important, then a blow-up map large enough to preserve those features faithfully would be a good idea.

Generalization of a base map is necessary, as shown above, to avoid the merging of features when they are photo-reduced. Furthermore, it is most appropriate to generalize the base for a *thematic* map, because its purpose is to convey a distribution, not to serve as a reference for coastline and boundary details. The method of generalization depends on whether the base map is in digital, i.e. machine-readable, form or exists instead as a conventional map image on paper. The degree of generalization depends upon the scale of the map being drawn and its intended purpose and style.

MACHINE-READABLE BASE MAPS VERSUS CONVENTIONAL

Modern maps made with the aid of computers depend upon map bases whose lines are defined by strings of points joined by very short line segments (see chapter 9). Generalization of a coastline defined this way can be accomplished by systematically eliminating a certain proportion of the points or, as an alternative, eliminating every second point (Fig. 5.17A). The rationale can be clearly defined, and thus make the "level" of generalization not only understandable but repeatable. The same treatment can be applied to a number of different map areas in order to render them all with the same degree of simplification.[4]

If, on the other hand, the base map is not in machine-readable form, the generalization must be done in a more subjective fashion. The process will vary from cartographer to cartographer and will be difficult to define. It has the advantage, however, of keeping in sight those map characteristics that make an area recognizable and distinctive.

THE AUTHENTIC VERSUS THE STYLIZED BASE MAP

For most maps, the need is for a base that has not lost its distinctive character in the process of simplification. Particularly for map themes that are literal and down-to-earth, an authentic base is essential: dot maps showing human or livestock populations, for instance, or maps of soil types or agricultural zones, must reveal how those occurrences relate to real-world features. Even if the map theme is more abstract and represented by symbols applied to data units such as counties, an authentic base map will be pleasing.

Three separate drawings of Ireland show one cartographer's approach to generalizing a base map while retaining authenticity (Fig. 5.17B).
- the deeply indented and complex southwestern coast is preserved, as is the smooth eastern coast
- major lakes are retained, even on the smallest of the three drawings
- distinctive features, such as the hooked promontory in the northeast, are retained.

If the map theme is abstract and demands no

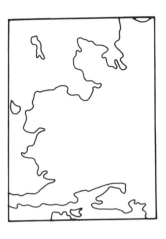

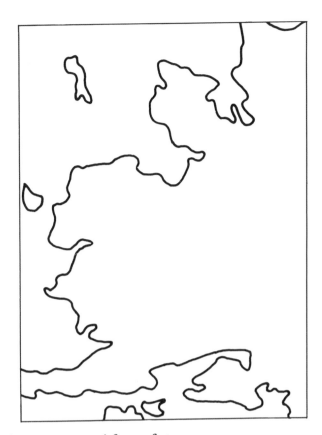

FIG. 5.15 Enlarging a small-scale source map leads to coarse, unsatisfactory features.

FIG. 5.16 Art work features that are too detailed will merge in the process of reduction. Generalization is needed.

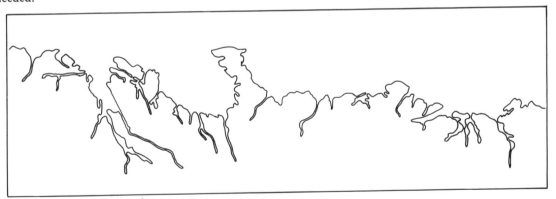

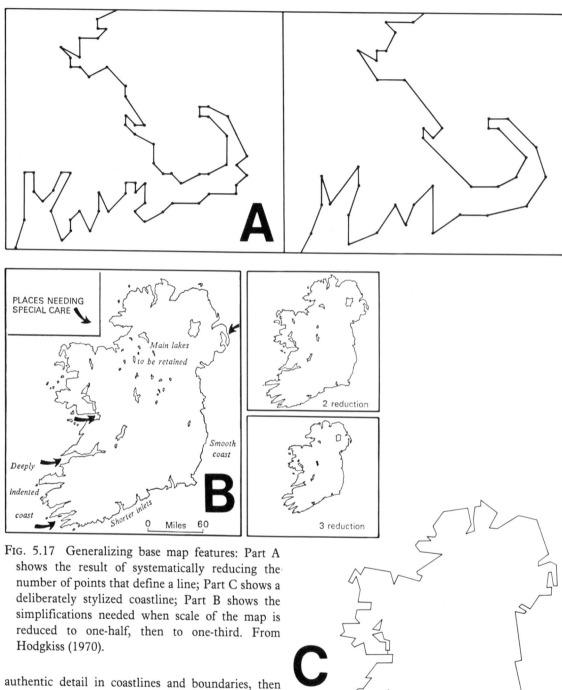

FIG. 5.17 Generalizing base map features: Part A shows the result of systematically reducing the number of points that define a line; Part C shows a deliberately stylized coastline; Part B shows the simplifications needed when scale of the map is reduced to one-half, then to one-third. From Hodgkiss (1970).

authentic detail in coastlines and boundaries, then base features may be generalized in the extreme by making a stylized outline that is obviously an approximation and has a "chiseled" look owing to its straight-line segments (Fig. 5.17C). This should be done only if the subject area is quite familiar to the reader. Within North America, for instance, either Canada or the United States could be treated this way for the sake of a dramatic illustration in the journalistic tradition.

What should be avoided in generalizing is a base map that is neither stylized nor authentic. A coastline that is simply a careless tracing will appear obviously so, and will detract from the map.

The matter of scale

Map scale is a statement of how distance on the map relates to distance on the ground, i.e. the extent to which reality has been reduced by the map. It is important to realize that the scale is usually not constant across a map. On a perfectly made globe, the scale *is* constant everywhere and in every direction: any given distance, such as an inch, will cover the same number of miles no matter where that inch is applied to the globe's surface. On a world map the inevitable distortions that occur in transforming the sphere to flat paper cause significant scale changes across the map. On Figure 5.11A, for instance, the scale at the equator is 1:240,000,000. At the 60th parallel, however, the scale is twice that, because that parallel circle is in reality only half the length of the equator, but is shown to be the same length. The scale of a world map should not be stated without noting where in the map that scale applies, the equatorial scale being the usual choice.

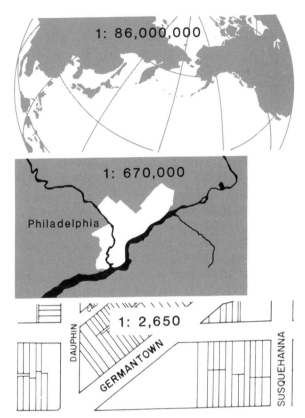

FIG. 5.19 Examples of small-, intermediate-, and large-scale maps, with their representative fractions.

EXPRESSIONS OF MAP SCALE

There are three common expressions of scale: verbal, representative fraction (RF), and graphic. The first expression is exemplified by "one inch (on map) represents one mile." The representative fraction (or RF) may be derived by first stating both sides of the expression in inches, thus one inch = 5280 x 12 or 63,360 inches. Then the units are dropped, and the representative fraction remains, as 1/63,360, or 1:63,360. Because it is stated without units, the fraction is universal and serves equally well the map reader who thinks in miles and the one who thinks in kilometers. A graphic scale is a line on which convenient ground distances are shown, as in Figure 5.18.

The terms, *large scale* and *small scale*, which may be used loosely in conversation, have very specific meaning in cartography. Large-scale maps are those on which features are large, as on a street plan or map of some part of a city. Small-scale maps are those in

FOR THEMATIC MAPS

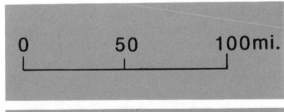

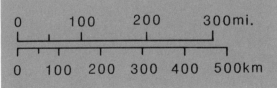

FOR REFERENCE MAPS

FIG. 5.18 Graphic, or linear, expressions of map scale.

which features are small (but large areas are covered) such as a map of a continent, a hemisphere, or the world. To reinforce the terms and to avoid confusion it is helpful to realize that for a large-scale map the RF may be 1:62,500, which is much *larger* as an arithmetic entity than the fraction 1:1,000,000 that applies to a small-scale map (Fig. 5.19).

It is not clear which map scales should be labelled as small, and which should be called large. An atlas map of the world may represent the entire length of the equator by only 12 inches of page. In that case, a foot represents roughly 25,000 (miles) x 5280 (feet per mile), or roughly 135,000,000 feet. A map with a scale of 1:135,000,000 certainly is a small-scale map. On a topographic map, one foot may represent less than 5 miles, for a scale of 1:24,000. That certainly is a large-scale map. The dividing line between small- and large-scale maps sometimes is put at 1:1,000,000. This would place most atlas and book maps in the small-scale group, along with smaller reference maps that cover entire continents. Topographic maps, county road maps, and the like, would be considered large-scale. It is more useful to make a three-way grouping that defines large-scale maps as those with scales larger than 1:250,000 (4 miles to the inch), small-scale maps as those with scales smaller than 1:1,000,000 (16 miles to the inch) and intermediate scale maps as those with scales between those limits (Muehrcke, 1978, p. 171).

THE SCALE AS IT APPEARS ON THEMATIC MAPS

There are two reasons to discuss the apparently simple matter of how the cartographer shows the scale of the map he is producing: first is ensuring an accurate statement of map scale; and second is the matter of the scale's visual prominence in the composition.

AN ACCURATE STATEMENT OF SCALE

The fact that scale changes across a small-scale map because of projection distortion has already been recognized. Another error can result from the fact that the cartographer's art work is *reduced* before photo print or printing plate is made. Obviously, if the art work states "one inch equals one mile" and is then reduced to half its size, the verbal statement of scale will be unchanged, while the map scale itself has been changed drastically. The Representative Fraction,

despite its unitless universality, is subject to the same error because it is nothing more than a restatement of the verbal expression. If either of these two expressions is to be used it must not refer to the art work scale but to the scale of the finished (usually reduced) product. On topographic maps such expressions are used, but instead of being part of the graphic work itself they are printed beyond the map frame and thus are unaffected by any reduction that has taken place.

On simple thematic maps for reproduction in journals and textbooks, it is usual to note map scale directly on the art work so the piece is self-contained once it leaves the draftsman's table. For this purpose the graphic scale is the best and *only* safe scale expression (Fig. 5.20). It is clear that the length of bar that represents some distance will shrink or grow as the map is reduced or enlarged, and will never be deceiving.

THE NEED FOR A PROMINENT EXPRESSION OF SCALE

Rarely does a thematic map deal with a subject in which distance itself is an important factor. When it *is* vital to the theme, then a graphic scale of adequate length and convenient subdivisions, such as those on road maps, should be provided. More often, the scale serves only for perspective to aid in the reader's orientation. If the study area is a small part of some obscure area, with no recognizable landmarks for the reader, then a graphic scale will be valuable. It should, however, be *simple and unobtrusive*.

There is a tendency among inexperienced cartographers to overdo the map scale, both in style and in frequency. Figure 5.21 shows what may be called *scale worship*, in which the scale is more bold and interesting than need be (diverting attention from the map theme) and appears for good measure on each of the small maps. Incidentally, an elegant north arrow is drawn doggedly on each map, although it is obvious that orientation does not change.

THE IMPACT OF SCALE UPON MAP FIDELITY

Maps of smaller scales are drawn with a very significant handicap: the map is so small that the cartographic marks and symbols occupy far more space than they should if the map were truly accurate.

Consider a very large-scale plan of a room. Rectangles for tables, chairs, and benches can be drawn

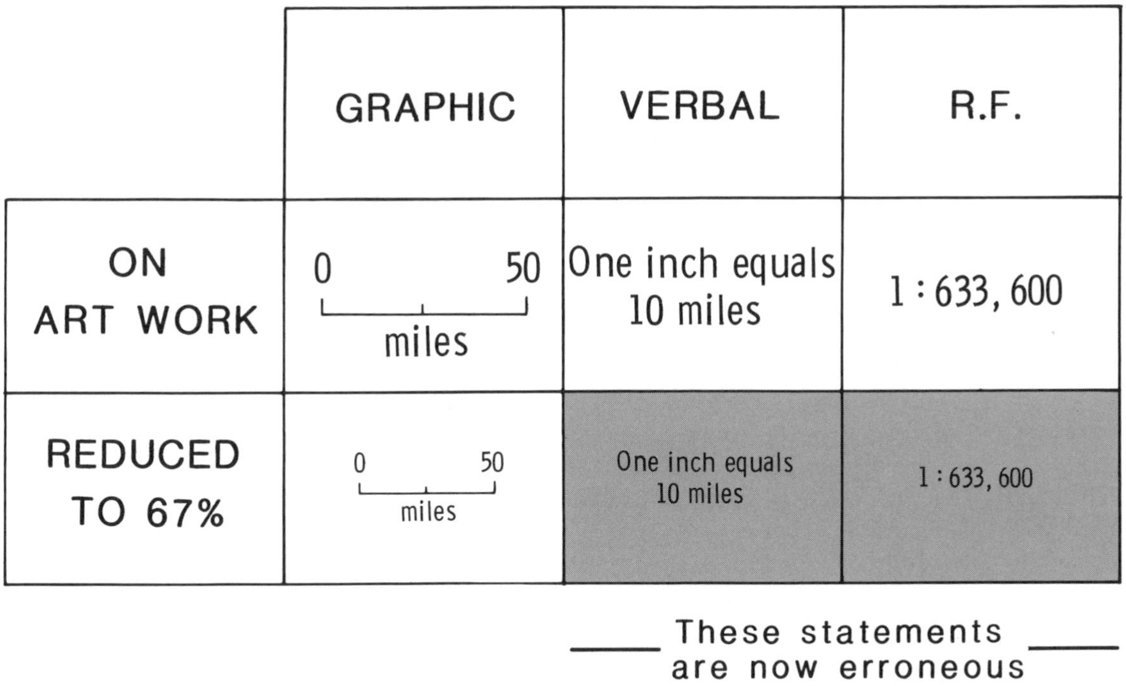

GRAPHIC
VERBAL
R.F.
ON
ART WORK
0 50
miles
One inch equals
10 miles
1 : 633, 600
REDUCED
TO 67%
0 50
miles
One inch equals
10 miles
1 : 633, 600
These statements
are now erroneous

FIG. 5.20 Only the graphic expression of map scale will remain accurate after photo-reduction.

FIG. 5.21 An example of graphic scale and north arrow that are far too bold and complex for their purposes.

Scale
0 300 600
Miles
N
0 300 600
Miles
N
Scale
0 300 600
Miles
N

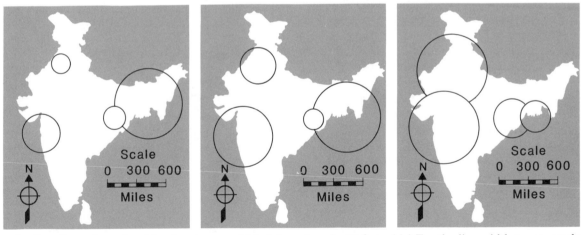

quite literally to the scale of the drawing on which 0.2 inches may represent one foot. All furniture and features can be shown easily so that various room arrangements can be visualized without any distortion.

On the other hand, consider a map with scale 1:250,000 (roughly, 1″ = 4 miles). To represent a road, the cartographer may draw a line of width 0.02 inches. At the scale of the map, that line corresponds to 0.02 x 4 miles, or 410 feet; but the road in actuality is only 40 feet wide! For the line width to accurately represent the road, the map scale would have to be 10 times greater, or 1:25,000, which is roughly that of the largest-scale topographic maps produced by the US Geological Survey.

On maps of small scale it is inevitable that map symbols will occupy more earth space than is appropriate. This may make it impossible to include all the features the cartographer would like to show. The problem is most often encountered when making topographic and reference maps whose purpose is to show earth features or a wealth of detail. In thematic mapping the limitation of scale is felt when the cartographer attempts to include a number of settlements as reference points. He may find there is space for very few such places if symbols for thematic material are given priority.

THE APPEARANCE OF LARGE- AND SMALL-SCALE MAPS

Map scale is indicated by using one or more of the *expressions of map scale* mentioned above. In addition, it may be argued that the cartographer should incorporate certain cues to indicate to the reader that a map is of a certain scale. The idea is that a reader should *not* have to seek the scale expression in order to get the impression that the map in question is markedly large or markedly small in scale. This goal is akin to the idea that if map symbolization is well-designed, then the reader may not have to refer to the legend, but can get the right general impression from the map itself.

The subject was explored in a provocative study by Arthur Robinson (1965) and pursued more recently in an experiment at Boston University (Eastman, 1981). That experiment suggests that if a map has *larger* lettering for place-names that are *less crowded*, the map is perceived to be of *larger scale*. Specifically, such maps were judged by readers to cover *less territory* than a certain map used as a standard. This suggests it is quite feasible to lend individual maps the "look" of either larger or smaller scale, so a map reader will be made aware immediately (and subliminally) that a change in scale has occurred in the map series he is using. The idea is especially interesting because the general and conventional practice is to choose lettering size with due regard for anticipated reduction so that lettering will appear more or less *the same on every map*!

★   ★   ★

Most, or all, of the work reviewed in this chapter pertains to planning and assembling map elements on the *work map* (symbols that represent thematic material must also be considered in planning, because in some cases the symbols will demand space that goes beyond the limits of the study area itself). The *finished art work* will usually be drawn on a fresh sheet of tracing paper laid over the work map: it is at this stage that decisions are made regarding visual emphasis and composition, which are discussed in the next chapter.

Notes

1 This ratio always refers to linear dimensions, not areal. If the art work is 2x the finished product, then it is said to require 50% reduction. To avoid any possible confusion, it is best to note (on the edge of the art work) what the final dimensions are to be.

2 For map sources in the United States, the summaries provided by Muehrcke (1978) and by Thompson (1979) are unsurpassed. For maps and reference information pertaining to Great Britain, the review by Hodgkiss (1970) is essential. For information and catalogues dealing with government maps in the United States, write to the Superintendent of Documents, US Government Printing Office, Washington, DC, 20402; and the National Cartographic Information Center, US Geological Survey, 507 National Center, Reston, Virginia.

3 This assumes the earth is perfectly spherical. In fact, the distance between parallels is slightly greater in high latitudes than in low ones.

4 Fundamental to this simplification process is the original work that translated a conventional map image into digital form: the scale of that original map and the density of points used to define its lines are most relevant to the accuracy of the simplified map.

References

Eastman, J. Ronald (1981) "The perception of scale change in small-scale map series," *The American Cartographer*, 8 (1), 5–21.

Hodgkiss, Alan G. (1970) *Maps for Books and Theses*, Newton Abbot, David & Charles.

Lawrence, G. R. P. (1979) *Cartographic Methods*, London, Methuen.

McDonnell, Porter W. (1979) *Introduction to Map Projections*, New York, Marcel Dekker.

Monmonier, Mark S. (1977) *Maps, Distortion, and Meaning*, Washington, DC, Association of American Geographers.

Muehrcke, Phillip C. (1978) *Map Use: Reading, Analysis, and Interpretation*, Madison, Wisconsin, J. P. Publications.

Robinson, Arthur H., "Designing maps for scale: a report," unpublished report for the advisory board of the World Book Atlas, University of Wisconsin, Madison. [For a summary of this report, see Eastman, 1981.]

Steers, J. A. (1965) *An Introduction to the Study of Map Projections*, London, University of London Press.

Thompson, Morris M. (1979) *Maps for America: Cartographic Products of the US Geological Survey and Others*, Washington, DC, US Government Printing Office.

6 Orientation and Composition

A map with appropriate symbolization, thoughtful lettering, and economical use of space may still be ineffective because it confronts the reader with visual puzzles and is therefore difficult to read. Two aspects of this question may be distinguished, though they are not entirely separate. One is the *locational puzzle*, which may be characterized by the reader's question, "Where is it?"; and the other is the *homogeneity puzzle*, characterized by the questions, "What is it?" or, "Where shall I look first?" These two puzzles may not be explicitly recognized by the map reader; they may be evident only in his failure to obtain the map message quickly, or in his decision to pass by the map completely because it does not appear attractive and readable. It is productive though, for the cartographer to anticipate both these *potential* puzzles and to ensure they are not allowed to reduce the map's effectiveness.

Orientation: avoiding the locational puzzle

Some study areas, such as the conterminous USA or the country of Canada, are so distinctive and at the same time so familiar to the readership, that they are instantly recognized even on a poorly designed map. Unfamiliar countries, and especially large-scale maps of some portion of unfamiliar countries, must be accompanied by abundant, yet unobtrusive, clues for orientation. In Figure 6.1A, the study area hangs as an isolated blob in a field of white, and although the title or caption informs the reader the country is Tanzania, the map is both unconvincing and misleading because the area seems to be surrounded by either land or ocean. Part B of the illustration shows a vital improvement: the coastline has been extended to the limits of the frame to make the setting more realistic.

In Part C, the addition of major political boundaries and names to the surrounding land mass further improves the setting. Part D uses an index map to place the country on its continent. Latitude and longitude ticks within the map frame or delicate parallels and meridians drawn across the study area would be appropriate if locational information were important to the theme.

Continuing coastlines until they reach the map frame can be *the* most important aid to reader orientation. Figure 6.2 shows how obscure forms become recognizable when the setting is made more complete. If the coastal lines are omitted, then there is great ambiguity about the areas adjacent to the study area. Are they land or ocean? The Dominican Republic, when presented as in the left side of Figure 6.2, is bounded in a way that is technically accurate; but it appears to be an island. When the coastlines are continued, and the political boundary given a line symbol different from the coastlines, then the locational puzzle is avoided. Only a few additional marks are made on the page; but the effect is profound.

Even if an area is familiar to the readership, selected portions of it can be confusing if they are presented in isolation. The economic regions of the United States (Fig. 6.2) need to be placed in their setting. Once again, it is the distinction between coastline and inland boundaries that is a critical factor.

If the whole of a familiar country is presented, then it may not be necessary to continue coastlines and thus distinguish surrounding land areas from surrounding ocean areas. For the United States as a whole, it might be assumed that the bordering land areas of Canada and Mexico are so well known that the country may be allowed to hang in space. If that is acceptable, then the country may be "raised" by the shadow effect to make the presentation more dramatic and interesting (Fig. 6.3).

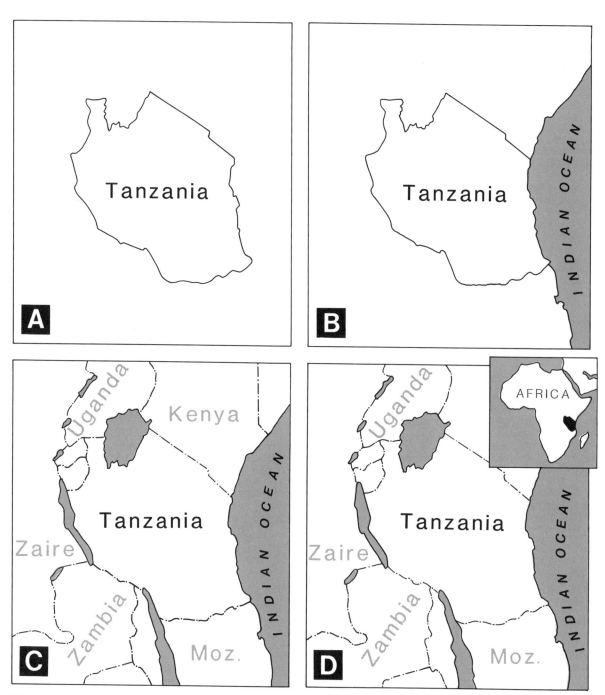

FIG. 6.1 Locational puzzle resolved by a series of changes that improve the setting of the subject area.

If the area mapped is quite obscure – as, for instance, a very large-scale map of some part of a country – then a statement of *map scale* is essential (see chapter 5). If the reader sees that the whole map covers a distance of only 50 miles (80 km) then a vital aspect of the orientation need has been dealt with.

Large-scale maps require *index maps* to forestall instantly any confusion about location of the study

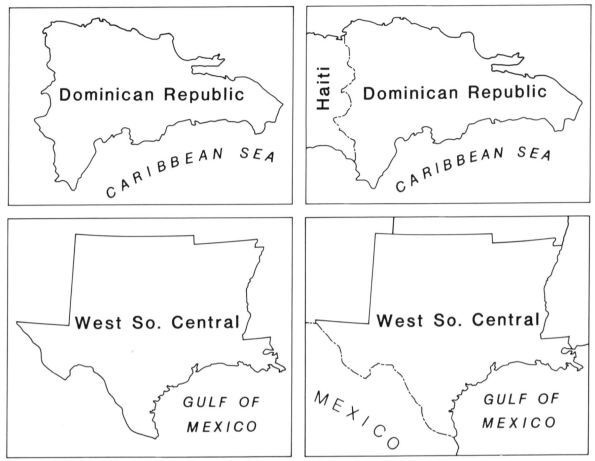

FIG. 6.2 Improving the setting of a study area, and clarifying which boundaries are coastlines and which are not.

area. In any survey of book and journal maps that prove puzzling to the reader the cause of puzzlement will frequently be the lack of index map. The usual index map shows the setting by using a small-scale map of continent or region (Fig. 6.4A). *Index maps* should be distinguished from *blow-ups*. Index maps are at small scale, and show the setting of the study area. A blow-up resembles an index map, because it is small and subsidiary to the main map on the page; but it is used for a large-scale view of some selected part of the study area (Fig. 6.4B). The term *inset map*, incidentally, refers only to the arrangement, and reveals nothing about the function of the smaller map. Either index map or blow-up may be inset within the main map or simply placed beside it.

Composition: recognizing the third dimension

The term *composition* is used here for the design aspects which make certain parts of the map more commanding and other parts more recessive. This concern is not entirely separate from the matter of orientation discussed above, nor is it divorced from the matter of *layout* dealt with in chapter 2. Whereas layout is concerned with effective use of the two-dimensional space available on a page, composition makes use of techniques that create *visual levels within the map*, and thus make use of an apparent third dimension. These techniques, especially if they deal with land–water differences, contribute to the reader's

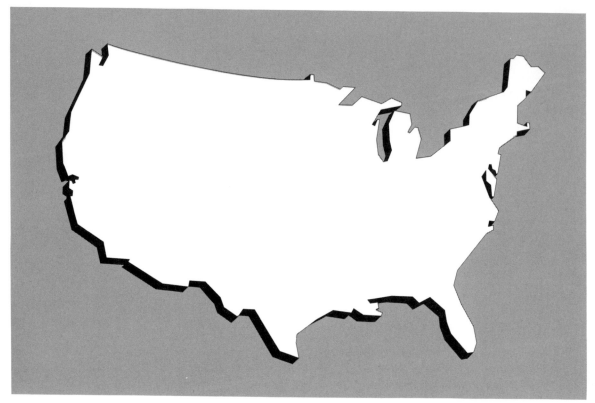

FIG. 6.3   A very familiar study area may be allowed to hang in space.

orientation. They also may affect the balance of the layout.

The term *composition* is used through analogy with written composition in which structure is so important to a reader's understanding. Ideally, a written essay has a beginning, a middle and an end; and, most important, a hierarchy of ideas revealed by headings of different status. Nothing is quite so formidable to the reader as unbroken pages of the written word without evidence of structure or headings. The visual counterpart is a map that is *homogeneous*. The eye swims through it, searching for something to cling to. Homogeneous lettering and lines are undesirable, of course, because logical distinctions in both size and style should be used to show differences in status. More important to the overall map, though, are *contrasts* in the *character of areas*; and very often the need is to distinguish land from water.

LAND–WATER DISTINCTIONS

Figure 6.5 Part A shows a large-scale map with homogeneous areas traversed by a line whose form suggests a coast. Which area is water, and which land is obscured by the fact that both are white and both have lettering on them. Close examination shows settlements are on the right side; but the ambiguity continues to be annoying even after the land is established. In Part B of the illustration, place-names are removed from the water, so it is now different from the land, and less interesting. The land is more complex and interesting and thus tends to be seen as *figure* rather than *ground*, to use the psychologist's terminology. Realize that the key is making water areas not only different from the land but *plain*. In Parts C and D, the ocean is patterned in ways that seem appropriate but in fact attract attention because of their

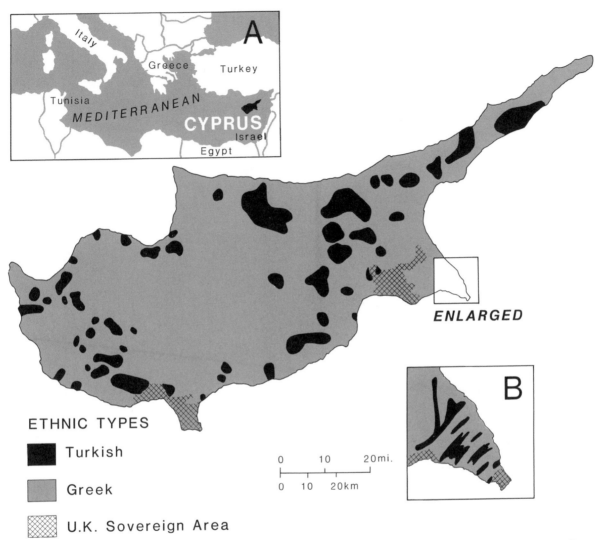

FIG. 6.4 Examples of index and blow-up maps: Part A, an index map to show the location of Cyprus; Part B, a blow-up to show part of Cyprus in greater detail.

relatively coarse and interesting texture. Similarly, the stippled pattern in Part E lends an interesting texture to the ocean and makes it compete with the land for the reader's attention.[1] In Part F, the ocean is given a fine grey tone which serves the purpose very well.

Because the land–water differentiation problem is such a good example of figure–ground relationships, it is appropriate to elaborate on the idea and to seek the cartographic applications of it. Psychologists tell us that the following traits tend to make an area seen as

figure (or subject area) not as background. Of course, the opposite traits should be given to areas that are to be recessive and serve as background.

Articulation, or complexity of markings As suggested above, this may be equated with coarse texture and with the inclusion of place-names and thematic materials. This factor tends to take care of itself in most maps, because the subject matter *is* on the land and in the study area as opposed to the land areas that

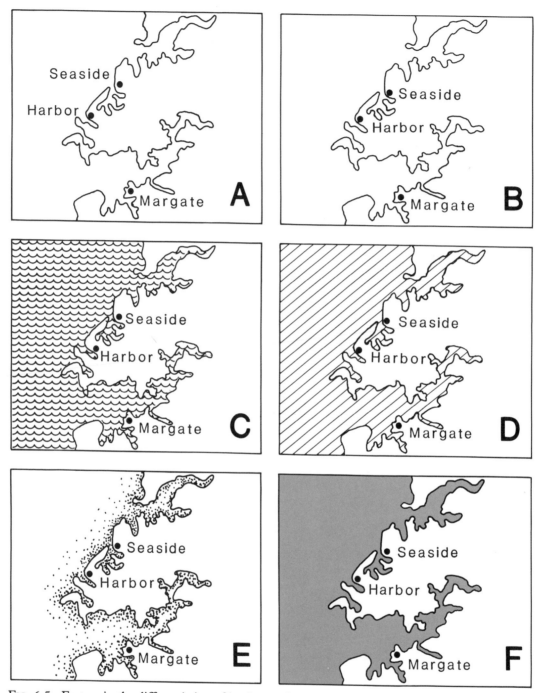

FIG. 6.5 Factors in the differentiation of land areas from water.

surround it. Care should be taken, however, to keep the place-names where they belong and, insofar as possible, to keep them off areas (such as oceans) where they do not belong.[2]

Closed or complete forms A form, such as that of a country, will be recognized and seen as figure more readily if it is complete (Fig. 6.6). Italy, for instance (Part A), is not readily evident because its extremities have been truncated. Adding a dull grey tone to water areas (Part B) helps to reduce the ambiguity, but making the form complete (Part C) is a more significant alteration.

Size of area Generally, smaller areas tend to emerge as figure; and there has been some cartographic research to identify the optimal ratio between areas of figure and areas of ground (Crawford, 1976). An important implication, surely, is that smaller areas tend to be *surrounded* by other areas, and thus perceived as figure.

Centrality This trait is extremely important. Areas that are central and surrounded by areas of a different character will tend to be the focus of the reader's attention. Even when an area is no more interesting in texture than its surroundings, it will be seen as figure because of its centrality (Part B). In another example, water is unintentionally made prominent by its central location, while the intended subject area is incomplete and off-center (Part D).

Darkness of area Darker areas will tend to be seen as figure, unless other traits, such as completeness or centrality, favor another area. This principle is consistent with ideas of visual hierarchy that are developed below.

VISUAL LEVELS WITHIN A SUBJECT AREA

Complementary to the idea of figure–ground relationships is the idea that the cartographer should establish distinctly different *visual levels* within the map in order to organize the various map components and to avoid homogeneity. In its most elemental form, the idea of visual hierarchy is extremely useful and is, in fact, the key to successful map compositions. When considered in light of land–water and figure–ground needs, however, there is a possible conflict in design guidelines, as will be shown below.

Different visual levels may be needed in order to separate thematic materials from features of a base map; or they may be needed to show a hierarchy that exists entirely within thematic materials. In any case, some system should be explicitly followed in designing a map that is complex. Figure 6.7 shows a system of organization in which white is the lowest level, grey rises above white, darker grey rises above that, and black rises above all other levels because it obscures them (Dent, 1972, 1973).

The principle is applied in Figure 6.8, where Part A

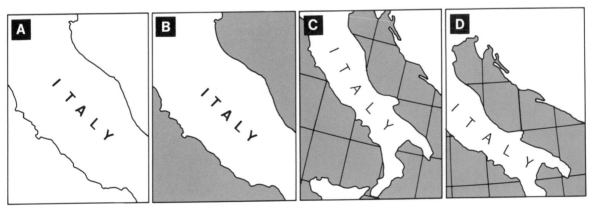

FIG. 6.6 Forms that are complete and forms that are central in the map will tend to be perceived as figure.

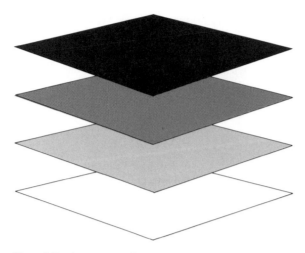

FIG. 6.7 A system of visual levels to conform to a hierarchy that exists in map features.

shows bold black boundary lines of the base conflicting visually with scaled circles. In Part B the boundaries are sufficiently light that the circles rise above them without confusion. A more complex hierarchy is established in Figure 6.9, in which the base map and routes of various status are rendered in lines that are progressively darker and more broad.

Despite the strong logic of darkest for the highest visual level, it is *not* essential that thematic symbols be dark in contrast to light base materials. In Figure 6.10, for instance, symbols are light grey and transparent, with the black base showing through. This is an interesting case to analyze: the grey circles do rise above the base, which is composed largely of white areas; and the circles rise above the black boundaries because the boundaries are viewed through the circles. Apparently map designs do not lend themselves to simple formulas.

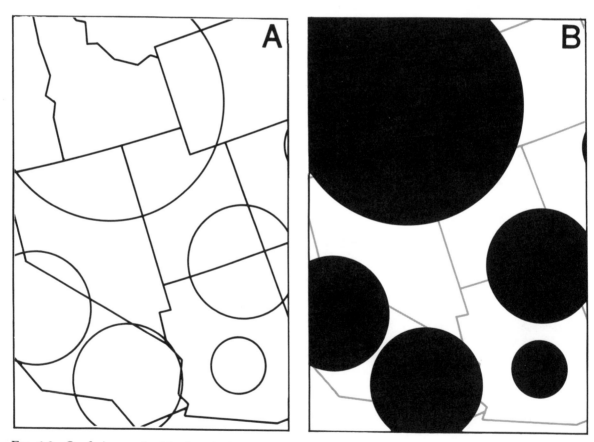

FIG. 6.8 Confusion resolved by introducing a second visual level.

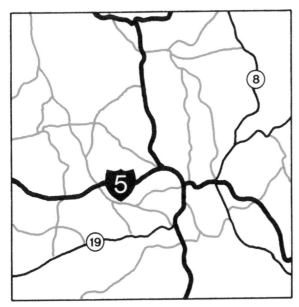

FIG. 6.9 A succession of visual levels consistent with the hierarchy that exists in routes of varying status.

VISUAL COUNTERPOINT: A STRUCTURE THAT WORKS FOR MANY MAPS

A potential conflict in guidelines should be recognized now. If the white to black visual hierarchy is a valid principle, then how can we defend the use of grey on ocean areas to help the reader focus on the land area as the subject? It would seem that grey on water areas would make them rise above the white land and be more conspicuous.

The first answer to this is to realize that other traits may strengthen the study area. Automatically, place-names and thematic materials will tend to make the study area more interesting. At the same time, the non-study area – whether it be land or water – will be at the edges of the composition, while the study area is more central.

The second answer to the apparent paradox is more gratifying, because it unifies the two ideas: figure–ground, on the one hand, and visual levels, on the other. There really is no paradox, because there are *two different visual realms* within many map compositions. In Figure 6.11, for instance, the relatively light study area is seen as figure despite the darker tones used on surrounding areas. As first priority, the surrounding areas are made different from the study

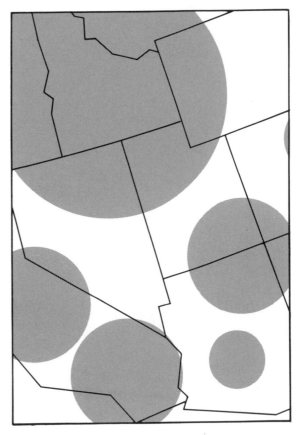

FIG. 6.10 Symbols made transparent appear to rise above the base map although the base has black elements in it.

area. Because they are darker, they serve to literally *highlight* the study area. Because they are fine textured and dull, and especially because they are *peripheral*, they are seen as background, not as figure. Within the more central realm, a number of visual levels are built by using progressively darker elements on the white field. This structure may be called *visual counterpoint* because there are two simultaneous and somewhat overlapping compositions within the whole.

EXCEPTIONS

The counterpoint structure cannot be applied in all cases; in fact, even the simple use of grey on water bodies may be not possible. Whenever a map theme is symbolized by shaded isarithmic patterns or by data

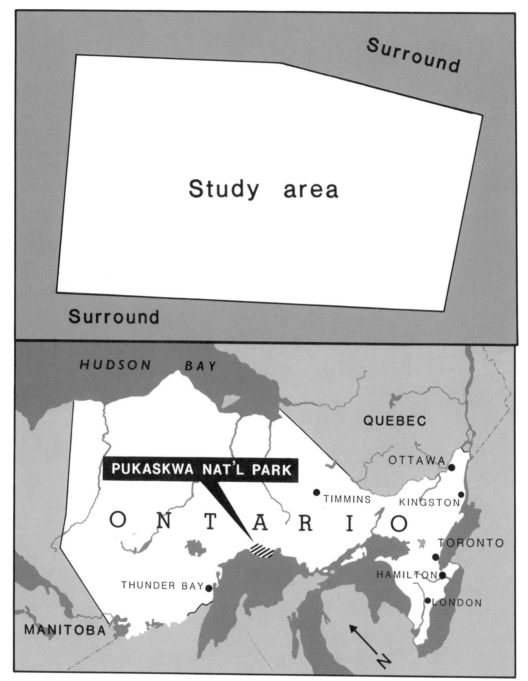

FIG. 6.11   An example of visual counterpoint. Peripheral dark areas serve to highlight the study area which is lighter; within the study area a hierarchy of white, grey, and black is used. Map designed and produced by Patrick Stocking, Philadelphia.

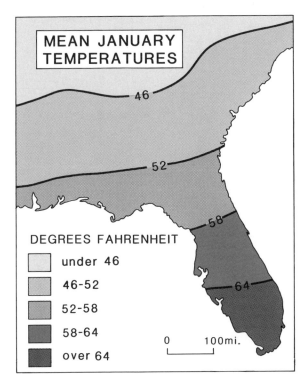

FIG. 6.12 Surrounding areas are necessarily left white when greys are used for symbolization throughout the study area.

areas shaded in choropleth fashion the study area is filled with grey tones that pre-empt the greys (and maybe even the black) that would otherwise be available for surrounding areas (Fig. 6.12).

Each thematic map will present a unique challenge for which there may be a number of compositions in black and white that will be satisfactory. While no single formula can be applied, there is one general principle of overriding importance: homogeneity is to be avoided. Logical use of *contrasts* is the essential tool for compositions that are pleasing and easily understood.

Notes

1 For consistent use of stippling for water areas, see maps in the *Geographical Review*. For results of testing different treatments of land versus water, see Head (1972).
2 If the subject were in the ocean (routes, depths, minerals, or drilling leases, for instance) then it would be logical to render land areas in a dull fine tone.

References

Crawford, Paul V. (1976) "Optimal spatial design for thematic maps," *The Cartographic Journal*, 13 (2), 134–44.

Dent, Borden (1972) "Visual organization and thematic map design," *Annals*, Association of American Geographers, 62, 79–93.

Dent, Borden D. (1973) "Simplifying thematic maps through effective design: some postulates for the measure of success," *Proceedings*, American Congress on Surveying and Mapping, Fall Convention, 243–51.

Head, C. G. (1972) "Land–water differentiation in black and white cartography," *The Canadian Cartographer*, 9, 25–8.

PART THREE

Reproduction and Production

The logical and psychological principles that suggest the most appropriate graphic and verbal content in a map and the most effective ways of presenting the map content have been given high priority and assigned to Parts One and Two of this book. In practice, however, matters of production and reproduction must be confronted very early in any illustration project, because the reproduction process chosen will determine what effects the cartographer can attain in the printed map.

Methods of *production* are best understood with some knowledge of the processes of *reproduction*. For that reason reproduction processes are reviewed in chapter 7, and production methods in chapter 8. Practical hints to ease the purchase of tools and materials and to expedite the production of graphics suitable for reproduction are reserved for chapter 9. That chapter will be most useful if it is referred to frequently during the work on exercises.

7 Reproduction Methods

The processes of reproduction constitute a most important aspect of the cartographic process. Except for certain unusual projects, such as posters or other displays, the materials produced on the cartographic drafting table are not end products. They must be reproduced if they are to appear on the pages of a book, a journal article, or a graduate thesis. The reproduction processes set some limits on what can be accomplished on a map: but, at the same time, they offer opportunities for quick and easy completion of the cartographer's work. Understanding what may happen to a piece after it leaves the drafting table is essential, because those processes may dictate what is done on the table. That is true whether the work is done with relatively simple and economical techniques or the more advanced and more expensive techniques. The many reproduction possibilities may be grouped as those most suitable for very limited numbers of copies versus those which produce a large number of copies by use of a printing press.

For a few copies

For the sake of a quick test of how materials will reproduce or how they will survive reduction it is very helpful to have one or two copies made by processes such as those in Figure 7.1. Some office copiers have the capacity to reduce, and can give the cartographer a good idea of how a map will look when its symbols and lettering are at finished size.

Photostats are fast, fairly inexpensive if the finished

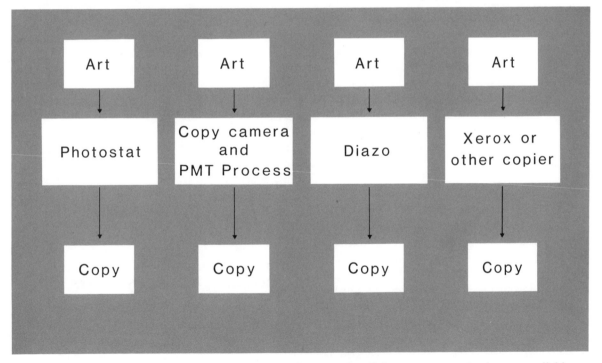

FIG. 7.1 Reproduction for single or a few copies, without a press. Enlargement or reduction are available.

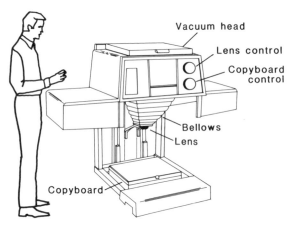

Vacuum head

Lens control

Copyboard control

Bellows

Lens

Copyboard

FIG. 7.2 A vertical copy camera suitable for a college cartographic laboratory. From a photo of a Kenro brand camera.

size is not large, and can be obtained in either positive or reverse (white on black) form. They may be used to reduce a base map or other source map by a given proportion, and are usually done by commercial photography shops or by establishments that specialize in photostats. Similar in effect, and often called photostats, are the prints made by a copy camera and PMT (brand name) materials. Instead of exposing and developing a negative, then making a photo print in a darkroom, a paper negative is made, applied to sensitive paper, and run through a special solution that makes a print in one step. Many print shops and a number of college departments now use copy cameras for quick prints and also for making negatives (Fig. 7.2).

Another process for a few copies is the *diazo* (ozalid) process used by survey or engineering firms that need inexpensive copies of large originals. Translucent or transparent art work is placed in contact with sensitive paper which is rolled through a processing machine where it is exposed to strong light and finally developed in ammonia fumes. The product usually is black-line or blue-line and, because it is made by a contact process, is the same size as the original art work. The process works by features on the art work *blocking* light in some areas, while light passes through in other areas to create white areas. Because of this, all map areas, other than desired marks, must be transparent; so stick-on labels or opaque correction

materials cannot be used. The lettering or other materials applied to the original must be heat-resistant or they will peel off as they roll through the machine. If a number of maps are to be drawn on the same base, then a series of sepia (brown-line) pieces can be produced in the machine from the original base map and used as "intermediates." Thematic materials can be added to these sepia copies, which themselves can be run through the machine to produce copies of the complete maps.

For many copies

If more than 20 or 25 copies are needed it pays to use a printing plate and press. Two major routes are summed up by Figure 7.3. One option is to use a plate-making machine found in many commercial copy shops (Fig. 7.4). The art work is illuminated on a copy board, and its image falls onto a sensitive paper material which then is immediately ready to serve as a printing plate good for at least 500 impressions. Reduction or enlargement of the original image is easy; and the process is quick and relatively cheap.

For longer press runs, for large art work, or for the sake of more professional-looking products (see chapter 8) it may be necessary to use a traditional copy camera (Fig. 7.5) to make a photographic negative(s) and from that negative(s) make a metal printing plate. Even for simple map products this process has an important advantage: any unwanted marks or features can be obliterated by *touching-up* with opaque materials applied to the negative. As suggested by Figure 7.3, a photographic print may be made from the negative(s) rather than a printing plate.

PRINTING PROCESSES AND THEIR CARTOGRAPHIC IMPLICATIONS

Among the various printing processes, there are two of main interest, letterpress printing and lithography.

LETTERPRESS PRINTING

This is the process by which many newspapers, some business cards, and some books with simple graphics

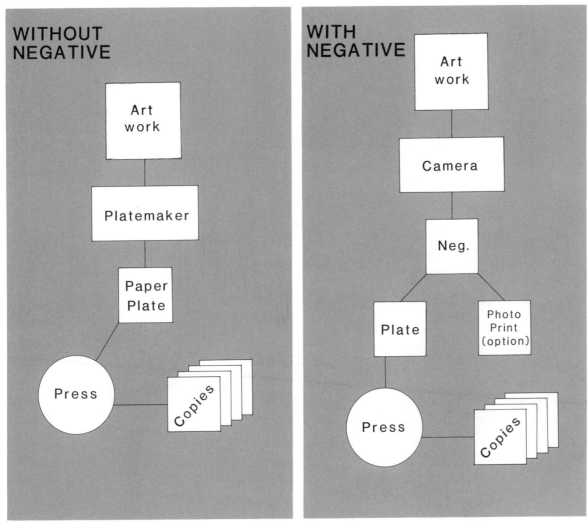

FIG. 7.3 Two methods of reproduction using printing plate and press.

are printed. On the printing plate are *raised areas* which pick up ink and transfer it directly to the paper. Since pressure is needed to transfer ink to paper in this process, there is some crushing or indentation of the paper. The implication for reproduction of maps and other graphics is important: fine lines and fine dot screens are not printed faithfully by letterpress, especially on a soft paper. The printing plate, incidentally will appear to be *wrong-reading* so that when the image is transferred to paper the result duplicates the original (Fig. 7.6).

LITHOGRAPHY, OR OFFSET, PRINTING

Lithography, as the name suggests, originally made use of limestone blocks with areas and lines to be printed drawn in a greasy substance. These lines and areas had affinity for ink, while the other areas were receptive to water. If the block was wetted, then inked, only the areas and lines drawn in grease retained the ink and transferred it to paper.

The modern version of lithography makes use of the same principle: some areas of the printing plate bear

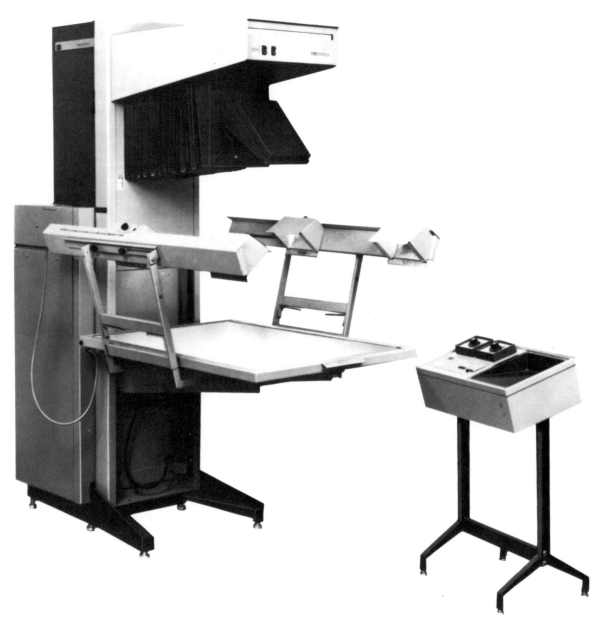

FIG. 7.4 Electrostatic plate-maker that makes a plate directly, without need for a negative. Copy board is 2 x 3 feet. Photo courtesy of Itek Corporation.

the image to be printed and are receptive to ink, while other areas are blank and are receptive to water, not ink. The distinctions are made by means of chemical or metallic coatings on a metal plate. When the map image is imposed photographically onto the plate the veneer material is altered or removed only in the areas to be inked. Remaining areas are unchanged and will

not be receptive to ink. Since the veneer is very thin, there is virtually no depth to the image on the plate. The image is transferred, therefore, not by pressing it into paper, but by rolling it gently onto the paper. In fact, most lithographic printing is done by *offset press* in which the image is transferred from printing plate to a rubber "blanket" cylinder which applies ink to

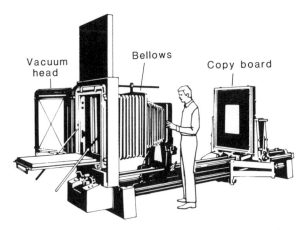

FIG. 7.5 Commercial-scale copy camera, showing copy board that will accommodate large pieces of art work, or a number of pieces for the same reduction. From International Paper Company, *Pocket Pal*.

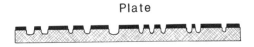

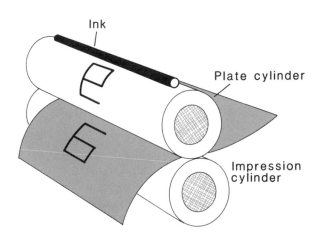

FIG. 7.6 Letterpress printing (schematic). Areas to be printed are raised on the plate in a pattern that is the reverse, or mirror image, of that on the printed product.

the paper. Because of the intermediate transfer, the image on the plate itself is not reversed but is *right-reading* and resembles the original art and, of course, the printed product (Fig. 7.7).

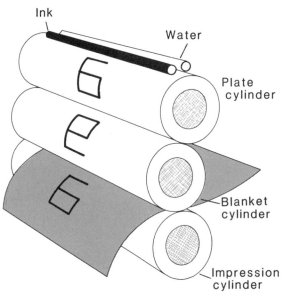

FIG. 7.7 Offset lithographic printing (schematic). The shallow image on the plate appears the same as the printed product.

A most important implication for cartographers is that offset lithography very effectively reproduces fine lines, grey tones, and other subtleties. It is widely used, therefore, for printing book and atlas maps in black ink and in color. The small press that prints on $8\frac{1}{2}$ x 11 inch sheets in a small copy shop and the giant four color press that prints eight pages at once in a large printing operation both make use of the offset method.

THE REPRODUCTION OF SUBTLE TONES AND IMAGES

Regardless of whether the printing is by letterpress or lithography, areas of the printing plates will either accept ink or they will not. There is, in most circumstances, no halfway or partial condition that would enable the plate to print lightly in one area and heavily in another. Fortunately, the plates – especially lithographic plates – are capable of retaining a very fine pattern of inked versus non-inked areas.

In general, the images imposed onto printing plates must be composed of quite absolute elements. Art work for a map, for instance, must comprise elements that are either black or white. If grey tones (or comparable tones in colored inks) are desired they must be simulated by the use of fine dots or closely spaced lines (Fig. 7.8).

Photographic portraits, views of scenery, or aerial photographs capture their subjects by means of *continuous tone* film that records subtle variations in darkness. If these are to be printed by either letterpress or lithographic method, the continuous tone image must be converted into the "on or off" condition that a printing plate can deal with. This conversion is done by the process of *halftoning* which renders the dark and light areas all as discrete dots of different sizes. The result is a remarkably faithful reproduction of the subject (Fig. 7.9).[1]

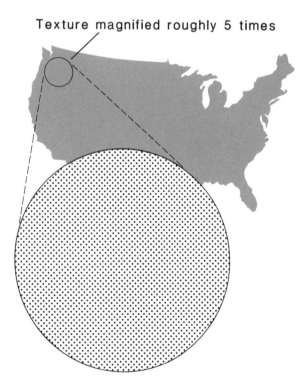

Texture magnified roughly 5 times

FIG. 7.8   Simulation of grey by printing a fine pattern of dots or lines.

Art work suitable for reproduction

There are a number of characteristics of the reproduction processes that dictate what should and should not be done on the drafting table.

SIZE OF CAMERA

If the art work is rather large, *it should be determined very early* in the project whether it will fit the copy board of the camera available. While commercial photographers and some printers have extremely large copy boards that accommodate art work 3 × 4 feet, many other establishments can deal with art work no larger than 1½ × by 2 feet. A slight adjustment in the size of the art work (see chapter 5 on use of space and layout) could make a big difference in the feasibility of reproduction.

THE RESPONSE OF PHOTOGRAPHIC FILM

Black and white film used for portraits or scenery will record slight variations in darkness and is called *continuous tone film*. The film used for reproduction of maps and similar graphics is *high-contrast film* (or line film) and responds in a more absolute fashion, either recording a mark or not recording it. Actually, it is the photographer who determines what will appear, as he controls the developing of the negative after the film has been exposed; but all he can achieve is either the presence or absence of features.

In order to make a clean sharp negative that will make a satisfactory print or printing plate, the photographer must be supplied art work on which the marks all are uniformly black and sharp-edged. Any lines, lettering, or other features that are grey (as when made with a pen not functioning well) will be very difficult to deal with in conjunction with other marks that are quite black.

If a grey is desired on the finished product, it must be simulated by closely spaced black dots or lines which will give the effect of grey when viewed at arm's length. To ensure reproducibility, dot or line screens *used on art work* should not be very fine in texture. A limit of 42½ lines per inch is a usable guideline; but if the work will be reduced *by a factor more than two*, then a coarser screen will be needed.

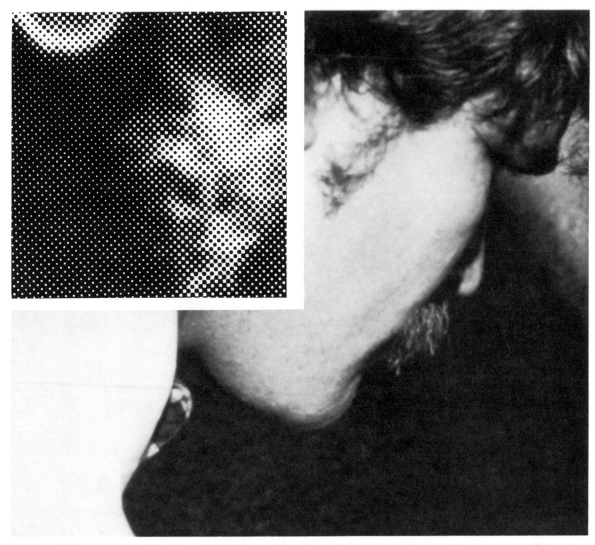

FIG. 7.9 Enlargement to show how halftoning converts a continuous-tone photograph to a pattern of dots that can be printed.

Photographically, red on art work has the same effect as black. Because of this, any large areas to be black may be covered with red material available at art supply houses (see chapter 9). This is much more convenient than painting large areas with ink or some other black substance. On the other hand, a certain blue color is photographically invisible. This means that notes and guidelines may be sketched onto the art work in a *non-reproducing blue* pen or pencil with no danger of their appearing on the product. Engineering supply stores can provide printed rolls or sheets of squared paper and perspective guidelines in blue. These greatly ease the drawing of graphs and perspective views.

The insensitivity, or rather the absolute response, of high-contrast film allows some extremely convenient short cuts:

- lettering, whether typed or produced by a more expensive process, may be applied in the form of labels. Label edges will not show unless the labels are so thick they cast shadows

- errors may be corrected with stenographers' white-out material applied with a brush or with correction tape
- more extensive errors can be corrected by splicing out the old and splicing-in a replacement. The edge of splice will not show
- overlays on clear acetate may be added to a base map with no fear that the acetate cover will show. In this way, one "base" can serve for more than one theme, whether it is a map base, the framework for a graph, or some other skeleton to which more than one addition may be made.

Note

1 In fact, it may be possible to print a continuous tone image without *halftoning* it. Trials have been conducted with aerial photographs in the hope that they can be printed without losing the detail that resides in their continuous tones (Keates, 1978).

References

International Paper Company (1979) *Pocket Pal: A Graphic Arts Production Handbook* (12th edn), New York.

Keates, Johns S. (1978) "Screenless lithography and ortho-photo maps," *The Cartographic Journal*, 15 (2), 63–5.

8 Production Methods

Two important distinctions exist in the preparation of materials to be reproduced. First, is the difference between *camera-ready* work and the *use of separations*; and second, the use of *positive art work* versus *negative art work*. A complete discussion of the techniques embraced by those four terms is not appropriate here; but a brief review is necessary if the student's work is to be seen in relation to mapping activities beyond the introductory level. Computers can be used to aid production either in camera-ready style or with the use of separations; and they can be used in the making of either positive or negative art work. Computer-aided production, therefore, is discussed after those distinctions have been clarified.

Camera-ready art versus the use of separations

The difference between using camera-ready art and using separations is extremely important because it is virtually synonymous with the distinction between low-cost and rather coarse-looking map products and higher-cost products that can be more subtle, more professional-looking, and can be printed in more than one color.

CAMERA-READY ART WORK

This is a piece of art work[1] which leaves the drafting table as a map, graph, or other illustration that is essentially complete. On it are all the lines, patterns, tones and other effects that are to appear on the final product (Fig. 8.1). Only one exposure and one photographic negative are needed to make a printing plate (Fig. 8.2). As an alternative, an inexpensive printing plate may be made directly, without the intervening negative. In either case, only the single piece of art work is used. Its features are simply *reproduced*, in the literal sense of the word, with little or no alteration.

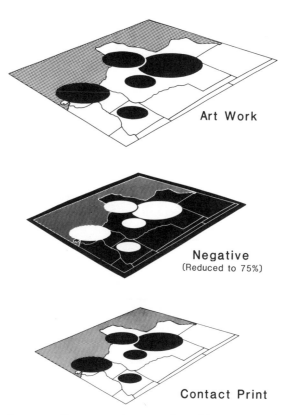

Art Work

Negative
(Reduced to 75%)

Contact Print

FIG. 8.1 Camera-ready art work, and its corresponding photographic negative and contact print.

There are some advantages to working this way. First, it is relatively inexpensive, since only one photograph is required, and the plate-making is very simple. Second, the cartographer is quite in charge of the process and can readily predict what the printed result will be.

There are, however, some serious disadvantages. All the elements placed on the art work must survive the photographic reduction that normally precedes the negative and the plate-making. All patterns and tones must, therefore, be relatively *coarse* (see chapter 9), a constraint that makes certain design goals impossible

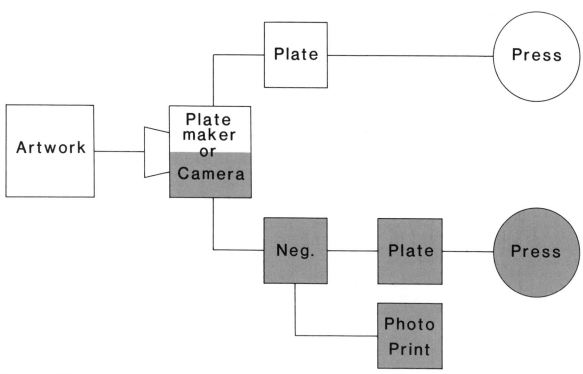

Fig. 8.2 The reproduction of camera-ready art work.

to attain. To create a variety of patterns and tones on the art work, the cartographer must stock, or have access to, a large variety of pre-printed art work materials. Perhaps the most serious restriction is in regard to the superposition of lines and patterns. This may be necessary to demonstrate the coincidence of two or more distributions (see chapter 3); or it may be necessary because some pattern or tone is imposed onto the physical and political features of the base map. In camera-ready art the superposition must be accomplished, of course, by ingenious and skilled work on the art itself. This is less true when using the alternative techniques mentioned below.

THE USE OF SEPARATIONS

Because a full discussion of the use of separations is not consistent with the needs of most introductory courses in thematic cartography, only a brief account is presented here.

When working with separations, the cartographic draftsman produces separate pieces of art that constitute different elements of the final product that is envisioned (Fig. 8.3). These pieces are photographed to make a series of negatives whose features are combined when the printing plate (or photographic print) is produced. Most of the patterns, grey tones, and superpositions desired in the printed product are accomplished in the photo lab or the print shop when the printing plate is made (Fig. 8.4). Obviously, the cartographer who is working this way must be thoroughly familiar with the potential of the graphic arts processes available in the photo lab and the print shop.

As implied in the above discussion of camera-ready art work, the important advantage in using separations is the ability to accomplish *fine textured* tones and superpositions − both of which are difficult through the use of camera-ready methods. Figure 8.5 shows a simple map produced in one case by camera-ready methods and in the second case by using separations.

FOR 100%   FOR 30%

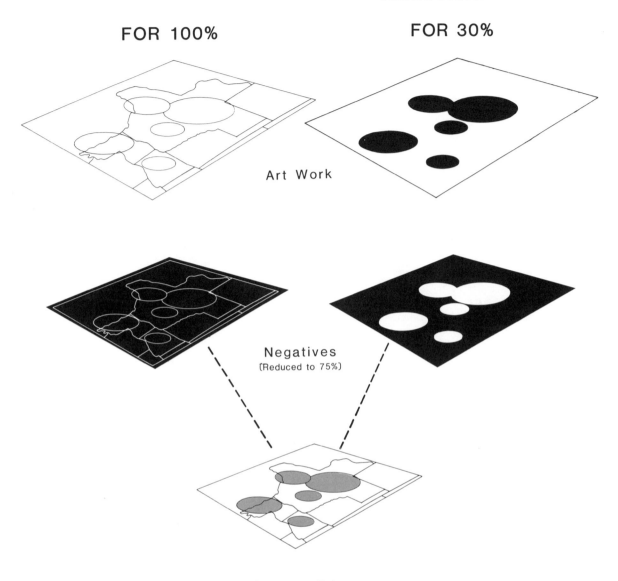

Art Work

Negatives
(Reduced to 75%)

Contact Print

FIG. 8.3 Two art work separates, and their corresponding negatives and composite contact print.

The difference in overall effect is quite pronounced. Throughout this book there is extensive use of fine grey tones accomplished by using separations.

Positive art work versus scribing and peelcoat methods

The foregoing discussion of reproduction and produc-

tion has assumed that the cartographic draftsman produces black (or red) lines and areas on the art work. Such black work drawn upon white or clear materials is called positive art work. It does not matter whether the production is being done by camera-ready methods or with use of separations.

The destiny of this positive art work is to make a printing plate; and in virtually all maps for journals, books, and atlases that means negatives must be made from those pieces of art. In large map production

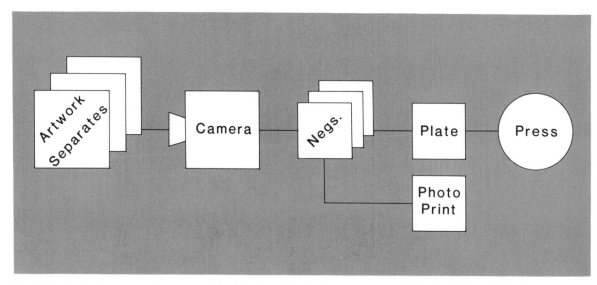

FIG. 8.4 Producing a map by means of separations. Vital effects are accomplished while making the photoprint or the printing plate. The single plate implies printing in only one ink.

FIG. 8.5 One map produced by camera-ready methods and also by use of separations.

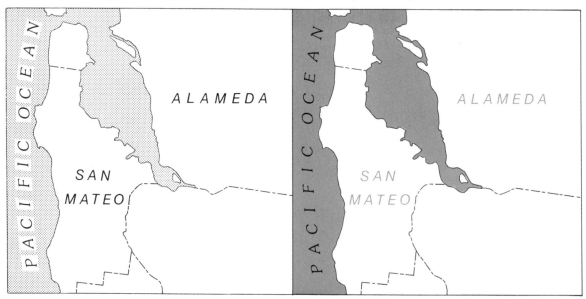

operations which use a lot of separations those negatives become very expensive. Rather than drawing positive art, the draftsman will produce a piece *that serves as a negative* and may be called negative art work. In this way the photography and the developing of a negative are avoided.

Line work is done in negative fashion by the process of scribing. Transparent drawing materials are veneered with an opaque material which then is carved away by the draftsman using a scribing tool of the desired width (Fig. 8.6). This opens up lines which are comparable to the open lines on a negative

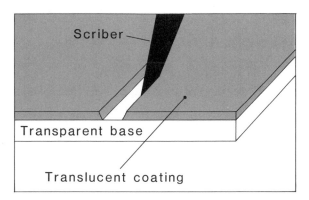

FIG. 8.6 Scribing to produce negative art work.

made from a black line drawing. Areas that are to have distinctive character, such as oceans or lakes, are "opened up" by a similar process, but using a slightly different material which is easily peeled off a transparent base after an outline has been traced with a blade or "burned" into the material photographically. This is the *peelcoat* method: there may be one separate for oceans and lakes, another for urban areas, and another for forested areas.

There is a significant advantage to this style of production – in addition to the fact that photography and negatives can largely be eliminated. Line work done by scribing can be of higher quality than that done by positive art, because an inked line tends to vary in width and in density, whereas a scribed line is more easily standardized. A significant disadvantage is that all work must be done *at finished size*, because the photographic step is by-passed.

In summary (Fig. 8.7) it is apparent that the use of scribing requires special tools and materials and is used mostly in large mapping operations. Similarly, the use of separations is more prevalent in high-volume production than in the average college geography department. It is quite accessible to any cartographer, however, since it can be accomplished quite easily with positive art work. Finally, the use of camera-ready (positive) art work is typical of maps to illustrate a thesis, a journal article, or a book that must be produced inexpensively.

Computer-aided map production

The use of computers for map production has, in recent years, evolved from a novelty to a technology that is relied upon for day to day map production. Automation has brought to cartography unprecedented speed of production, reliability, flexibility in design, and ease of revision. Some of the technical advances have eased and speeded the production of conventional-looking map products. But in addition, automation has made widely accessible some interesting graphics that are difficult to produce without the aid of machines.

The ability to produce maps quickly from information stored on magnetic tapes or discs has substantially changed the concept of the *map*. No longer are maps limited to precious paper copies – the products of much labor in compiling, drafting, photography, plate-making, and printing. In some applications the permanent map is being replaced by *the ephemeral*

	CAMERA–READY	USE OF SEPARATIONS
POSITIVE ARTWORK	Usual for low-cost illustrations for theses , journal articals, or books printed in one ink	For superior maps in journals, books, or atlases printed in one or more inks
NEGATIVE ARTWORK	(This combination not practical)	Usual in high-volume government mapping operations using black and colored inks

FIG. 8.7 Summary of the four possible modes of cartographic production.

map – a short-lived image on a cathode ray tube, subject to immediate revision in its geographic scope, its scale, or its symbolization.

Some of the traits of computer-aided map production can be understood by analogy with separation techniques described earlier in this chapter. A base map, for instance, exists as a record of digitally coded coastlines, rivers, and political boundaries. All or part of the base map may be summoned and associated with some selected data which, too, are stored and await use or revision. If there is a data revision to be made, only the data file need be altered. If some feature of the base map needs improvement, only the base file need be dealt with. The difference between the traditional map separates and the computerized version is that revisions are made only to the electro-magnetic record – not to a paper copy, negative, or scribed sheet. The physical maps are seen as just temporary and perhaps out-of-date expressions of the mappable data. The latest and most suitable map resides in some combination of base features and data that exist in digital form.

It is through the multiple use of one base that computerized map production really justifies the effort of converting base maps into digital form. This is equally true in a large government mapping agency and in a college where computers are used, not for high-volume map production, but for teaching and research. In a well-equipped and well-conceived mapping facility a cartographer can quickly combine a number of different variables with one base to make a series of maps. Or, he can experiment with different presentations of the same data set – changing first the map scale, next the map projection, and finally the symbolization or its scaling factor.

This capability to manipulate digital map bases (base files) and combine them at will with old and new data sets converted to symbolic form is not common-place. It exists only at facilities that have the necessary *hardware* (equipment) and the necessary *software*, that is the digital base maps and the computer programs to make the mapping system run.

HARDWARE

The equipment needed for computer-aided map production can be grouped into three categories: devices for input, for processing, and for output.

INPUT DEVICES

In general, these include card readers and tape readers for loading digital information into a processor or into storage. But for cartographic applications, input devices are those pieces of equipment that convert images into digital form so they can be stored, manipulated, and mapped.

One type of equipment is the scanner used to convert photographic (or other) images into numerical form. A photograph will be scanned by the device which records every line scan as a horizontal string of picture cells (pixels) each with a certain darkness level.[2] Once in numerical form, the various map areas can be classified according to their darkness character so that areas of a certain land use, for instance, can be mapped separately.

More relevant to the creation of digital base maps and to the storage of thematic map information are devices called *digitizers* (Fig. 8.8). These machines are essential to any high-volume computer-aided map production because they convert the elements of an existing map into numerical form. All computer mapping depends on having points and lines defined by X–Y coordinates. When a conventional map is placed on a digitizing table, an operator can system-atically convert any desired points or any chosen lines into X–Y coordinates by placing a cursor on a point and pushing a button. The device instantly senses the cursor's position in terms of the table's X and Y coordinates and records the position on tape or a punched card. A line can be followed by the operator, or by a semi-automatic cursor, and represented by a string of X–Y coordinates. In this way, certain cate-gories of map information, such as contours, coast-lines, political boundaries, or drainage features, can be committed to digital form.

For small experimental maps, as might be made in a college geography department, a digitizer is neither necessary nor economical. The structure of a map can be converted to coordinate form quite easily by using an overlay of translucent squared paper on which the coordinate system is clearly evident.

PROCESSING DEVICES

In general, the processor is a computer in which data can be sorted and subjected to mathematical operations

FIG. 8.8 Digitizing table, showing the cursor that is moved from feature to feature. Photos courtesy of ALTEK.

before being mapped. The processor may alter certain parts of the raw base map – for the purpose of generalizing a coastline, for instance. Another base map manipulation might be to alter systematically all the X–Y coordinates that define the base in order to change the map from one *projection* to another. Or the processor might be called upon to select a certain part of a large base map (the part defined by a specified coordinate field) so that it can be displayed. Finally, the processor might be called upon to associate a list of data values with certain parts of the base, to create symbols or shadings in appropriate areas, and to produce instructions that will direct an output unit to produce the map image. All of these operations, incidentally, are directed by computer programs (software) especially written with the cartographic needs in mind.

OUTPUT DEVICES

The output device dictates the overall appearance and character of the map or graphic that is produced. Some devices will produce images that are obviously computer products, while others imitate conventional maps.

Line printers

Patterns and pictures have been produced on the line printer ever since the device became available, so its potential for making maps is apparent (Fig. 8.9). Although the alphabetic and numeric characters of the printer are not square, the array of character locations can readily be associated with a system of X–Y coordinates. The printer output is rather coarse-looking, and because of its coarseness has low resolution, which is to say it is incapable of recording fine details on a map. The visual coarseness can be dealt with by reducing the output photographically. The resolution, however, can be improved only by making large-scale output. If a wall-sized map is built from many 13-inch panels of printer output, then a span of 10 units in the coordinate system may be represented by six character locations, whereas on a page-sized map that same coordinate range may be represented by only one character location.

Plotters

The plotter may be the most fascinating of all the output devices because it is a robot draftsman – actually holding a pen in its grasp, and moving it across paper, with startling speed in the X and the Y directions. It is commanded by a program that views

FIG. 8.9 Non-map graphic produced on a line printer.

all lines and lettering elements as a series of increments or steps.[3] In the drum plotter, which is more compact than the flatbed, one component of motion is provided by moving the pen, while the other is provided by rolling the paper under the pen (Fig. 8.10).

Some versions of the flatbed plotter can not only

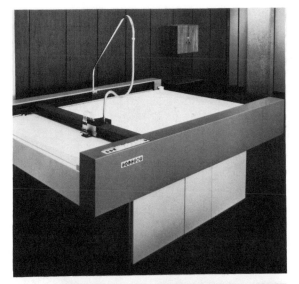

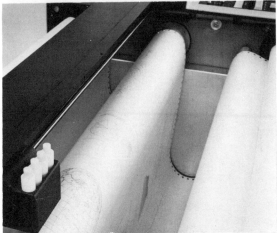

FIG. 8.10   Flatbed and drum plotters. Photos courtesy of California Computer Products Inc. (CALCOMP).

Cathode ray tubes

The cathode ray tube (CRT) is essentially the same large vacuum tube used in an oscilloscope or a television set. An electron beam paints images onto the face of the screen in response to commands from graphic programs. On one form of CRT (the *storage* type, as opposed to the *refresh* type) the map image can be altered, rearranged, and augmented until the desired product is seen. The map represented by that temporary image can then be stored, or it can be output on paper by a plotter or by an electrostatic *hard copy* machine connected to the CRT (Fig. 8.11). The ability to manipulate the map image this way, called *interactive* computer mapping, is possible only with extensive programming. It is the speed and flexibility of the CRT device, though, that makes the process technically feasible.

Electrostatic printers

Just as an image may be maintained on a CRT by very rapid sweeps of an electron beam, so a map image can be built line by line by a scanning device. The principle has been used for years on office copiers that slowly scan a map image and simultaneously transfer the alternation of blacks and whites on the original into blacks and whites on a printing stencil. Similarly, a weather map can be transmitted by radio as a succession of signals derived from scanning the original. Images from satellite "photography" are coded and transmitted by means of the same principle.

Electrostatic printers, making use of the same technique of building an image line by line, can produce large and small maps with remarkable speed, regardless of their complexity. As a sheet of sensitive paper, up to six feet wide, rolls through a long electrostatic "head" it receives a succession of *on or off* signals, first along one very thin line, then along the next, in an electronic progression that is matched to the speed of the paper (Fig. 8.12). The resolution can be quite high – up to 100 elements per inch; and the speed of production can be up to 2 inches per second. Producing a large complex map image this way is far more efficient than directing a mechanical plotter to chase here and there across the map as it traces the various lines and lettering elements that make up the map.

draw with a pen, but can also *scribe* linework (as for contours on a topographic map) or can draw such lines onto photographic film with a beam of light. They are especially well-suited to high-speed production of very accurate line work, but are not very efficient in drawing separates for areas to appear in certain shades of grey or colored inks. Plotters clearly are output devices that mechanize the drafting work involved in the production of conventional cartographic products in mapping operations such as those of the US Geological Survey. In this sense they are quite different from the line printer.

FIG. 8.11 A large (19-inch diagonal) cathode ray tube terminal with over 16 million addressable points. The maps on the screen can be printed on an electrostatic hard copy unit or instead can be routed to a pen plotter. Photo courtesy of Tektronix Inc.

Computer on Microfilm (COM) units

Cartographers at the US Bureau of the Census have devised a method for high-speed production of separations to be used in making printing plates for books and atlases (see Broome, 1974; and Meyer, Broome, and Schweitzer, 1975). The COM unit uses electron beams to paint open areas onto 35 mm photographic film, in response to computer programs that have stored the coordinate descriptions of data areas and have assigned those areas to certain categories for mapping in choropleth style. The electron beam is directed to turn *on* as it sweeps across the coordinate field of a county that is to be included in a separate,

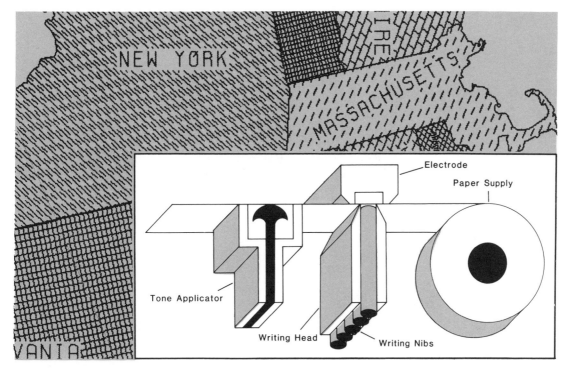

FIG. 8.12   Electrostatic printer and its product. The full map is 3 feet by 5 feet, and was produced in about one minute. Courtesy of Versatec.

and to turn *off* as it sweeps through the fields of counties excluded from that separate.

In this production work, the Census Bureau uses negative art work *much smaller* than the finished product. This opposes the usual practices of making art work larger than the finished product, or making it same size as is done when scribing. It works because the high resolution of the COM unit makes film images precise enough to be enlarged. The final printed products are of high quality and show no evidence of the unique methods used in their production. The Bureau has used this technique for production of published maps, including the Census of US Agriculture (US Bureau of the Census, 1973) and the series of urban atlases that can be found in most large libraries.

SOFTWARE

This discussion will deal briefly with both digitized base maps (base files) and computer mapping programs − both of which may be considered under the heading of *software*.

BASE MAPS

Some base maps for unique mapping needs are small enough to be digitized by hand. Others are very large and complex, and therefore difficult to translate to numerical form without a staff and the use of a digitizer. At the same time, these large bases are sufficiently popular that they now are available for purchase.

A prime example of such a base map is World Data Bank I or World Data Bank II available from the CIA on magnetic tapes. These files hold all the coastlines, rivers, and political boundaries of the world map. With the proper computer programs, the cartographer can direct a plotter or a CRT to draw all or part of the base at a selected map scale and on a chosen map projection. The CIA uses this base file itself for quick maps "in-house," and for its published maps and atlases.

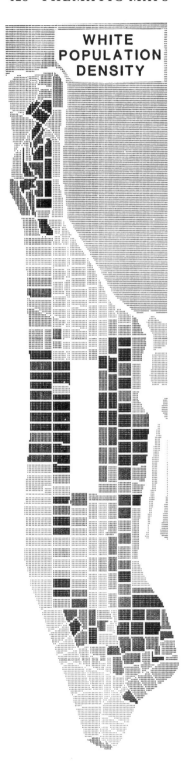

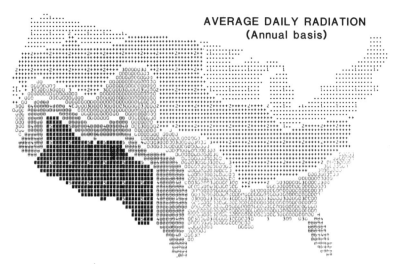

FIG. 8.13 Isarithmic and choropleth maps produced on a line printer by use of the SYMAP program. The Manhattan map is from the Harvard Lab for Computer Graphics. Both maps show the benefit of photographic reduction.

The US Bureau of the Census also makes available the base maps it has digitized for its own work. Most noteworthy are its base for all the US counties (as used in its atlas of agriculture) and the twenty base maps for census tracts in twenty metropolitan areas of the USA (the Urban Atlas files). These also can be purchased through the Harvard Laboratory for Computer Graphics and Spatial Analysis.

MAPPING PROGRAMS

A great many programs have been written and circulated by individuals, by government agencies, and by enterprising institutions such as Harvard. Only a few will be dealt with here in order to give some idea of the kinds of maps and graphics that can be produced.

For printer maps

A versatile mapping program that now enjoys wide distribution is SYMAP from the Harvard Laboratory. It is capable of producing isoline maps, choropleth maps, proximal (nearest-neighbor) maps, and in its latest version can perform trend-surface analysis. Examples of SYMAP output are in Figure 8.13. More specialized programs only for choropleth maps are C-MAP and SCANGEN from the US Census Bureau. If the purpose of mapping is mainly to summarize information, such as land use assigned to small map "cells," then the Composite Mapping System (CMS) developed for the US Department of Commerce may be appropriate. It has the capacity to take various kinds of information that are stored by map cell and combine them, or to map only those cells which have certain combinations of attributes (see Marsh, 1976).

For various types of map on plotter or CRT

In choropleth mapping, a program directs a plotter to shade areas by drawing line or dot patterns. One such

program is CALFORM from the Harvard Lab (Fig. 8.14). Another is GIMMS from the University of Edinburgh. Unlike printer maps, these plotter-drawn maps have a conventional look that is due to the automated drafting procedure. Instead of being drawn by plotter, they can, at many installations, be produced on a CRT, then printed on paper very quickly by an electrostatic hard copy unit.

Maps using spot symbols can be produced with programs that scale the symbols and direct a plotter to draw them. One program with this capability is GIMMS (Fig. 8.15) which can draw a variety of circles, circle segments, and squares.

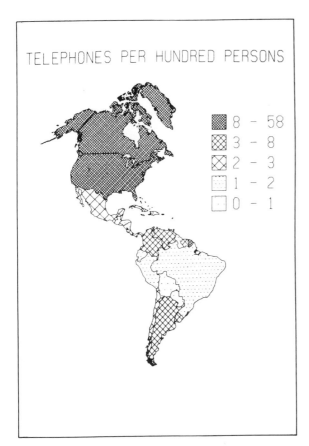

FIG. 8.14 Choropleth map produced on a pen plotter by use of the CALFORM program. From Harvard Lab for Computer Graphics.

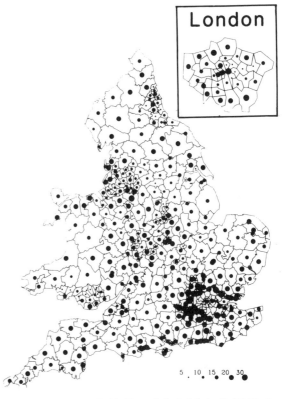

FIG. 8.15 Scaled circle map prepared using GIMMS program from the University of Edinburgh. Taken from a GIMMS brochure.

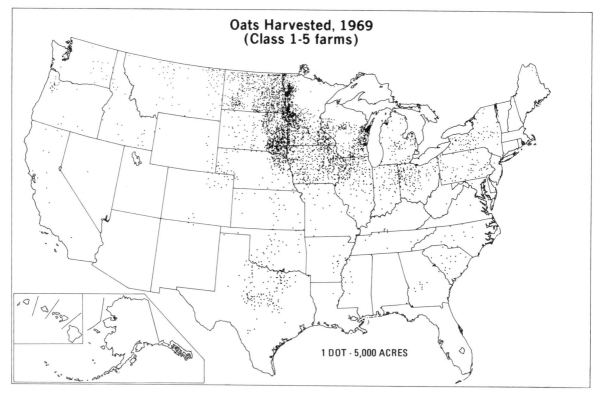

Oats Harvested, 1969
(Class 1-5 farms)

1 DOT - 5,000 ACRES

FIG. 8.16 Dot map prepared by the US Census Bureau, using programs written by Wendell Beckwith while associated with the University of Wisconsin at Madison. From US Census Bureau (1973).

Even the dot map can be automated (Fig. 8.16). The example shown used programs that calculated the density of dots per county, and placed the dots in certain parts of counties according to land-use information.

For smooth or stepped statistical surfaces

Drawing a stepped surface by hand is an easy task (see chapter 9). The smooth surface, on the other hand, requires a great deal of skill, and would be out of reach for most cartographers if it were not for plotters or CRT units and some very clever programming. Again, the Harvard Lab has a program available for drawing surfaces. In its older form, it is SYMVU; in its latest and interactive form it is called ASPEX (Fig. 8.17). These programs provide for different vertical scales and the selection of various viewing directions

and viewing elevations. The fishnet version of a smooth surface may be produced by using the program SURFACE II available from the Kansas State Geological Survey (Fig. 8.18). A stepped surface is visually more pleasing when the data area prisms are drawn straight-sided, rather than with sloping sides and complex faces as in the SYMVU plot. One program that will produce a stepped surface with straight-sided prisms was written by Waldo Tobler a number of years ago (Tobler, 1974) and is available from him (Fig. 8.19). With the right hardware arrangement and the necessary programming, any of these three-dimensional plots can be previewed on a CRT, and then produced by plotter or hard copy unit.

FIG. 8.17 Smooth and stepped statistical surfaces ► produced on a pen plotter by use of the SYMVU program.

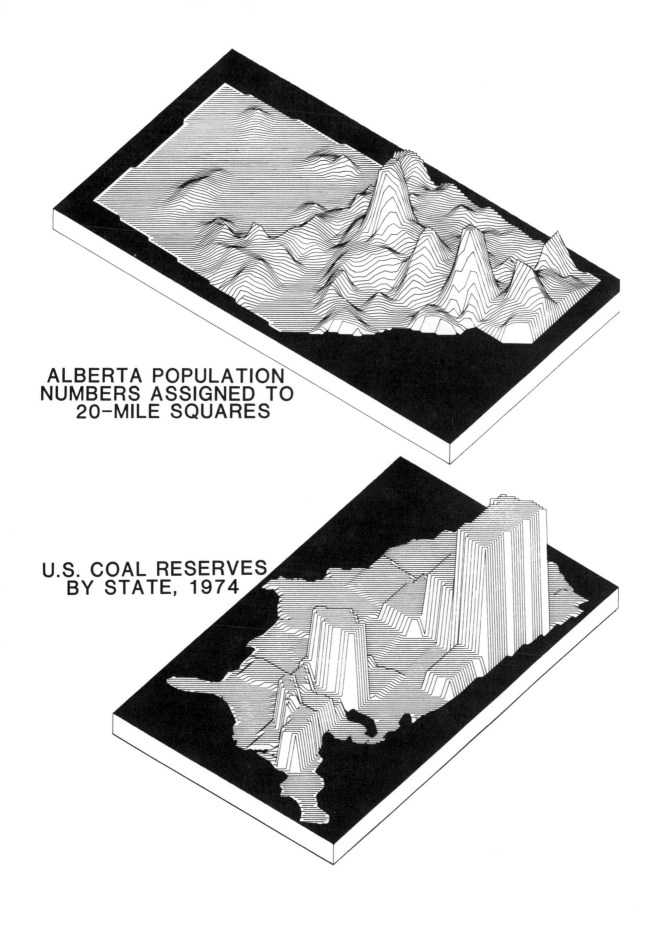

ALBERTA POPULATION
NUMBERS ASSIGNED TO
20-MILE SQUARES

U.S. COAL RESERVES
BY STATE, 1974

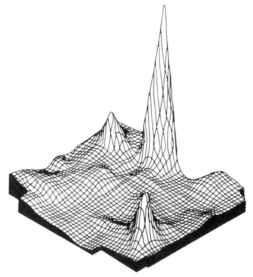

FIG. 8.18 Smooth statistical surface in fishnet style, produced on pen plotter by use of SURFACE II program. From Jenks (1963).

FIG. 8.19 Stepped statistical surface with straight-sided prisms, produced on pen plotter. Black added to prism faces. Part of Michigan is shown: the variable is unknown. From Tobler (1974).

Notes

1 The trade term *art work* (or simply "the art") is applied to the piece or pieces that leave the drafting table and go to photography, or possibly to plate-making without need for a photographic negative (see chapter 7). The term, *camera-ready*, is not ideal for the purpose, because the art work used for separations is also ready for the camera. *Single-piece* art work is a more expressive term that may be substituted for *camera-ready*.
2 This procedure is analogous to the method by which a satellite records a "picture" of Mars, then transmits it to earth.
3 The most recent plotters are capable of continuous-curve motions that are not limited to successive steps along the X or the Y directions.

References

Broome, Frederick R. (1974) "Micrographics: a new approach to cartography at the Census Bureau," *Proceedings*, American Congress on Surveying and Mapping, Fall Convention, Washington, DC, 1–14.

Jenks, George F. (1963) "Generalization in statistical mapping," *Annals*, Association of American Geographers, 53 (1), 15–26.

Lab-Log (1980) Catalogue from Harvard Laboratory for Computer Graphics and Spatial Analysis.

Marsh, Elizabeth R. (1976) *Computer Mapping in a Rural County*, Pomona, NJ, Stockton State College (copies available from Professor Marsh).

Meyer, M. A., F. R. Broome, and R. H. Schweitzer (1975) "Color statistical mapping by the US Bureau of the Census," *The American Cartographer*, 2, 100–17.

Tobler, Waldo R. (1974) "A computer program to draw perspective views of geographical data," *The American Cartographer*, 1 (2), 124.

US Bureau of the Census (1973) *1969 Census of Agriculture: Graphic Summary*, part 15 of vol. 5, *Special Reports on the 1969 Census of Agriculture*, Washington, DC, US Government Printing Office.

9 Production Hints

Anyone starting in thematic cartography will encounter a dazzling array of tools and materials for sale in engineering supply and art supply stores, and will need assistance when using the tools and materials. This chapter provides guidance for selection of tools and materials, and describes methods that will streamline production work and lead to products that have a professional look.

The suggestions about methods are of two kinds. Hints that deal with line work, lettering, and corrections are of general application. Other hints, such as those for producing spot symbols, area symbols, and unconventional graphics, are directly related to concepts of symbolization outlined in earlier chapters and are intimately connected to exercises for those kinds of symbolization. The chapter can serve, therefore, as a *handbook* to be referred to during work on exercises.

All the ideas in this chapter apply to making *positive* art work: nothing is provided on the use of scribing or peel coat methods. Many of the hints apply to completing satisfactory art work, regardless of whether it is camera-ready art or a series of separates. It is assumed, however, that the student will be working mostly with camera-ready art; and for this reason the chapter does not begin to discuss the many useful effects that can be achieved through superposition of images from art work separates.

Drawing materials

For most thematic cartography only two classes of drawing materials need to be considered: tracing papers and synthetic materials such as mylar and acetate.

TRACING PAPERS

Papers in a great range of quality will be encountered in an art supply store. The flimsy papers are good only as cover sheets for finished art work. For the drawings themselves, only higher-grade papers, i.e. *vellum*, with 100 per cent rag content, should be used. Albanene brand, from Keuffel and Esser Company is an excellent choice; though a roughly equivalent paper is sold under the Clearprint label. If the price is much less than 10 cents per $8\frac{1}{2}$ x 11 inch sheet (as of 1981) the paper will not accept ink evenly, and will wrinkle excessively when ink is applied to areas.

In general, tracing papers are for page-sized drawings, and can be used for larger work only if there is no need for two or more drawings to fit one another precisely. All papers will stretch or shrink with changes in humidity and therefore lack the *dimensional stability* which is essential if two or more pieces of art are used as separations from which the final map is produced (see chapter 8). The effects of shrinking or stretching are much greater in larger sheets of paper and would be very slight in sheets that are $8\frac{1}{2}$ x 11 inches. Tracing papers can be purchased in rolls, loose sheets, and pads. Rolls are most economical if they can be cut into useful sheets. Pads are most convenient and easiest to store.

Special mention should be made of the papers printed with a blue grid (Albanene or Clearprint brands, for instance). These tracing papers are ideal for preparation of graphs and special symbols without need for an underlying guideline sheet. Drawing can be done directly on the gridded tracing paper because the lines are printed in a *non-reproducing* blue ink which will not affect photographic film.

SYNTHETICS

The major alternative to tracing papers is drafting film made of *polyester* or *mylar* (brand names Herculene, or Technifax). It is tough, accepts ink uniformly, can be erased repeatedly, and is dimensionally stable. It is, therefore, the ideal material for inked work used as separations which must fit one another precisely.

Various thicknesses of drafting films are available, but a thickness of *3 mil* (3 thousandths of an inch) is adequate for most work. The film needs to be only *single matte*, that is, with a frosted drawing surface on one side, not both. At those specifications, the material is roughly twice the price of high-grade tracing papers. On a very large job the difference in price would be significant; but if a job requires only 10 sheets of 11 x 17 inch size the price would be around $5.00 for mylar and $2.50 for tracing paper – a difference that is very slight when the benefits of mylar are considered. If extensive work is done on this material, there will be surprising wear on the technical pens. The matte surface, or *tooth*, on the film will erode pen tips and alter the width of line eventually, unless special wear-resistant tips are used.

Acetate is clear plastic film without a frosted drawing surface. If perfectly clean, it will accept an inked line beautifully, but will make the line slightly wider than on mylar. Acetate does not have the dimensional stability of mylar. Its unique characteristic is transparency. A drawing on acetate can be applied as an overlay to another drawing for photographic exposure, then removed for a second photograph in order to make multiple use of one base. This would not be possible with any other material. Both mylar and acetate films must be kept very clean if ink is to adhere to the surface. Commercial erasing and cleaning liquids can be used; but cleaning pads and inking powders such as *pounce* are more convenient. They are sprinkled on, rubbed around, then brushed off thoroughly to avoid clogging a pen. Special inks are available for working on mylar and acetate films, though they are not essential. Those same inks are versatile, and may be used on tracing papers as well.

Tools

From the vast variety of tools available for engineering and cartographic drawing, a few essentials have been selected.

PENCILS

Careful drawings in pencil are preliminary to most thematic maps. The drawing materials, and especially frosted mylar, demand that *hard* leads be used. A soft lead will make a clumsy line that varies in width and is easily smudged. On tracing paper, a 4H lead is needed. Mylar demands a 5H or 6H. There are two devices that make it easy to maintain a sharp point. One is the *mechanical pencil* with slim leads (0.5 mm) that need no sharpening. A more dependable alternative is the engineer's *lead holder* with a supply of leads and a sharpener (the soft leads that may be in the mechanical pencil or the lead holder at time of purchase should be set aside). A wooden pencil with blue non-reproducing lead will be useful for making notes on art work to be photographed.

PENS

The universal tool for most line work is the technical pen supplied by Mars-Staedler, Rapidograph, or Castell-Faber (Fig. 9.1). The different pen points allow for a great range of line widths, each of which can be replicated by using the same pen point, so long as the drawing material and the drawing technique are not varied. Pens of this type all have tubular tips and create lines with round ends. Each point has its own cylindrical ink reservoir with a large supply of ink which means the pen can be in a ready-to-work condition for weeks. After a few weeks the pen should be taken apart and washed, using a commercial pen cleaner (ink solvent) if necessary.

An alternative style of pen that accomplishes similar effects is a series of reservoir-points with one wooden holder (brand names Leroy or Wrico). These are excellent for freehand drawing of curved lines. Prompt cleaning *after each use* is essential, however.

For square-ended lines it is necessary to use a set of special ruling nibs which are attached, interchangeably, to a fountain-style pen with reservoir (brand: Pelican-Graphos).

For irregular lines such as rivers, the best tools are nibs such as the *mapping nib* or *crowquill* which are flexible enough to make a fine line with light pressure, and broader line with heavier pressure (Fig. 9.1).

KNIVES

A knife is extremely valuable in cartographic production. It is essential for trimming and handling labels,

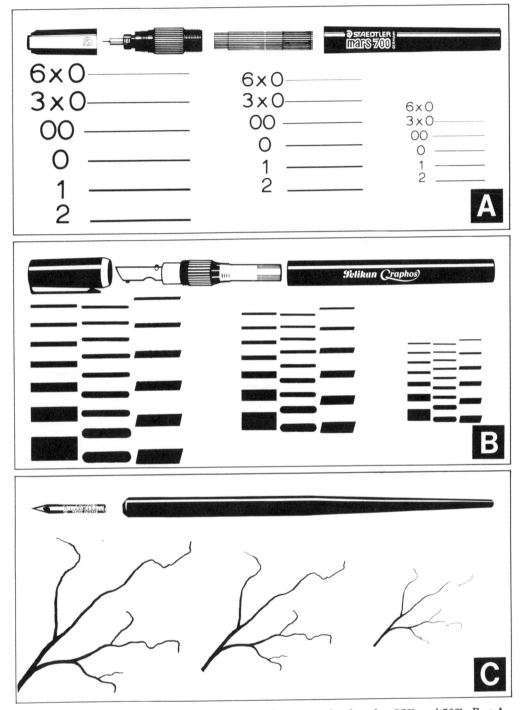

FIG. 9.1   Three pens, showing their products at full size and reduced to 75% and 50%: Part A, technical pen; Part B, Pelican-Graphos; Part C, crowquill.

for making corrections, and for slicing and applying films and graphic tapes. Any good hobby knife with replaceable blades (X-acto) will do the job.

STRAIGHT DRAWING EDGES

For inking, a plain 15- or 18-inch wooden ruler with steel edge is perfectly adequate. Its raised edge prevents ink from running underneath. Plastic triangles have the advantage of transparency; but their edges may soon become marred. They should not be used for knifing. To prevent ink from running underneath, it may be necessary to slightly raise a plastic triangle with several layers of tape applied near the edge of the underside.

For knifing it is best to have a solid steel rule – preferably three feet or longer. The same rule can be used for inking longer lines.

The traditional T-square will be very useful when working with inked lettering and when drawing certain unconventional graphics. A steel or steel-edged model can double as a knifing edge and reduce the number of tools required.

CURVED DRAWING EDGES

For regular curved lines drawn in ink, some sort of special edges are needed. A set of plastic French curves will serve for most small-scale mapping needs if their range of sizes is great enough. Another approach is to use one of the lead-cored flexible curves which can, in theory, be fitted to any shape; in practice, the flexible curve is not easy to use. For larger-scale mapping and for more careful work on parallels and meridians, a set of *ship curves* should be available.

COMPASSES

For most inked circles a compass of six-inch length is suitable. The better grades of compass will have an inking tip that resembles an old-style ruling pen and can be interchanged with a tip that holds a lead (the same kind of lead used in the lead holder pencil mentioned above). For ease of use and for the sake of standardized line widths it is best to have a compass that holds a technical pen point. Some compasses are designed expressly for technical pens (Ko-I-Noor brand, for instance). Others can be equipped with an adapter to hold the technical pen (Fig. 9.2). If very

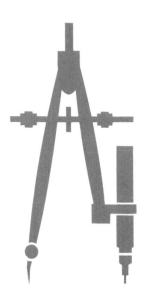

With adapter for technical pen

Designed for technical pen

Drop bow type

Drop bow designed for technical pen

FIG. 9.2 Compasses of varying styles, for ink work.

small circles must be inked, then a *drop-bow compass* is invaluable. Very large inked circles must be drawn with the aid of a beam extension fitted to a traditional compass.

AIDS FOR DRAWING SYMBOLS AND FOR LETTERING

Tools for these purposes will be discussed in the sections that deal with "Spot symbols-inked" (pp. 138–9) and with "Execution of lettering" (pp. 147–8).

ITEMS FOR THE STUDENT'S KIT

The following tools and materials are suggested for the student engaged in making small-scale thematic maps. Brand names are mentioned only to expedite the selection of suitable tools. For many of the items listed there are equivalent tools or materials in other brands.

- *Technical pens.* Rapidograph, Mars-Staedler, or Castell brands. A minimal set would have sizes 00, 0, 1, and 2
- *Compasses* with capacity to hold technical pen. Mars-Staedler brand can be fitted with an adapter. Rapidograph is designed expressly for technical pens
- *Templates.* For circles and other symbols. Berol brand has an excellent selection of symbols on their R-965 model
- *Protractor.* Circular or square, 4-inch diameter
- *French curves.* A set including small and large sizes
- *Scale.* Graduated in tenths of inch and in millimeters
- *Wooden ruler with steel edge.* For inking. Cheap 15-inch or 18-inch grade-school ruler will do splendidly
- *Lead holder.* The engineer's pencil. One with pocket clip will be handy. Also, leads of hardness 4H, and a sharpener
- *X-acto knife.* The no. 1 knife is adequate. Also a package of no. 11 blades
- *Tracing paper.* One pad of Albanene brand or equivalent, in size 11 x 17 inches

EQUIPMENT AND TOOLS FOR THE CARTOGRAPHIC LAB

The room for cartographic work will contain drafting tables, one or two light tables, and large drawers for projects and for drawing materials. In addition, a device for enlarging and reducing maps is essential (see chapter 5). The tools listed below will be needed frequently, but should not be purchased by every student:

- dispensers with masking and cellulose tapes
- a waxer for stick-on lettering
- a lead pointer (table model)
- ship curves for long curves in map projections
- long steel rules for knifing
- steel triangles
- a circle cutter for graphic films
- Leroy system lettering sets; and lettering guides

Line work

Line work can be executed either in ink or with graphic tapes, depending on the specific needs. Both are reviewed below.

INKED LINES, AND THE USE OF PENS

If inked lines are to be uniform and reproducible they must maintain their *dimension* and their *density*. The dimension (width) of line will not be constant unless the technical pen is held *vertical to the drawing surface*. That technique is important to line density also; but density will be most seriously affected if any of the following occur when using technical pens:

- the pen is drawn too quickly across the surface
- the point is clogged with old ink
- the ink is diluted with water remaining in the pen after washing
- the ink level in the reservoir is too low to encourage flow
- the inner wire that controls ink flow is bent
- the drawing surface is coated in some areas by oil from the skin

Dashed or dotted lines (with technical pen or with Pelican-Graphos nib) will be more regular if a sheet of squared guideline paper is placed under the work. Lines drawn against a straight edge or a curve are more easily drawn if the work is turned so the line is drawn from left to right, not in a vertical direction. Conversely, a line drawn freehand, such as a coastline, is better drawn *toward* the body, not from left to right.

INKLESS LINES, USING GRAPHIC TAPES

A variety of graphic tapes exists for the artist and cartographer. Chartpak is the dominant brand (see Fig. 9.3). These should not be confused with *border tapes* which are rather wide with fancy designs not suited to cartographic work.

The best application for graphic tapes is for lines that are curved or wandering, or for *short* straight lines. A long straight line is better done with pen and straight edge. There are tapes with dashed and dotted lines that are appropriate for symbolizing political boundaries or routes of different status. The most useful, though, are the plain black tapes in matte finish, and in a number of widths from $\frac{1}{64}$ inch. These are ideal for isarithmic lines or boundaries of natural areas such as physiographic provinces. They are especially useful for creating flow arrows or for wide lines that may be needed when art work is exceptionally large. When trimmed with a knife, their ends are sharp and square and distinctive from lines drawn with technical pen. A further advantage of all graphic tapes is that they can be applied on a surface, such as computer printer paper, that will not accept ink.

When applying tapes, the following hints should be followed:

- tapes should not be *stretched* when applied. If they are stretched they will soon assert themselves, shrink back, and leave gaps in the work
- they should be burnished into place, but not squashed
- they should be applied *after* ink work has been finished, because:
  (1) inking over them is impossible
  (2) the procedure of applying and knifing the tapes leaves oil and knife cuts on the drawing material
- for curved lines in black (the most important use for graphic tapes) the tape to buy is the *flex*, or *crepe* variety which has a matte finish. This is the only tape that will bend sharply and stay in place.

Spot and area symbols

The execution of spot and area symbols is extremely important, since the map message may depend upon these symbols being clear and without distracting flaws. To ensure that symbols are not compromised by unwanted overlap with features of the base map, it may be best to ink the base map *after* certain symbols have been completed. Both spot and area symbols may be created by traditional pen and ink methods or by use of dry materials now available in art supply and engineering supply stores. The discussion below deals first with the use of ink, then with dry materials.

SPOT AND AREA SYMBOLS USING INK

A useful distinction is between those spot symbols that are simply made distinctive in size and shape (non-scaled) and those that are carefully sized to represent quantities (scaled).

FIG. 9.3 Some of the effects attainable with graphic tapes.

NON-SCALED SPOT SYMBOLS

The small symbols used to differentiate towns from other sites such as mines or weather stations need not be drawn to specific sizes and therefore can be executed by inked or inkless methods. When drawn with pen and ink these should have the benefit of either squared guideline paper or templates in order to ensure a regular appearance. A poor rendering of a well-known geometrical form is very distracting. Squares, diamonds, and triangles are easily accomplished with the aid of guideline paper. Hexagons and circles are best drawn with a template which may include circles, squares, hexagons and triangles (Fig. 9.4). Incidentally, it is not wise to use both circles and hexagons on the same map because they tend to be very similar when reduced to small size. Small circular dots are difficult to make, even with the aid of a template. It is best, therefore, to apply the ready-made perfect dots that can be purchased in dry-transfer materials (see p. 142).

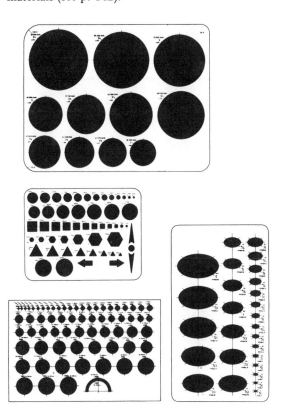

FIG. 9.4   A few of the templates available for drawing symbols.

SCALED SPOT SYMBOLS

Spot symbols that are scaled literally to the values being symbolized (non-grouped vs. grouped approach as described in chapter 2) must be drawn in ink on a custom-made basis. This applies to symbols scaled geometrically and those of the accumulated type.

Circles

The preceding section on tools mentions traditional inking compasses and the newer types that hold technical pen points. Whichever tool is used, it is a good idea to practice extensively before beginning on the art work.

One design matter that must be confronted is the overlap of circles. If the smaller circles are to be large enough, some circles are likely to overlap. This is not a flaw, so long as the overlap is neatly accomplished. There are essentially three methods for drawing the overlap (Fig. 9.5). First, the circles are left empty and intact, so every part of every circle is visible. This appears rather busy, but tests show that readers can interpret such a presentation without difficulty. A second treatment is to allow small circles to obliterate larger ones and thus rise to the foreground. Notice that applying grey tone to the circles is easy in this case because the pattern can be applied over entire clusters: black, however, cannot be applied to such a cluster because the edges of the foreground circles would disappear. A third treatment is similar to the second, except that white halos are made by swinging arcs from the centers of the foreground circles. This allows all circles to be made black, but it complicates the procedure of applying grey to the circles.

Squares and cubes

Both of these symbols are best drawn with the aid of guideline paper. The square needs no explanation. Cubes of small and moderate size can be drawn without actual perspective, simply using squared guideline paper to ensure the sides are parallel (Fig. 9.6). If a cube is very large then its horizontal lines should converge to make it look natural. Perspective guideline paper for this purpose is available at art supply stores.

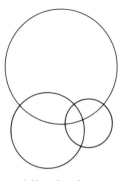

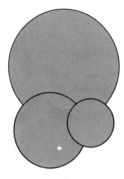

FIG. 9.5 Three methods of dealing with circle overlap.

All circles complete

Small circles in foreground

Small circles in foreground, with halos

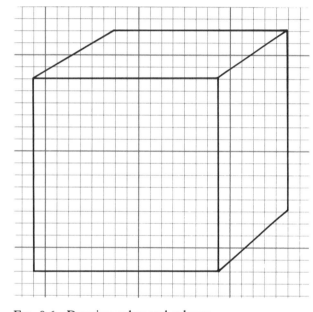

FIG. 9.6 Drawing cubes and spheres.

Spheres

The illusion of sphericity can be accomplished by drawing a circle and modifying it by either the graticule or the billiard ball approach. In the first case, parallels and meridians are drawn onto a circle to make it resemble a globe. This is challenging. The illusion can be created, instead, by simulating the highlight seen on a polished ball. It is most effective on a circle that is solid black, or is made solid grey by means of graphic films (see pp. 143–4).

Accumulated symbols

Blockpiles are drawn with the aid of squared guideline paper (non-perspective). It is necessary to keep the style and arrangement consistent. Front faces, for

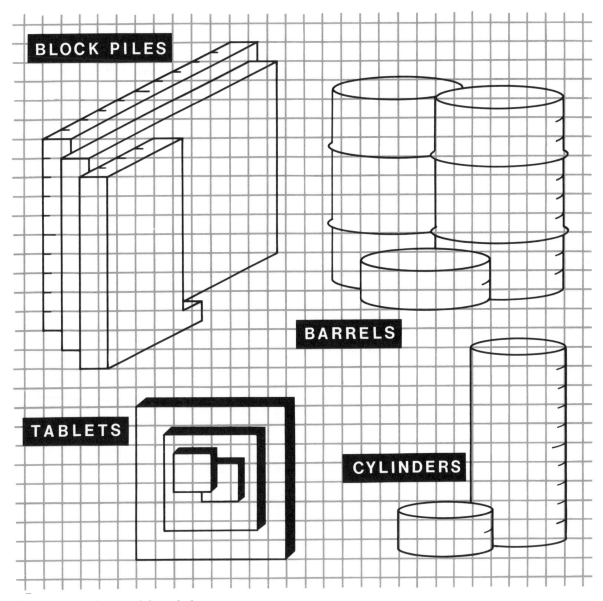

FIG. 9.7 Drawing special symbols.

instance, are kept clean and simple by always placing odd amounts in the rear. If using a group of slabs, it is necessary to draw the front slabs first, because they obscure those in the rear.

Barrels and cylinders are drawn with the aid of an ellipse template and squared paper.

The tablet used by *Oxford* atlases to symbolize urban populations is simply a square with a shadow created by slipping an inked square diagonally away from an underlying model square, and then tracing the exposed portion of that underlying square (see Fig. 9.22). The area of shadow must be black if the symbol is made entirely by hand. The shadow can be dark grey, however, if graphic film of the dot-screen type is used (see "Area symbols," below). Tablets of two or more sizes may be accumulated to represent numbers such as the populations of metropolitan areas.

AREA SYMBOLS

The patterns used to indicate qualitative differences such as swampland versus forest (see chapter 1) are time-consuming and very challenging to execute with a pen (for many patterns, incidentally, an old-fashioned nib, rather than a technical pen, is the preferred tool). Nevertheless, the skillful cartographer may draw such patterns by hand in order to "customize" them for the job at hand, rather than applying some pre-made patterns that may not be appropriate.

The same comments can be made about area symbols that are more quantitative in nature, such as a series of line patterns or stippled patterns that are progressively more dense to symbolize increasing value or intensity in the measure mapped. It is difficult to draw such patterns well, and virtually impossible to duplicate the fine textures available in pre-made patterns.

Hand-drawn patterns tend to look rather coarse and unfinished. Largely because of this coarseness, however, they reproduce very well and in this regard are safer than the fine dot screens available in pre-printed materials (see below). Making patterns by hand is *economical* in the sense that no materials need to be purchased and no time spent on trips to the supply store. All the work can be done without budging from the drafting table. It is far *slower*, though, than working with ready-made patterns, and entails, for the beginner, the hazard of spoiled lines and serious errors that are difficult to repair. In this sense it may be *far less economical* than using dry materials.

SPOT AND AREA SYMBOLS USING DRY MATERIALS

As suggested above, there are some advantages to using dry materials. Generally, they are speed of execution, uniformity, and repeatability of the pattern, and the freedom from hazards of the ink-spill kind. Skill with the knife is essential, however; and there may be serious difficulties with reproduction if care is not taken.

The dry materials are in two broad categories, *dry-transfer materials* and *graphic films*. The dry-transfer materials allow a letter or a symbol to be transferred from carrier sheet to the art work by simply rubbing it on while the sheet is held in position. Graphic films, on the other hand, must be peeled off their backing sheet, applied to the art work, then trimmed.

SPOT SYMBOLS

Symbols that are scaled literally (non-grouped) must have their outlines drawn with a pen in order to accomplish the desired sizes. They can be filled-in and made black, if that is desired, by means of *red block-out film* (see p. 143). This may be cut easily with a knife to fit squares and cubes, and also may be cut to fit any circle by means of a *circle cutter*. This is important, because large areas painted with ink will wrinkle tracing papers and distort the art work.

Geometric symbols used for data grouped into categories need not be precisely sized. For this purpose, dry-transfer materials are ideal, especially if the symbols are not very large. The better dry-transfer materials are on a carrier sheet that does not buckle and distort the letter or symbol during the transfer. In this regard, two of the best brands are Chartpak-Velvetouch and Geotype. An excellent selection of symbols is provided by Copyaid brand. The most expensive brand may be the British import, Letraset. Most brands offer the option of buying a sheet that holds a variety of symbols and sizes or a sheet that holds only circles, for instance, in a few sizes (Fig. 9.8). Some symbols are available also in graphic film or dry-transfer rolls that contain one symbol repeated over and over. Among the most useful items in dry-transfer materials are arrowheads in a variety of sizes. One of these can be applied at the end of a length of graphic tape to make a most professional arrow.

For dot maps and for data points on isarithmic maps it is essential to have perfectly round dots. Dry-transfer sheets are ideal for the purpose. It is more economical, though, to find a graphic film that offers a very coarse dot screen. The dot elements on such a sheet may be large enough to be used singly for many purposes if the degree of photo-reduction is not great. These dots from a graphic arts film cannot be used for a dot map, because the film material will overlap the film of neighboring dots, making a thick and visible accumulation of material.

When applying dry-transfer dots and symbols it is important to:

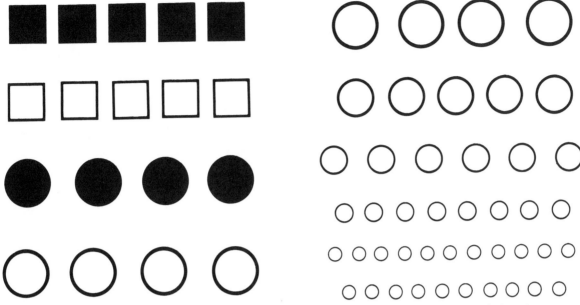

Fig. 9.8 Dry-transfer sheets offer variety in symbol and size, or variety in size for one symbol.

- maintain a square relationship between geometric symbols and map frame
- cover map areas not being worked on, to minimize the accidental transfer of symbols to the map
- burnish the transferred symbols thoroughly, using the glossy paper that accompanies each sheet of material
- spray the finished map with a clear matte fixative, if permanence is necessary
- avoid excessive bending of the art work, because this will encourage the symbols to flake off.

AREA SYMBOLS

Grey tones and patterns can be accomplished by the use of separations or by working directly on the art work on a camera-ready basis (see chapter 8). This section of production hints assumes the use of camera-ready methods.

One of the most useful of dry materials is the red film used in place of ink to render areas black. It is especially appropriate for large areas with straight boundaries that can be quickly sliced with a knife. It can also be used, though, for black circles and other symbols. For the usual camera-ready positive art work:

- choose red block-out film which is supplied with a waxed paper backing *and can be transferred*, like other graphic films from backing paper to art work
- avoid buying rubylith or amberlith, which resemble block-out film but come on a clear mylar backing. The red or amber film is designed to be peeled off and discarded, and will not stick satisfactorily to art work.

For qualitative patterns and for grey tones that suggest quantitative differences, graphic films are extremely useful. While a typical graphic film catalogue includes many film patterns not suitable for cartographic work, nevertheless there are many films that are appropriate. There is one for swamps, another for forested areas, and some to symbolize limestone and granite. Each of these would be time-consuming and very difficult to draw by hand. Also, the same simple parallel lines and cross-hatching that might be drawn by hand with almost-perfect spacing are drawn perfectly on pre-printed films. After some practice, most people can work more effectively with these films than with the hand-drawn counterparts.

Regardless of the type of pattern, the following procedure is used when applying graphic films: (1) cut a piece slightly larger than needed; (2) place it on the art work, and rub gently along the intended trim line; (3) trim to fit with a cut on the edge of the bounding line (if a bounding line is used); (4) discard waste, and burnish the area thoroughly.

The following procedures will help to avoid trouble when using films:
- cover map areas that are not being worked on, so that materials applied earlier will not be lifted off by the new material
- burnish the outline of the patterned area so the film does not move while being trimmed
- align any obvious grain or linearity in a pattern with that of other patterns on the map to avoid discordant effects. This applies even to the mechanical dot screens used for greys
- do not splice two pieces of film together in order to cover a large area. The join may be difficult to see; but the *camera will discern it*. This applies especially to mechanical dot screens used for greys
- burnish away all bubbles, and prick stubborn ones with a needle. The camera will find even the bubbles not obvious to the eye
- burnish from the *reverse* side of the art work so the pattern itself is not damaged
- always use a new blade for trimming films so it can be done with a light touch and with no danger of dragging and tearing the film
- for curved cuts, use a swivel X-acto knife, if the work is extensive
- apply films before applying graphic tapes
- avoid damaging the line work when trimming along an inked boundary.

Mechanical dot screens

These are the ready-made fine dot screens that simulate greys and are used for light to dark shadings symbolizing differences in density or intensity on choropleth and dasymetric maps, shaded isarithmic maps, or maps showing ranked data for areas. They are specified according to two measures: the percentage of black, or darkness, of the screen; and the texture, or number of lines per inch (see Fig. 9.9). The illustration does not show the full range of screens available. Most brands offer textures of 27.5, 30.0, 32.5, 42.5, 55.0, 60.0, 65.0, and 85.0 lines per inch. Each of these is available in 10, 20, 30, 40, 50, 60, and 70 per cent black.

The texture of screen used on art work must be coarse enough (few enough lines per inch) so dots will survive photographic reduction and plate-making. Because of variation in photographic skill and equipment it is difficult to specify how coarse the screens must be in order to avoid difficulty. A fairly conservative limit is 85 lines per inch. If the work is to be reduced to half its size (reduction factor of 50 per cent) then screens no finer than $42\frac{1}{2}$ lines per inch should be used on the art work.

Differences in percentage of black must be great enough to be discernible by the reader. For choropleth maps whose patterns are complex, it is necessary to use a series of screens in increments of 20 per cent, so the greys will be distinctive even against a complex and variable background. For shaded isarithmic maps that have simple patterns, obvious gradients, and are augmented by isoline labels, it is possible to use a series with 10 per cent increment, but the reader may have difficulty identifying the individual greys and relating them to the legend.

Combining dot screens with lettering and lines The relatively coarse texture of dot screens that will survive reduction makes superposition with lettering and lines very hazardous, because the dots tend to become visually attached to letters and lines and make them fuzzy (Fig. 9.10).

When lettering is combined with dot screens darker than 10 per cent the lettering cannot be dry-transfer applied directly to the screen, but must be on an opaque label that will obliterate the screen. These labels should be trimmed closely, and should be quite rectangular or the white patch will be distracting (Fig. 9.11).

Screens darker than 10 per cent cannot be safely placed over lines. This is important to know in choropleth mapping, because a great deal of knifing time *can* be saved by running light screens across the boundaries of data units, but darker screens must be trimmed back from the lines. The same principle applies when a shaded area includes features like roads or rivers. Screens should be sliced to make elongated windows for the line work (Fig. 9.12).

A DESIGN HINT FOR USE OF GRAPHIC FILMS

When used to show simple areas of occurrence, such

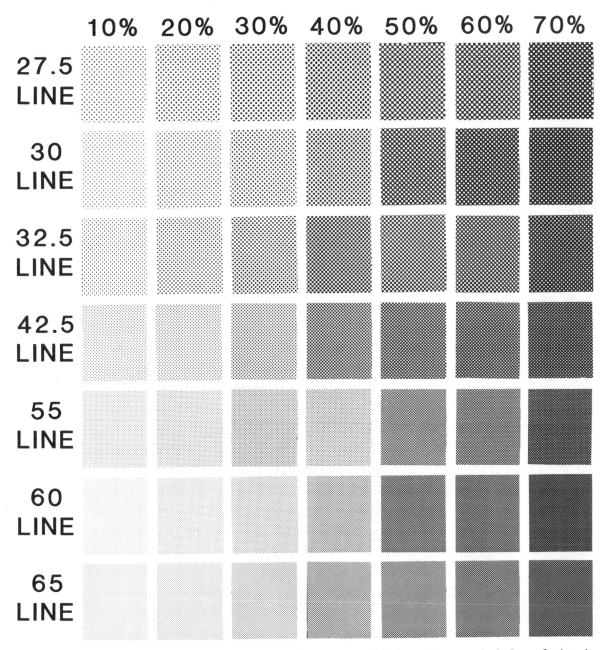

Fig. 9.9 Mechanical dot screens are specified according to percent black, and lines per inch. Imperfections in the darkness gradations often occur.

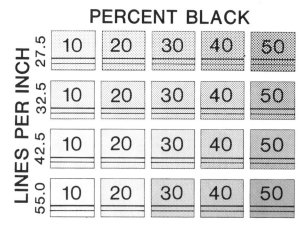

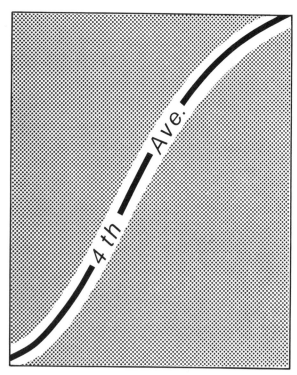

Fig. 9.10 Only the lightest dot screens can be successfully combined with lettering and line work.

Fig. 9.12 Windows must be sliced through darker dot screens to reveal rivers or roads.

as areas with elevation over 2000 feet, or areas affected by tree blight, graphic films can be used most effect-ively *without a bounding line*. The pattern or dot-screen material is applied, then trimmed to the correct size and shape. Because it has no hard bounding line the patch is pleasing and will not conflict with map features that must be represented by black lines (see Fig. 9.13). A similar treatment can be used for flow lines: the broad and slim arrows are created by trim-ming graphic film that has been applied to the art work. A *dual cutter* can be purchased to facilitate the slicing of parallel edges.

Execution of lettering

Either inked or dry methods can be used, the inked being the more traditional method. Having the ability

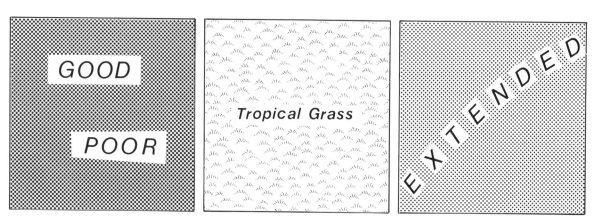

Fig. 9.11 Opaque labels successfully obliterating dot screens and patterns. Labels must be trimmed to consistent rectangles.

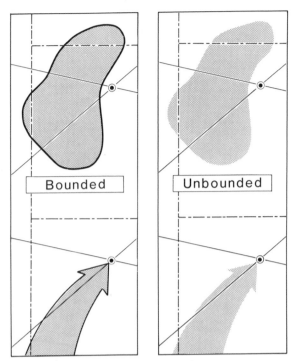

FIG. 9.13 Unbounded areas of occurrence or flow lines will be distinct and separate from black-line features.

and the equipment for inked lettering can be advantageous because the work can be done economically and without depending on material supply store or a typesetting service. On the other hand, the inkless methods offer greater speed and a full range of professional-looking type faces.

INKED LETTERING

Free-hand lettering, when done skillfully, is appropriate for sketch maps and views of landscapes. It lends the work a traditional look that is very pleasing; but it demands a great deal of practice.

Even the beginner can make regular and inoffensive lettering with the aid of *lettering guides* that resemble stencils and are designed to accommodate technical pens such as Rapidograph or Mars-Staedler brands (Fig. 9.14). More refined, and more expensive, are mechanical aids such as the Leroy system which offers

various styles in many sizes, and the capacity for slant as well as upright letters. To avoid errors on the art work itself, all inked lettering can be done on separate sheets of opaque paper, *then attached as labels.*

The lettering guides and the Leroy system should be used with a T-square taped into place while a line of lettering is executed. In this way, the position of the letters will be fixed on a horizontal line, and only the letter and word spacing must be attended to. Labels, whether inked or dry in their lettering, can be attached by:
- using pre-gummed address labels
- *waxers:* these electrically heat a reservoir of paraffin wax and allow it to be rolled onto a label
- *rubber cement:* this, like the waxer, is especially useful for larger labels
- *double-stick tape* (Scotch brand) or *adhesive transfer tape:* this should be applied to a fairly large sheet of

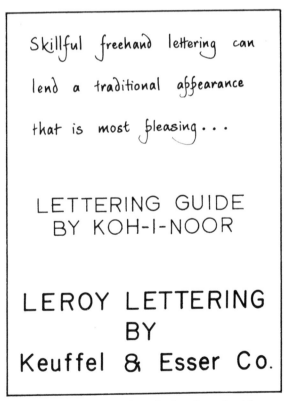

FIG. 9.14 Inked lettering: freehand, and with two mechanical aids.

completed lettering, then trimmed to make labels. *Do not* trim to label size, then attempt to apply double-stick tape.

INKLESS LETTERING

Both beginners and professionals can make good use of the various forms of lettering done with dry materials. There are two approaches. In the first, words are built, letter by letter, directly on the map (or on a separate sheet) using dry-transfer materials. In the second case, some machine is used to create words or blocks of words which are applied to the map as labels.

WORKING WITH ALPHABETS IN DRY-TRANSFER MATERIALS

The same firms that supply dry-transfer symbols also sell alphabet sheets with lettering all of the same style, variant, and point size. Both capitals and lower case letters are included, along with numerals (Fig. 9.15). When purchasing alphabets for a map, realize that two contrasting styles (or fonts) will usually be the limit. The necessary variety can be attained by different variants and sizes (see chapter 4).

As with inked lettering, the dry-transfer letters may be applied directly to the maps or may be assembled on pre-gummed address labels, or attached with wax, rubber cement, or double-stick tape. Whichever of the two methods is used, the following procedures should be followed:

- use squared paper as guidelines for both horizontal alignment and for letter and word spacing. *Check the alignment carefully*
- transfer letters by rubbing with a small burnishing tool, not with a ball-point pen
- remove errors with eraser, or by picking up the offending letter with cellulose tape
- burnish the finished lettering thoroughly, using the glossy paper that accompanies the alphabet sheet
- for permanence, cover the letters with clear cellulose tape or a fixer spray.

A handy label can be made by this procedure:

FIG. 9.15 Part of an alphabet sheet in dry-transfer lettering.

1 rub letters onto high-grade tracing paper with blue grid lines (or onto mylar with guidelines underneath)
2 apply clear cellulose tape of convenient length
3 strip the words off the drafting surface by removing tape and words together
4 apply label to art work.

A label with white letters on black can be made conventionally, if white lettering is available in the desired type style and variant. If only black dry-transfer lettering is available, the following procedure can be used to obtain white letters on black:

1 rub black letters onto tracing paper or mylar film
2 paint the letters and the surface thoroughly with black ink
3 apply cellulose tape, and burnish
4 strip lettering away from the black surface by removing the tape
5 trim and apply the label.

When purchasing dry-transfer lettering (and dry-transfer symbols) avoid brands that have very flexible backing sheets that tend to crack the letters as they are transferred. If the map is to be reproduced by Diazo (blueprint-style) process, then select lettering that is *heat resistant*. Geotype brand offers heat-resistant letters on a firm backing sheet that is easy to use.

The dry-transfer lettering is extremely convenient for making a few labels, especially for the student without access to other dry methods. Its disadvantages are its fragility and expense: in any one project, only small parts of any alphabet sheet will be used, leaving unused letters and numerals to age and deteriorate.

USING LABELS COMPOSED TO ORDER

It is far easier to apply a ready-made label than to build each word letter by letter on the map with either inked or dry-transfer lettering.

Typewriters can produce quite satisfactory lettering for many purposes, *but only if the machine has a carbon film (expendable) ribbon.* Machines with reusable cloth ribbons make lettering that is grey, textured, and will not reproduce well. Certain IBM Selectric machines use the carbon film ribbon and also have the capacity for both elite and pica sizes with adjustable spacing to suit the two sizes. For larger lettering, in one style only, an IBM Executive machine with large type is most useful in the cartographic lab (see Fig. 9.16).

One Executive type face

SAME EXECUTIVE TYPE FACE

WITH EXPANDED LETTER AND WORD SPACING

Prestige Pica--
Capitals and Lower Case

PRESTIGE PICA--
ALL CAPITALS

FIG. 9.16 A few of the lettering possibilities from IBM typewriters.

For truly professional lettering it is necessary to use a machine with styles, sizes, and quality of product that surpass those of the typewriter. Such lettering can either be obtained from typesetting services or can be produced "in-house" if the cartographic establishment can purchase and maintain a lettering machine.

Professional typesetting services offer a wide range of type styles and variants; and they can produce a large lettering job quickly by using advanced electronic equipment that will allow an operator at a keyboard to select any style, variant, and size, and to edit and modify the product on a cathode ray tube before printing. They also can compose large *blocks of lettering* that would be most tedious to assemble word by word on the drafting table. The main disadvantage of working with an outside typesetting service is the inflexibility. The order and its execution must be perfect, or the job is delayed while mistakes are corrected or missing labels produced by placing a second order. Having a machine within the cartographic laboratory is a great advantage.

There are a number of moderately priced lettering machines suitable for a small mapping facility. This review mentions only two.

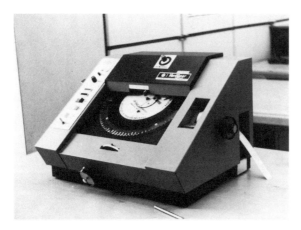

FIG. 9.17 The Headliner machine from Addressograph-Multigraph.

FIG. 9.18 The Kroy lettering machine by Kroy Industries.

One machine found on a number of college campuses − either in a visual aids service department, or in a cartographic laboratory − is the Varityper, by Addressograph-Multigraph (Fig. 9.17). This uses "type-masters" (one for each variant and size) with letters in negative form on a black plastic disc. Words are built, one letter at a time, by allowing light to pass through the chosen letter onto 35 mm photographic film. When a number of words have been composed, the film is led through three small tanks within the machine which develop, fix, and wash the product. The machine can be loaded with clear film or white paper, either plain-backed or with adhesive. A very large variety of type styles can be purchased for this machine, which is a feature that recommends it. Also it has the capacity to build small blocks of lettering (using some of the smaller type sizes) so the chore of assembling such blocks word by word can be reduced. Also in favour of the machine is the durability of the product: although it may yellow in time, the letters are an integral part of the film or paper and will not be accidentally smudged or scratched off. The machine has some serious disadvantages, though, for the college cartographic laboratory. It can easily be put out of commission by inexperienced operators, and its tanks and chemicals must be well maintained. These factors practically dictate that the machine be maintained and operated by a staff technician. Furthermore, there is considerable inertia whenever a job is to be done, because tanks must be washed and chemicals mixed at every start-up.

A new machine that is very well suited to a college cartographic laboratory, is the Kroy machine by Kroy Industries of St Paul, Minnesota (Fig. 9.18). It prints from a carbon film ribbon onto strips of paper or film, using a plastic type disc for each style and variant. As with the Varityper, the type disc must be rotated into position for each letter desired as the words are built letter by letter. Although the machine has no capacity for composing blocks of lettering, it makes a product that is extremely convenient for the single-line labels so prevalent in the usual mapping job. The words appear on a narrow strip of transparent film that is very easy to align and attach.

The range of Kroy type styles is not very extensive, and currently (1981) lacks a classic (with serif) style suitable for physical features such as drainage and mountain ranges. Within the type styles available, however, the range of variants and sizes provides abundant variety. What recommends the Kroy most is its simplicity and relatively low cost. Because the mechanism is simple it is not necessary for the machine to be off-limits to students. And because there are no chemicals to mix, a large or small batch of labels can be produced at once. With nothing to inhibit the production of small batches, the cartographer can experiment with different sizes; and most important, he can produce those few labels that may have been overlooked or misspelled in an earlier batch. Despite the limitations mentioned, the Kroy machine is the better choice for use in college cartographic facilities.

It is worth noting there are no significant differences in the clarity of products from a professional service as opposed to the products from machines in the cartographic laboratory. Which mode of production to adopt should depend, therefore, on whether blocks of words will be needed, and how important is the ability to produce small batches of lettering on impulse.

PLANNING THE LETTERING

The student should realize that, although he may need to produce his own lettering during course work, in practice the cartographer should design the map, the cartographic draftsman should execute it, and others should produce the lettering.

Regardless of whether the student or some service will produce the lettering, there is need to define carefully what is needed by listing all items with their style, variant, and size while referring to the catalogue of possibilities. It is at this stage that the logic of qualitative and hierarchical differences is specified. It is beneficial, therefore, to list all lettering in one sitting in which the verbal content of the map is given full attention.

A review of production priorities

In earlier chapters and in this chapter on production hints, suggestions have been made as to which steps should be completed before others. Those ideas are brought together here in a master check list.

APPLICABLE TO ALL MAPS

1 Define the publication space available for the graphic.
2 Select source map on a map projection suited to the theme.
3 Fit base map and other elements into a balanced layout within scaled-up space proportional to space available in the target publication.
4 Complete the pencilled work map, which will include symbolization, lettering with suitable hierarchy of sizes and styles, and specification of line widths and area shadings. At this stage the map has been designed, and could be completed by someone else.

APPLICABLE ESPECIALLY TO CAMERA-READY ART WORK

5 Complete symbols (inked or dry-transfer).
6 Complete any inked lettering that is directly on the art work (so it will be unaffected by area shadings or base map features).
7 Finish area shadings in ink or graphic films.
8 Ink the base map, omitting those portions of coastline or boundaries that conflict with symbols, lettering, or area shadings.
9 Apply any graphic tapes and dry-transfer lettering. The adhesive or wax from these materials would make inking difficult if they were applied earlier.
10 Apply opaque labels.
11 Add note specifying dimensions of finished product, or specifying percentage reduction needed.

Corrections

It is not practical to scrap an entire piece of art work because of an error. The amateur may insist that the work look perfect, and redraw the whole thing: the professional will quickly make corrections that are noticeable to the eye but not discernible by the camera when high-contrast film is used. There are three methods for corrections, arranged below in order of the intractability of the error: erasing, eradicating, and splicing.

ERASING

Pencil lines can be removed, of course, with a soft eraser such as Pink Pearl or Magic Rub. Ink can be removed from mylar drafting material with a plastic eraser slightly moistened. Solvents can be used, too, on mylar: there are commercial fluid erasers for the purpose, but ordinary alcohol or office Ditto machine fluid will do as well. A sharp X-acto blade, carefully applied, is an effective eraser and one of the best tools for removing small ink errors from tracing paper.

ERADICATING

Tracing paper is not tough enough for ink erasing. Unless the error is small enough to be scraped off with a blade, it should be eradicated or spliced away.

White *correction fluid* can be used for small errors. Ink can be applied over the eradicated area if the fluid is applied smoothly, then covered with clear cellulose tape or Scotch Magic Mending tape.

For extensive errors, especially long lines, eradication can be accomplished quickly with white *correction tape*. This will not take ink; but Scotch brand "colored" cellulose tape in *white* can be used for the same purpose and will accept ink.

SPLICING

For many errors it is advantageous to splice. This applies especially to work done on tracing paper because with that material erasing is difficult, but splicing is easy.

SPLICING THE PAPER

An error not intimately connected to the sound work (such as an ink blot near the edge of the map) can be cured by simply slicing away the offending blot and replacing it with a fresh piece of tracing paper. Ink must be kept away from the join, of course.

SPLICING THE IMAGE

The more interesting challenge is the inked error that occurs in a complex of line work or symbols and appears to have spoiled the map irrevocably. It can be corrected by the procedure shown in Figure 9.19. The line or symbol at fault is redrawn, *along with features that surround it*, on a separate piece of tracing paper taped over the original to ensure the newly drawn features are precisely aligned with their continuations on the underlying map. Then, with the piece still taped firmly in place, a number of cuts are made to excise the offending area and at the same time create a patch that exactly fits the opening. When taped on the reverse side, such a patch is nearly invisible, and will not be discerned by the camera using high-contrast film.

Drawing unconventional graphics

As pointed out in chapter 2, the cartogram is an alternative to more conventional maps for the symbolization of absolute amounts that occur at areas. The

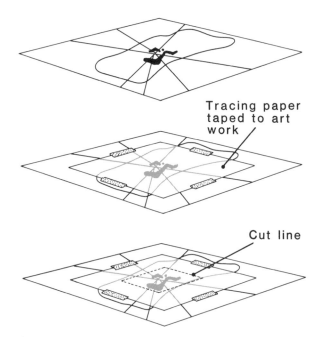

Tracing paper taped to art work

Cut line

FIG. 9.19   Splicing the image when an inked error necessitates redrawing of map features.

stepped surface is an alternative to the choropleth map for ratios and density measures gathered for areas, just as the smooth statistical surface is an alternative to an isarithmic map. Smooth statistical surfaces are difficult to draw without the aid of computer programs and a plotter. Both the cartogram and the stepped surface, though, are surprisingly easy to construct.

CARTOGRAMS

In general, cartograms show the (absolute) amounts of some variable assigned to data areas by using the data areas *as symbols*, and drawing them *with areas in proportion to the amounts*.

The task is relatively easy if the data areas are simply enlarged or reduced by some optical device or similar squares procedure and then arranged in a pattern that corresponds to their real-world arrangement. The result is called a non-contiguous-area cartogram.

THE CONTIGUOUS-AREA CARTOGRAM

Greater dramatic impact is gained if the distorted data areas are fitted together to form a coherent whole.

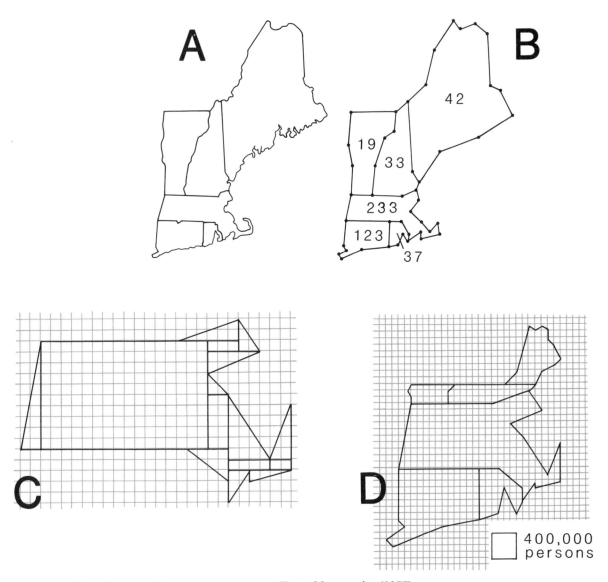

FIG. 9.20 Drawing a contiguous-area cartogram. From Monmonier (1977).

Drawing this *contiguous* type of cartogram is more challenging, but it requires only a conventional base map, a sheet of squared paper, a straight edge, a pencil and an eraser. The following steps should be taken while referring to Figure 9.20.[1]

1 *Simplify the boundaries.* Base map features (Part A of the figure) are reduced to a few straight line segments (Part B).

2 *Select a scaling factor.* The scaling factor will convert the values to be symbolized into the number of

grid squares to be occupied by each data area. In the example, the 1975 state populations (Part A) are divided by an arbitrary factor of 25 to yield 19 squares for Vermont, 33 squares for New Hampshire, and 233 for Massachussets (Part B). For your particular map, select a scaling factor that leads to reasonable sizes for the data areas with the largest and smallest values.

3 *Build the distorted data areas.* Beginning with the data area near the center of the region, draw an

approximation of the area's shape that encloses the right number of squares. A data unit can be constructed through the accretion of rectangles and triangles as in Part C. Triangles are especially useful, since their diagonal boundries help to avoid shapes that are too blocky. The area of any triangle, incidentally, is exactly half the area of the rectangle that encloses it.

In the example illustrated, Connecticut and Rhode Island are added below Massachussets without difficulty. Vermont and New Hampshire are problems, because population density is lower there than in Massachussets. To preserve contiguity, these two states must be drawn without their characteristic north–south extent, but preserving New Hampshire's Atlantic coastline. Since Maine is contiguous only to New Hampshire, the essence of its shape can be preserved with little difficulty.

4 *Add a legend.* A simple square is an effective guide by which the reader can estimate the values represented by state areas. In this example, one grid represents 25,000 persons, so a convenient block of 16 squares will represent 400,000 (Part D).

Not all contiguous cartograms can be constructed as readily as this one. Extreme variations in density make the preservation of both shape and contiguity impossible. For example, a cartogram based on the populations of Canadian provinces and territories cannot portray adequately the Yukon and the Northwest Territories. The Northwest Territories have such a great east–west extent and such a small population that it would be reduced to a mere sliver along the northern edge of the provinces.

THE STEPPED STATISTICAL SURFACE

The stepped surface is constructed by creating a perspective-style view of the mapped area, then raising each data area to a height proportional to the value being symbolized for that data area. The procedure described below is illustrated by Figure 9.21.

1 *Choose a viewpoint.* On the basis of the raw data themselves, determine the viewpoint which will place highest values toward the background and thus minimize the blocking of lower areas.

2 *Grid the source map.* Draw a regular grid (of roughly 1 inch spacing) on the source map – making sure

that *one corner* of the grid system coincides with the viewpoint chosen in the previous step. This may be the southwest or the northeast corner of the original source map, but it need not be: a corner of the grid system can be placed *anywhere* along the edge of the source map (Part A).

3 *Make an isometric grid.* Using a 30 degree angle, as shown in Part B of the illustration, draw an isometric grid based on a line parallel to the paper's bottom edge. Use a spacing less generous than that on the source map ($\frac{1}{2}$ inch, for instance) if you wish to reduce the map size. As an alternative to drawing the grid, buy a sheet of isometric–orthographic guideline paper at an engineering supply store.

4 *Draw a skewed base map.* Transfer map features from the gridded source map to the isometric grid, preserving only essential details (Part C). A sharp pencil is needed.

5 *Add scaling device.* At one edge of the skewed base map sheet, draw a vertical line with ticks showing the values to be symbolized. The values will progress *down* the vertical line from least to greatest (Part C). The spacing of values along this linear scale will determine whether the resulting stepped surface appears either exaggerated or suppressed, so choose the scale with care. Add another vertical line on the opposite side of the sheet to serve as a guide to keep the drawing square with the base line of the isometric grid.

6 *Draw the raised surfaces.* Place a fresh sheet of tracing paper over the skewed base, and draw two vertical guidelines that coincide with the vertical scale and the guideline on the skewed base sheet (Part D). On the guideline that coincides with the scale, make a short horizontal mark to serve as height indicator. With the mark set on zero, draw some foreground base features, and the outlines of foreground areas whose values are zero. Be sure this portion of the drawing is near the bottom of the overlay sheet. Draw lightly with sharp pencil.

For each area to be raised, slide the overlay *down* until the marker reaches the desired value on the scale (Part E). Make sure the guidelines coincide (to ensure the drawing will have true verticals) then trace the outline of the data area and drop tentative vertical lines to the zero level. If the near areas are raised first it will be apparent which lines in the rear should not be drawn.

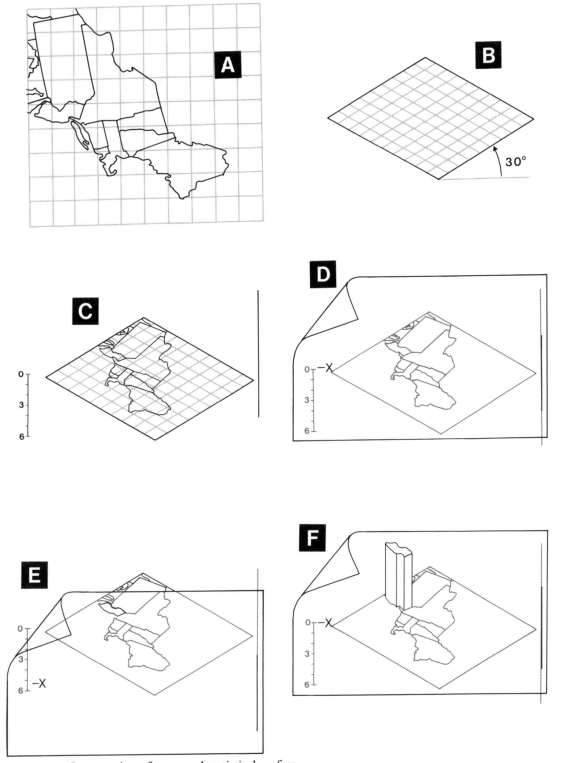

FIG. 9.21 Construction of a stepped statistical surface.

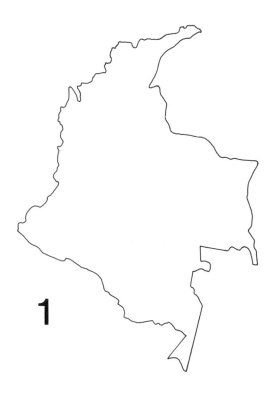

1

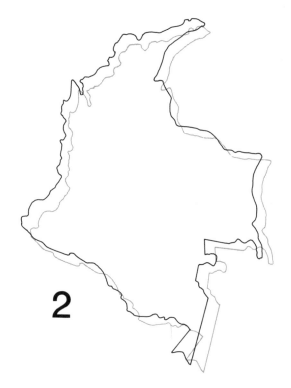

2

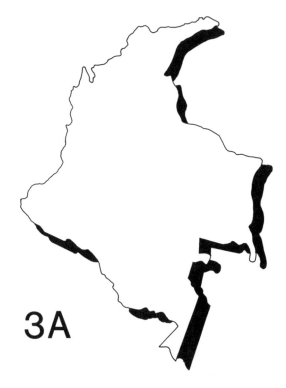

3A

Shadow effect

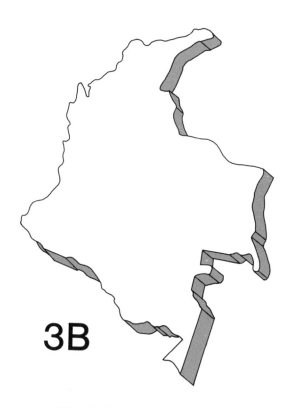

3B

Tablet effect

FIG. 9.22 Raising a base map.

7 *Complete the drawing (Part F).* Drop verticals from prominent corners of the data areas, and finish the lower parts of exposed data areas, making sure to draw only the lines that would be exposed, not obscured, if the surface were a real three-dimensional model.

8 *Add a vertical scale.* Choosing some convenient, rhythmically spaced values, draw a vertical scale to serve as legend, and head the scale with carefully chosen words.

RAISING THE BASE MAP

A map that rises dramatically from the page can be accomplished either by adding a shadow to the map's edge or by drawing the map as if it were a tablet. The procedures listed below are illustrated in Figure 9.22.

1 Trace the base map, and shift the tracing diagonally upward 45 degrees.

2 Trace the exposed edge of country or continent.

3A For the shadow effect, simply shade or blacken the shadow produced in step 2.

3B For the tablet effect, join the pairs of promontory or re-entrant points that serve to define corners. The resulting tablet edge can be left white, or can be filled in with grey or black.

Note

1 That illustration, as well as the procedures described here, are taken with little modification from Monmonier (1977), with permission of the Association of American Geographers.

Reference

Monmonier, Mark S. (1977) *Maps, Distortion, and Meaning*, Washington, DC, Association of American Geographers, 19–20.

Appendix:
Additional Readings

The books and journal articles listed here are arranged by topic. Some topics, such as quantitative symbolization, have been dealt with in the present book: others, such as remote sensing and air photos, have not. A few of the books under the general heading will appear again under other headings because certain chapters in them deal thoroughly with specific topics such as history of cartography or map projections. For a more comprehensive bibliography, the items on this list of additional readings should be integrated with the items in *References* at the end of each chapter.

These additional readings include the major reference works on the subject, some of the older articles and monographs that may be considered classics, and some recent journal articles that indicate the trend of current research and thought in thematic cartography. Not included are the many atlases – world, national, state, and provincial – that can be found in most college libraries. They offer a happy hunting ground for anyone seeking examples of layout, projection choices, or methods of symbolization.

In the event that the local library does not subscribe to the cartographic journals listed here, the nearest North American library that does hold them can be found in *The Union List of Serials*. As well, books and copies of articles can be obtained with ease from distant libraries through interlibrary loan services.

General

Balchin, W. G. V. (1976) "Graphicacy," *The American Cartographer*, 3 (1), 33–8.

Bertin, Jacques (1979) "Visual perception and cartographic transcription," *World Cartography*, 15, 17–27.

Birch, T. W. (1964) *Maps: Topographical and Statistical* (2nd edn), London, Oxford University Press.

Board, C. (1967) "Maps as models," in R. J. Chorley and P. Haggett (eds) *Models in Geography*, London, Methuen, 671–725.

Brandes, D. (1976) "The present state of perceptual research in cartography," *The Cartographic Journal*, 13 (2), 172–6.

Dickinson, G. C. (1969) *Mapping and Air Photographs*, London, Edward Arnold.

Dickinson, G. C. (1973) *Statistical Maps and the Presentation of Statistics* (2nd edn), London, Edward Arnold.

Dury, G. H. (1972) *Map Interpretation* (4th edn), London, Pitman.

Gould, Peter, and R. White (1974) *Mental Maps*, Baltimore, Penguin Books.

Greenhood, D. (1971) *Mapping*, Chicago, University of Chicago Press.

Guelke, Leonard (1976) "Cartographic communication and geographic understanding," *The Canadian Cartographer*, 13 (2), 107–22.

Guelke, Leonard (ed.) (1977) *The Nature of Cartographic Communication*, Cartographica Monograph, 19, Toronto, University of Toronto Press.

Hodgkiss, Alan G. (1970) *Maps for Books and Theses*, Newton Abbot, David & Charles.

Keates, John S. (1973) *Cartographic Design and Production*, New York, Halsted Press (Wiley).

Kolacny, A. (1969) "Cartographic information – a fundamental term in modern cartography," *The Cartographic Journal*, 6, 47–9.

Lawrence, G. R. P. (1979) *Cartographic Methods* (2nd edn), London, Methuen.

Leverenz, J. M. (1974) "The private cartographic industry in the United States, its staff and educational requirements," *The American Cartographer*, 1, 117–23.

McCleary, George F. (1970) "Beyond simple psychophysics: approaches to the understanding of map perception," *Proceedings*, American Congress on Surveying and Mapping, Annual Meeting, Washington, DC, 189–209.

Meine, Karl-Heinz (1979) "Thematic mapping: present and future capabilities," *World Cartography*, 15, 1–16.

Monkhouse, F. J., and H. R. Wilkinson (1973) *Maps and Diagrams: Their Compilation and Construction* (3rd edn), London, Methuen.

Monmonier, Mark S. (1977) *Maps, Distortion, and Meaning*, Washington, DC, Association of American Geographers.

Morrison, Joel L. (1974) "Changing philosophical–technical aspects of thematic cartography," *The American Cartographer*, 1 (1), 5–14.

Morrison, Joel L. (1976) "The science of cartography and its essential processes," *International Yearbook of Cartography*, 16, 84–97.

Muehrcke, Phillip C. (1972) *Thematic Cartography*, Washington, DC, Association of American Geographers.

Muehrcke, Phillip C. (1973) "Beyond abstract map symbols," *The Journal of Geography*, 73 (8), 35–52.

Muehrcke, Phillip C. (1978) *Map Use: Reading, Analysis and Interpretation*, Madison, Wisconsin, JP Publications.

Muehrcke, Phillip C., and J. O. Muehrcke (1974) "Maps in literature," *The Geographical Review*, 64 (3), 317–38.

Olson, Judy M. (1975) "Experience and the improvement of cartographic communication," *The Cartographic Journal*, 12 (2), 94–108.

Raisz, Erwin, *General Cartography* (1948) New York, McGraw-Hill.

Raisz, Erwin, *Principles of Cartography* (1962) New York, McGraw-Hill.

Robinson, Arthur H., and Barbara B. Petchenik (1975) "The map as a communication system," *The Cartographic Journal*, 12, 7–15.

Robinson, Arthur H., and Barbara B. Petchenik (1976) *The Nature of Maps: Essays Toward Understanding Maps and Mapping*, Chicago, University of Chicago Press.

Robinson, Arthur H., Randall D. Sale, and Joel L. Morrison (1978) *Elements of Cartography* (4th edn), New York, Wiley.

Salichchev, K. A. (1978) "Cartographic communication: its place in the theory of science," *The Canadian Cartographer*, 15 (2), 93–9.

Tyner, J. A. (1973) *The World of Maps and Mapping*, New York, McGraw-Hill.

Wilford, J. N. (1981) *The Mapmakers*, New York, Knopf.

Wood, M. (1972) "Human factors in cartographic communication," *The Cartographic Journal*, 9, 123–32.

Regular cartographic journals in English showing address for subscription information

The American Cartographer. American Congress on Surveying and Mapping, 210 Little Falls Street, Falls Church, VA 22046.

The Cartographic Journal. British Cartographic Society, c/o J. K. Wilcox, 9 Kenilworth Close, Boreham Wood, Hertfordshire, WD6 1QF, England.

Cartographica (journal and monograph series, replacing *The Canadian Cartographer* and *Cartographica* monographs), Canadian Cartographic Association. Order from University of Toronto Press, Journals Dept, 5201 Dufferin Street, Downsview, Ontario, M3H 5T8.

Cartography. Australian Institute of Cartographers, GPO Box H592, Perth, Western Australia, 6001, Australia.

New Zealand Cartographic Journal. New Zealand Cartographic Society Inc., PO Box 9331, Courtnay Place, Wellington, New Zealand.

SUC Bulletin. Society of University Cartographers, c/o Department of Geography, King's College, The Strand, London, WC2R 2LS.

International Yearbook of Cartography. International Cartographic Association, Kirschbaum-Verlag, Siegfriedstrasse 28, D-5300 Bonn, Federal Republic of Germany.

For information on irregular and specialized cartographic serials, see John D. Stephens (1980) "Current cartographic serials: an annotated international list," *The American Cartographer*, 7 (2), 123–38.

History of cartography

Bagrow, L. (1964) *History of Cartography* (revised and enlarged by R. A. Skelton), London, C. A. Watts.

Baldock, E. D. (1966) "Milestones of mapping," *The Cartographer*, 3, 89–102.

Brown, L. A. (1949) *The Story of Maps*, Boston, Little, Brown.

Crone, G. R. (1979) *Maps and Their Makers* (7th edn), Hamden, Connecticut, Archon Books.

Hodgkiss, Alan G. (1981) *Understanding Maps: A Systematic History of their Use and Development*, Folkestone, William Dawson.

Lynam, Edward (1953) *The Map Maker's Art, Essays on the History of Maps*, London, The Batchworth Press.

Raisz, Erwin, *General Cartography* (1948) New York, McGraw-Hill.

Ristow, W. (1957) "Journalistic cartography," *Surveying and Mapping*, 17, 369–90.

Ristow, W. (1973) *Guide to the History of Cartography*, Washington, DC, Library of Congress.

Robinson, Arthur H. (1955) "The 1837 maps of Henry Drury Harness," *The Geographical Journal*, 121, 440–50.

Robinson, Arthur H. (1971) "The genealogy of the isopleth," *The Cartographic Journal*, 8, 49–53.

Robinson, Arthur H., Randall D. Sale, and Joel L. Morrison (1978) *Elements of Cartography* (4th edn), New York, Wiley.

Skelton, R. A. (1952) *Decorative Printed Maps of the 15th to 18th Centuries*, London, Staples Press.

Thrower, Norman J. W. (1972) *Maps and Man*, Englewood Cliffs, NJ, Prentice-Hall.

Tooley, R. V. (1952) *Maps and Map Makers* (2nd edn), New York, Bonanza Books.

Quantitative symbolization

Armstrong, R. W. (1969) "Standardized class intervals and rate computation in statistical maps of mortality," *Annals*, Association of American Geographers, 59, 383.

Blumenstock, David I. (1953) "The reliability factor in the drawing of isarithms," *Annals*, Association of American Geographers, 43, 289–304.

Chang, Kang-tsung (1978) "Visual aspects of class intervals in choroplethic mapping," *The Cartographic Journal*, 15 (1), 42–8.

Crawford, Paul V. (1971) "Perception of grey-tone symbols," *Annals*, Association of American Geographers, 61 (4), 721–35.

Cuff, David J. (1972) "Value versus chroma in color schemes on quantitative maps," *The Canadian Cartographer*, 9, 123–40.

Cuff, David J. (1973a) "Shading on choropleth maps: some suspicions confirmed," *Proceedings*, Association of American Geographers, Annual Meeting, 50–4.

Cuff, David J. (1973b) "Colour on temperature maps," *The Cartographic Journal*, 10, 17–21.

Dahlberg, R. E. (1967) "Towards the improvement of the dot map," *International Yearbook of Cartography*, 7, 157–66.

Dent, Borden D. (1972) "A note on the importance of shape in cartogram communication," *Journal of Geography*, 71, 393–401.

Dent, Borden D. (1975) "Communication aspects of value-by-area cartograms," *The American Cartographer*, 2 (2), 154–68.

Dickinson, G. C. (1973) *Statistical Mapping and the Presentation of Statistics* (2nd edn), London, Edward Arnold.

Dixon, O. M. (1972) "Methods and progress in choropleth mapping of population density," *The Cartographic Journal*, 9 (1), 19–29.

Forster, F. (1966) "Use of a demographic base map for the presentation of areal data in epidemiology," *British Journal of Preventive and Social Medicine*, 20, 165–71.

Flannery, J. J. (1971) "The relative effectiveness of some common graduated point symbols in the presentation of quantitative data," *The Canadian Cartographer*, 8, 86–109.

Hsu, Mei-Ling (1968) "The isopleth surface in relation to the system of data derivation," *International Yearbook of Cartography*, 8.

Jenks, George F. (1963) "Generalization in statistical mapping," *Annals*, Association of American Geographers, 53, 15–26.

Jenks, George F. (1967) "The data model concept in statistical mapping," *International Yearbook of Cartography*, 7, 186–8.

Jenks, George F. (1970) "Conceptual and perceptual error in thematic mapping," American Congress on Surveying and Mapping, Annual Meeting, Washington, DC, 174–88.

Jenks, George F. (1976) "Contemporary statistical maps – evidence of spatial and graphic ignorance," *The American Cartographer*, 3, 11–18.

Jenks, George F., and F. Caspall (1971) 'Error on choropleth maps: definition, measurement, reduction," *Annals*, Association of American Geographers, 61, 217–44.

Jenks, George F., and M. R. C. Coulson (1963) "Class intervals for statistical maps," *International Yearbook of Cartography*, 3, 119–33.

Jensen, John R. (1978) "Three-dimensional choropleth maps: development and aspects of cartographic communication," *The Canadian Cartographer*, 15 (2), 123–41.

Kimmerling, A. J. (1975) "A cartographic study of equal value grey scales for use with screened grey areas," *The American Cartographer*, 2, 119–27.

Mackay, J. R. (1949) "Dotting the dot map," *Surveying and Mapping*, 9, 3–10.

Mackay, J. Ross (1951) "Some problems and techniques in isopleth mapping," *Economic Geography*, 27, 1–9.

Meihofer, Hans-Joachim (1973) "The visual perception of the circle in thematic maps: experimental results," *The Canadian Cartographer*, 10 (1), 63–84.

Monkhouse, F. J., and H. R. Wilkinson (1973) *Maps and Diagrams: Their Compilation and Construction* (3rd edn), London, Methuen.

Monmonier, Mark S. (1974) "Measures for pattern complexity for choroplethic maps," *The American Cartographer*, 1, 159–69.

Monmonier, Mark S. (1975) "Class intervals to enhance the visual correlation of choroplethic maps," *The Canadian Cartographer*, 12, 161–78.

Monmonier, Mark S. (1977) "Regression-based scaling to facilitate the cross-correlation of graduated circle maps," *The Cartographic Journal*, 14 (2), 89–98.

Morrison, Joel, L. (1971) *Method-Produced Error in Isarithmic Mapping*, American Congress on Surveying and Mapping, Washington, DC.

Muehrcke, Phillip C. (1976) "Concepts of scaling from the map reader's point of view," *The American Cartographer*, 3 (2), 123–41.

Muller, Jean-Claude (1975) "Definition, measurement and comparison of map attributes in choroplethic mapping," *Proceedings*, Association of American Geographers, 7, 160–4.

Muller, Jean-Claude (1976) "Objective and subjective comparison in choroplethic mapping," *The Cartographic Journal*, 13 (2), 156–66.

Muller, Jean-Claude (1980) "Visual comparison of continuously shaded maps," *Cartographica*, 17 (1), 40–52.

Olson, Judy M. (1972) "Class interval systems on maps of observed correlated distributions," *The Canadian Cartographer*, 9, 122–31.

Olson, Judy M. (1975) "The organization of color on two-variable maps," *Proceedings*, AUTO-CARTO II, International Symposium on Computer-Assisted Cartography, American Congress on Surveying and Mapping, 289–94.

Olson, Judy M. (1976) "Noncontiguous area cartograms," *The Professional Geographer*, 18, 371–80.

Olson, July M. (1977) "The rescaling of dot maps," *International Yearbook of Cartography*, 17, 125–36.

Olson, Judy M. (1981) "Spectrally encoded two-variable maps," *Annals*, Association of American Geographers, 71 (2), 259–76.

Patton, Jeffrey C., and Paul V. Crawford (1977) "The perception of hypsometric colours," *The Cartographic Journal*, 14 (2), 115–27.

Robinson, Arthur H. (1961) "The cartographic representation of the statistical surface," *International Yearbook of Cartography*, 1, 53–61.

Storrie, M., and C. I. Jackson (1967) "A comparison of some methods of mapping census data of the British Isles," *The Cartographic Journal*, 46, 38–43.

Williams, R. L. (1956) *Statistical Symbols for Maps: Their Design and Relative Values*, New Haven, Yale University Map Laboratory.

Williams, R. L. (1958) "Equal-appearing intervals for printed screens," *Annals*, Association of American Geographers, 48, 132–9.

Worth, Christopher (1978) "Determining a vertical scale for graphical representations of three-dimensional surfaces," *The Cartographic Journal*, 15 (2), 86–92.

Wright, John K. (1936) "A method of mapping densities of population with Cape Cod as an example," *The Geographical Review*, 26, 103–10.

Wright, John K. (1944) "A proposed atlas of diseases," *The Geographical Review*, 34, 642–52.

Numerical methods and correlation

Barry, R. G. (1973) "An introduction to numerical and mechanical techniques," Appendix to Monkhouse and Wilkinson, *Maps and Diagrams*, London, Methuen.

Blalock, H. M. (1972) *Social Statistics* (2nd edn), New York, McGraw-Hill.

Chorley, R. J., and P. Haggett (1965) "Trend-surface mapping in geographic research," *Transactions and Papers of the Institute of British Geographers*, 37, 47–67.

Cole, C. A. M., and J. P. King (1968) *Quantitative Geography*, New York, Wiley.

Davis, J. C., and M. J. McCullagh (eds) (1975) *Display and Analysis of Spatial Data*, NATO Advanced Study Institute, New York, Wiley.

Dickinson, Gordon C. (1973) *Statistical Mapping and the Presentation of Statistics* (2nd edn), London, Edward Arnold.

Draper, N. R., and H. Smith (1975) *Applied Regression Analysis*, New York, Wiley.

Ebdon, D. (1977) *Statistics in Geography: A Practical Approach*, Oxford, Basil Blackwell.

Haggett, Peter (1977) *Locational Analysis in Human Geography* (2 vols), New York, Halsted Press.

Lewis, Peter (1977) *Maps and Statistics*, New York, Halsted Press.

Monkhouse, F. J., and H. R. Wilkinson (1973) *Maps and Diagrams: Their Compilation and Construction*, London, Methuen.

Monmonier, Mark S. (1978) "Modification of the choropleth technique to communicate correlation," *International Yearbook of Cartography*, 18, 143–58.

Monmonier, Mark S. (1979) "An alternative isomorphism for mapping correlation," *International Yearbook of Cartography*, 19, 77–88.

Moroney, M. J. (1956) *Facts from Figures* (3rd edn), Baltimore, Penguin Books.

Neft, D. S. (1966) *Statistical Analysis for Areal Distributions*, Philadelphia, Regional Science Research Institute.

Norcliffe, G. B. (1969) "On the use and limitations of trend-surface models," *The Canadian Geographer*, 13, 338–48.

Olson, Judy M. (1972) "Class interval systems on maps of observed correlated distributions," *The Canadian Cartographer*, 9, 122–31.

Olson, Judy M. (1975) "The organization of color on two-variable maps," *Proceedings*, AUTO-CARTO II, International Symposium on Computer-Assisted Cartography, American Congress on Surveying and Mapping, Washington, DC, 289–94.

Schnell, G. A., and M. S. Monmonier (1976) "U.S. population change, 1960–70: simplification, meaning, and mapping," *The Journal of Geography*, 5, 280–91.

Tarrant, J. R. (1970) "Comments on the use of trend surface analysis in the study of erosion surfaces," *Transactions, Institute of British Geographers*, 51, 221–2.

Taylor, P. J. (1977) *Quantitative Methods in Geography: An Introduction to Spatial Statistics*, Boston, Houghton Mifflin.

Thomas, Edwin N. (1968) "Maps of residuals from regression: their characteristics and uses in geographical research," in Berry, B. J. L., and D. F. Marble (eds) *Spatial Analysis*, Englewood Cliffs, NJ, Prentice-Hall.

Lettering

Bartz, Barbara S. (1970) "An analysis of the typographic legibility literature," *The Cartographic Journal*, 7, 10–16.

Bockemuehl, Harold W., and Paul B. Wilson (1956) "Minimum lettering size for visual aids," *The Professional Geographer*, 28, 185–9.

Hodgkiss, Alan G. (1970) *Maps for Books and Theses*, Newton Abbot, David & Charles.

Imhof, Eduard (1975) "Positioning names on maps," *The American Cartographer*, 2, 128–44.

Keates, John S. (1958) "The use of type in cartography," *Surveying and Mapping*, 18, 75–6.

Keates, John S. (1973) *Cartographic Design and Production*, New York, Halsted Press (Wiley).

Robinson, Arthur H. (1950) "The size of lettering for maps and charts," *Surveying and Mapping*, 19, 37–44.

Robinson, Arthur H., Randall D. Sale, and Joel L. Morrison (1978) *Elements of Cartography* (4th edn), New York, Wiley.

Generalization

Jenks, George F. (1981) "Lines, computers, and human

frailties," *Annals*, Association of American Geographers, 71 (1), 1–10.

Lundquist, Gosta (1959) "Generalization – a preliminary survey of an important subject," *The Canadian Surveyor*, 14, 466–70.

Marino, Jill S. (1979) "Identification of characteristic points along naturally occurring lines: an empirical study," *The Canadian Cartographer*, 16 (1), 70–80.

Miller, O. M., and Robert J. Voskuil (1964) "Thematic map generalization," *The Geographical Review*, 54, 13–19.

Morrison, Joel L. (1974) "A theoretical framework for cartographic generalization with emphasis on the process of symbolization," *International Yearbook of Cartography*, 14, 115–27.

Pannekoek, A. J. (1962) "Generalization of coastlines and contours," *International Yearbook of Cartography*, 2, 55–74.

Steward, H. J. (1974) *Cartographic generalization: some concepts and explanations*, Cartographica Monograph, 10, Toronto, York University.

Topfer F., and W. Pillewizer (1966) "The principles of selection, a means of cartographic generalization," *The Cartographic Journal*, 3, 10–16.

and white cartography," *The Canadian Cartographer*, 9, 25–38.

Keates, John S. (1962) "The perception of colour in cartography," *Proceedings*, Edinburgh Cartographic Symposium, Glasgow.

Keates, John S. (1973) *Cartographic Design and Production*, New York, Halsted Press (Wiley).

Keates, John S. (1982) *Understanding Maps*, New York, Halsted Press (Wiley).

Monmonier, Mark S. (1980) "The hopeless pursuit of purification in cartographic communication: a comparison of graphic-arts and perceptual distortions of graytone symbols," *Cartographica*, 17 (1), 24–39.

Petchenik, Barbara B. (1974) "A verbal approach to characterizing the look of maps," *The American Cartographer*, 1, 63–71.

Robinson, Arthur H. (1952) *The Look of Maps: An Examination of Cartographic Design*, Madison, University of Wisconsin Press.

Robinson, Arthur H. (1967) "Psychological aspects of color in cartography," *International Yearbook of Cartography*, 7, 50–9.

Robinson, Arthur H., Randall D. Sale, and Joel L. Morrison (1978) *Elements of Cartography* (4th edn), New York, Wiley.

Wood, M. (1968) "Visual perception and map design," *The Cartographic Journal*, 5, 54–64.

Graphic design

Arnheim, R. (1976) "The perception of maps," *The American Cartographer*, 3, 5–10.

Board, Christopher, and R. M. Taylor (1977) "Perception and maps: human factors in map design and interpretation," *Transactions, Institute of British Geographers* (new series), 2 (1), 19–36.

Castner, Henry W. (1980) "Printed color charts: some thoughts on their construction and use in map design," *Proceedings*, American Congress on Surveying and Mapping, Annual Meeting, St Louis, 370–8.

Castner, H., and G. McGrath (eds) (1971) *Map Design and the Map User*, Proceedings, 1970 Queen's Symposium on Map Design and the Map User, Cartographica Monograph, 2, Toronto.

Castner, Henry W., and A. H. Robinson (1969) *Dot Area Symbols in Cartography: The Influence of Pattern on Their Perception*, American Congress on Surveying and Mapping, Washington, DC.

Crawford, Paul V. (1971) "Perception of grey-tone symbols," *Annals*, Association of American Geographers, 61 (4), 721–35.

Crawford, Paul V. (1976) "Optimal spatial design for thematic maps," *The Cartographic Journal*, 13 (2), 134–44.

Dent, Borden D. (1972) "Visual organization and thematic map communication," *Annals*, Association of American Geographers, 62, 79–93.

Head, C. G. (1972) "Land–water differentiation in black

Production and reproduction

Bach, Daniel N. (1973) "Non-press proofing methods," *Proceedings*, American Congress on Surveying and Mapping, Fall Convention, Lake Buena Vista, 32–41.

Eastman Kodak Company (1977) *Basic Photography for the Graphic Arts* (3rd edn), Rochester, New York.

International Paper Company (1980) *Pocket Pal* (12th edn), New York.

Keates, John S. (1973) *Cartographic Design and Production*, New York, Halsted Press (Wiley).

Keates, John S. (1978) "Screenless lithography and orthophotomaps," *The Cartographic Journal*, 15 (2), 63–5.

Loxton, John (1980) *Practical Map Production*, New York, Wiley.

Mertle, J. S., and G. Monsen (1957) *Photomechanics and Printing*, Chicago, Mertle.

Moore, Lionel C. (1968) *Cartographic Scribing Materials, Instruments, and Techniques* (2nd edn), American Congress on Surveying and Mapping, Washington, DC.

Robinson, Arthur H., Randall D. Sale, and Joel L. Morrison (1978) *Elements of Cartography* (4th edn), New York, Wiley.

Stoessel, O. C. (1971) "Standard printing color screen tint systems for the Department of Defense Mapping, Charting, and Geodetic Services," *Proceedings*, American Congress on Surveying and Mapping, Annual Meeting.

Computer-aided cartography

Aalders, H. J. G. L. (1980) "Computer mapping: I want to start ... but how?" *The Cartographic Journal*, 17 (1), 21–5.

American Congress on Surveying and Mapping, *Proceedings* of a series of international conferences on Automation in Cartography: AUTO-CARTO I, 1974; AUTO-CARTO II, 1975; AUTO-CARTO III, 1978; and AUTO-CARTO IV, 1979.

Bickmore, D. P. (1980) "Future research and development in computer-assisted cartography," in Taylor, D. R. F. (ed.) *The Computer in Contemporary Cartography*, New York, Wiley, 235–49.

Bie, Stein W. (1980) "Computer-assisted soil mapping," in Taylor, D. R. F. (ed.) *The Computer in Contemporary Cartography*, New York, Wiley, 123–50.

Bowen, Major D. R., and Capt. J. J. Charland (1981) "Interactive computer cartography at West Point," *Bulletin*, American Congress on Surveying and Mapping, 25–30.

Boyle, A. R. (1974) "Automated cartography," *World Cartography*, 15, 63–70.

Boyle, A. R. (1980) "Development in equipment and techniques," in Taylor, D. R. F. (ed.) *The Computer in Contemporary Cartography*, New York, Wiley, 39–57.

British Cartographic Society (1974) *Automated Cartography*, papers presented at Annual Symposium of the British Cartographic Society, Southampton, 1973.

Broome, F. R. (1974) "Micrographics: a new approach to cartography at the Census Bureau," *Proceedings*, American Congress on Surveying and Mapping, Washington, DC, Fall Convention, 1–14.

Broome, Fredrick R., and S. W. Witiuk (1980) "Census mapping by computer," in Taylor, D. R. F. (ed.) *The Computer in Contemporary Cartography*, New York, Wiley, 191–217.

Diello, J., K. Kirk, and J. Callander (1969) "The development of an automated cartographic system," *The Cartographic Journal*, 6, 9–17.

Douglas, D. H. (1972) "VIEWBLOCK: a computer program for constructing perspective view block diagrams," *La Revue de Géographie de Montreal*, 26 (1), 102–4.

Experimental Cartography Unit, Royal College of Art (1971) *Automatic Cartography and Planning*, London, Architectural Press.

Gold, Christopher (1980) "Geological mapping by computer," in Taylor, D. R. F. (ed.) *The Computer in Contemporary Cartography*, New York, Wiley, 151–90.

Harris, Lewis J. (1980) "The application of computer technology to topographical cartography," in Taylor, D. R. F. (ed.) *The Computer in Contemporary Cartography*, New York, Wiley, 59–92.

Hsu, Mei-Ling, and Philip W. Porter (1971) "Computer mapping and geographic cartography," *Annals*, Association of American Geographers, 61, 796–9.

Hsu, Shin-Yi (1979) "Automation in cartography with remote sensing methodologies and technologies," *The Canadian Cartographer*, 16 (2), 183–94.

International Cartographic Association (1973) *Automation Terms in Cartography*, American Congress on Surveying and Mapping, Washington, DC.

LeBlanc, A. (ed.) (1973) *Computer Cartography in Canada*, Toronto, York University.

Liebenberg, Elri (1976) "SYMAP: its uses and abuses," *The Cartographic Journal*, 13 (1), 26–36.

Marble, Duane F. (editor for IGU Commission on Geographical Data Sensing and Processing) (1980) *Computer Software for Spatial Data Handling* (a three-volume inventory), Washington, DC, US Geological Survey.

Meyer, M. A., F. R. Broome, and R. H. Schweitzer, Jr (1975) "Color statistical mapping by the US Bureau of the Census," *The American Cartographer*, 2, 100–17.

Moellering, Harold (1980) "Strategies of real-time cartography," *The Cartographic Journal*, 17 (1), 12–15.

Monmonier, Mark S. (1978) "Modifications of the choropleth technique to communicate correlation," *International Yearbook of Cartography*, 18, 143–58.

Monmonier, Mark S. (1981) *Computer-Aided Cartography: Principles and Prospects*, Englewood Cliffs, NJ, Prentice-Hall.

Monmonier, Mark S., and D. M. Kirchoff (1977) "Choroplethic mapping for a small minicomputer," *Proceedings*, American Congress on Surveying and Mapping, Annual Meeting, Washington, DC.

Morrison, Joel L. (1980) "Computer technology and cartographic change," in Taylor, D. R. F. (ed.) *The Computer in Contemporary Cartography*, New York, Wiley, 5–23.

Ottoson, Lars, and B. Rystedt (1980) "Computer-assisted cartography: research and applications in Sweden," in Taylor, D. R. F. (ed.) *The Computer in Contemporary Cartography*, New York, Wiley, 93–122.

Peuker, Thomas K. (1972) *Computer Cartography*, Washington, DC, Association of American Geographers.

Peuker, Thomas K., and N. Chrisman (1975) "Cartographic data structures," *The American Cartographer*, 2 (1), 55–9.

Rhind, David (1980) "The nature of computer-assisted cartography," in Taylor, D. R. F. (ed.) *The Computer in Contemporary Cartography*, New York, Wiley, 25–37.

Rhind, David W. and T. Trewman (1975) "Automatic cartographic and urban data banks: some lessons from the UK," *International Yearbook of Cartography*, 15, 143–57.

Rhind, David W., I. S. Evans, and V. Visvalingam (1980) "Making a national atlas of population by computer," *The Cartographic Journal*, 17 (1), 3–11.

Riordan, William T. (1971) "Digital data bases: the wave of the future," *Bulletin*, American Congress on Surveying and Mapping, 11–12.

Rosing, K. E., and P. A. Wood (1971) *Character of a Conurbation* (an atlas), Sevenoaks, Hodder & Stoughton Educational.

Schofer, J. P. (1975) "Computer cartography and professional geographers," *The Professional Geographer*, 27, 335–9.

Schweitzer, Richard H. (1973) "Mapping urban America with automated cartography," *Proceedings*, American

Congress on Surveying and Mapping, Fall Convention, Walt Disney World, 265–83.

Shepard, Donald (1968) "A two-dimensional interpolation function for irregularly-spaced data" (on the SYMAP interpolation algorith), *Proceedings*, National Conference of the Association for Computing Machinery, 517–23.

Smith, Richard M. (1980) "Improved areal symbols for computer line-printed maps," *The American Cartographer*, 7 (1), 51–7.

Southard, Rupert (1980) "The changing scene in surveying and mapping," *Surveying and Mapping*, 15 (4), 397–403.

Statistics Canada (1978) *1976 Census of Canada: Agriculture, Graphic Presentation*, Ottawa.

Taylor, D. R. F. (1971) *A Computer Atlas of Kenya*, Ottawa, Carleton University (*also see* Hsu and Porter, 1971).

Taylor, D. R. F. (ed.) (1980) *The Computer in Contemporary Cartography*, New York, Wiley.

Taylor, D. R. F., and D. Douglas (1970) *A Computer Atlas of Ottawa-Hull*, Ottawa, Carleton University.

Thomlinson, R. F. T. (1976) *Computer Handling of Geographic Data*, Paris, The UNESCO Press.

US Bureau of the Census (1969) *Computer Mapping*, Census Use Study Report, 2, Washington, DC.

US Bureau of the Census (1973) *1969 Census of Agriculture: Graphic Summary*, Washington, DC.

Waugh, T. C. (1980) "The development of the GIMMS computer mapping system," in Taylor, D. R. F. (ed.) *The Computer in Contemporary Cartography*, New York, Wiley, 219–34.

Williams, Anthony V. (1978) "Interactive cartogram production on a microprocessor graphics system," *Proceedings*, American Congress on Surveying and Mapping, Fall Meeting, Albuquerque, 426–31.

Wittick, Robert L. (1977) "The past, present and future of computers in cartography," in *Applications of Geographic Research*, East Lansing, Department of Geography, Michigan State University.

Worth, Christopher (1978) "Determining a vertical scale for graphical representation of three-dimensional surfaces," *The Journal of Geography*, 15 (2), 86–92.

Remote sensing and airphotos

Avery, T. E. (1977) *Interpretation of Aerial Photographs*, Minneapolis, Burgess.

Barret, E. C., and L. F. L. Curtis (1976) *Introduction to Environmental Remote Sensing*, New York, Wiley.

Blair, C. L., and Gutsell, B. V. (1974) *The American Landscape: Map and Air Photo Interpretation*, New York, McGraw-Hill.

Canby, T. Y. (1974) "Skylab, outpost on the frontier of space," and "Skylab looks at earth," *National Geographic*, 146 (4), 441–9 and 470–93.

Colwell, Robert N. (1968) "Remote sensing of natural resources," *Scientific American*, 218 (1), 54–69.

Eastman Kodak Company (1974) *Aerial Photography as a Planning Tool*, Rochester, New York.

Estes, J. E., and L. W. Senger (1974) *Remote Sensing*, Santa Barbara, Calif., Hamilton.

Fink, Daniel (1973) "Monitoring earth's resources from space," *Technology Review*, 32–41.

Holz, Robert K. (1973) *The Surveillant Science: Remote Sensing and the Environment*, Boston, Houghton Mifflin.

Howard, John A. (1970) *Aerial Photo-Ecology*, New York, Elsevier.

Jensen, Homer, L. C. Graham, L. J. Porcello, and E. M. Leith (1977) "Side-looking airborne radar," *Scientific American*, 237 (4), 84–95.

Lillesand, T. M., and R. W. Kiefer (1979) *Remote Sensing and Image Interpretation*, New York, Wiley.

Lintz, Joseph and D. Simonett (eds) (1976) *Remote Sensing of Environment*, Reading, Mass., Addison-Wesley.

Lo, C. P. (1976) *Geographical Applications of Aerial Photography*, Newton Abbott, David & Charles.

NASA (1976) *Mission to Earth: Landsat Views the World*, Washington, DC, US Government Printing Office.

NASA (1977) *Skylab Explores the Earth*, Washington, DC, US Government Printing Office.

Paul, Charles K. (1979) "Satellites and world food resources," *Technology Review*, 18–29.

Reeves, R. G. (1975) *Manual of Remote Sensing* (2 vols), Falls Church, Va., American Society of Photogrammetry.

Robinson, Arthur H., Randall D. Sale, and Joel L. Morrison (1978) *Elements of Cartography* (4th edn), New York, Wiley.

Rudd, Robert D. (1974) *Remote Sensing: A Better View*, Belmont, Calif., Duxbury Press.

Sabins, F. F. (1978) *Remote Sensing: Principles and Interpretation*, San Francisco, W. H. Freeman.

Scovel, J. L., E. J. O'Brien, J. C. McCormack, and R. B. Chapman (1965) *Atlas of Landforms*, New York, Wiley.

Siegal, Barry S., and A. R. Gillespie (eds) (1980) *Remote Sensing in Geology*, New York, John Wiley.

Thrower, N. J. W., and J. R. Jensen (1976) "The orthophoto and orthophotomap: characteristics, development, and applications," *The American Cartographer*, 3 (1), 39–52.

Townshend, J. R. F. (ed.) (1981) *Terrain Analysis and Remote Sensing*, London, Allen & Unwin.

Weaver, Kenneth F. (1969) "Remote sensing: new eyes to see the world," *National Geographic*, 47–73.

Williams, D. L., and L. D. Miller (1979) *Monitoring Forest Canopy Alteration Around the World with Digital Analysis of Landsat Imagery*, Greenbelt, Md, NASA Goddard Space Flight Center.

Williams, R. S., and W. D. Carter (1976) *ERTS 1: A New window on Our Planet*, Washington, DC, US Geological Survey.

Surveying and map projections

Burkard, Capt. R. K. (1968) *Geodesy for the Layman*, Rancho Cordova, Calif., Landmark Enterprises.

Cartensen, V. (1976) "Patterns of the American land," *Surveying and Mapping*, 36, 303–9.

Chamberlin, W. (1947) "The round earth on flat maps: a description of the map projections used by cartographers," *National Geographic*, 39–126.

Deetz, C. H., and O. S. Adams (1945) *Elements of Map Projection*, Washington, DC, US Coast and Geodetic Survey.

Fisher, I., and O. M. Miller (1944) *World Maps and Globes*, New York, Essential Books.

Garner, Clement L. (1954) "Geodesy – a framework for maps," *Surveying and Mapping*, 14, 154–8.

Goode, J. Paul (1925) "The homolosine projection: a new device for portraying the earth's surface entire," *Annals*, Association of American Geographers, 15, 119–25.

Greenhood, D. (1971) *Mapping*, Chicago, University of Chicago Press.

Johnson, H. B. (1976) *Order Upon the Land: The US Rectangular Land Survey and the Upper Mississippi Country*, London, Oxford University Press.

Mainwaring, J. (1943) *An Introduction to the Study of Map Projections*, New York, St Martin's Press.

Maling, D. H. (1973) *Coordinate Systems and Map Projections*, London, Philip.

Marschner, F. J. (1944) "Structural properties of medium and small-scale maps," *Annals*, Association of American Geographers, 34, 1–46.

Muehreke, Phillip C. (1978) *Map Use: Reading, Analysis, and Interpretation*, Madison, Wisconsin, JP Publications.

O'Keefe, John A. (1952) "The Universal Transverse Mercator Grid and Projection," *The Professional Geographer*, 4, 19–24.

Raisz, Erwin (1948) *General Cartography*, New York, McGraw-Hill.

Raisz, Erwin (1962) *Principles of Cartography*, New York, McGraw-Hill.

Richardus, P., and R. K. Adler (1972) *Map Projections for Geodesists, Cartographers, and Geographers*, New York, American Elsevier.

Robinson, Arthur H. (1949) "An analytical approach to map projections," *Annals*, Association of American Geographers, 39, 283–90.

Robinson, Arthur H., Randall D. Sale, and Joel L. Morrison (1978) *Elements of Cartography* (4th edn), New York, Wiley.

Steers, J. A. (1965) *An Introduction to the Study of Map Projections*, London, University of London Press.

Stewart, J. Q. (1963) "The use and abuse of map projections," *The Geographical Review*, 33, 589–604.

Tobler, Waldo R. (1963) "Geographic area and map projections," *Geographical Review*, 53, 59–78.

University of Wisconsin Cartographic Laboratory (1980) *Handbook on Projections*, Madison.

US Department of the Army (1967) *Grids and Grid References*, Washington, DC.

Vanicek, Peter and E. J. Krakiwsky (1978) "Geodesy reborn," *Surveying and Mapping*, 23–6.

Landform mapping

Baldock, E. D. (1971) "Cartographic relief portrayal," *International Yearbook of Cartography*, 11, 75–8.

Clarke, J. I. (1966) "Morphometry from maps," in Dury, G. H. (ed.) *Essays in Geomorphology*, London, Heinemann.

DeLucia, A. (1972) "The effect of shaded relief on map information accessibility," *The Cartographic Journal*, 9, 14–18.

Dornbach, John E. (1956) "An approach to design of terrain representation," *Surveying and Mapping*, 16, 41–4.

Gilman, Clarence R. (1981) "The manual/photomechanical and other methods for relief shading," *The American Cartographer*, 8 (1), 41–53.

Hammond, Edwin H. (1954) "Small-scale continental landform maps," *Annals*, Association of American Geographers, 44, 33–42.

Hammond, E. H. (1964) "Analysis of properties in land form geography: an application to broad scale land form mapping," *Annals*, Association of American Geographers, 54, 11–19.

Irwin, D. (1976) "The historical development of terrain representation in American cartography," *International Yearbook of Cartography*, 16, 70–83.

Keates, John S. (1961) "Techniques of relief representation," *Surveying and Mapping*, 21, 459–63.

Keates, John S. (1962) "The small-scale representation of the landscape in colour," *International Yearbook of Cartography*, 2, 76–82.

Keates, John S. (1972) "Symbols and meaning in topographic maps," *International Yearbook of Cartography*, 12, 168–81.

Keates, John S. (1973) *Cartographic Design and Production*, London, Longman.

Lobeck, Armin K. (1956) *Things Maps Don't Tell Us: An Adventure into Map Interpretation*, New York, Macmillan.

Lobeck, Armin K. (1958) *Block Diagrams and Other Graphic Methods Used in Geology and Geography* (2nd edn), Amherst, Mass., Emerson-Trussel.

Miller, O. M., and C. H. Summerson (1960) "Slope-zone maps," *The Geographical Review*, 50, 194–202.

Monkhouse, F. J., and H. R. Wilkinson (1973) *Maps and Diagrams: Their Compilation and Construction*, London, Methuen.

Phillips, Richard J., A. DeLucia, and N. Skelton (1975) "Some objective tests of the legibility of relief maps," *The Cartographic Journal*, 12, 39–46.

Raisz, Erwin (1931) "The physiographic method of representing scenery on maps," *The Geographical Review*, 21, 297–304.

Raisz, Erwin (1962) *Principles of Cartography*, New York, McGraw-Hill.

Ridd, M. K. (1963) "The proportional relief landform map," *Annals*, Association of American Geographers, 53, 569–76.

Robinson, Arthur H., Randall D. Sale, and Joel L. Morrison (1978) *Elements of Cartography* (4th edn), New York, Wiley.

Robinson, Arthur H., and Norman J. W. Thrower (1957) "A new method of terrain representation," *The Geographical Review*, 47, 507–20.

Scovel, J. L., E. J. O'Brien, J. C. McCormack, and R. B. Chapman (1965) *Atlas of Landforms*, New York, Wiley.

Sherman, J. C. (1964) "Terrain representation and map function," *International Yearbook of Cartography*, 4, 20–23.

Smith, Guy-Harold (1935) "The relative relief of Ohio," *The Geographical Review*, 25, 272–84.

Stacy, John R. (1958) "Terrain diagrams in isometric projection – simplified," *Annals*, Association of American Geographers, 48, 232–6.

Tanaka, K. (1950) "The relief contour method of representing topography on maps," *The Geographical Review*, 40, 444–56.

Thrower, Norman J. W. (1963) "Extended uses of the method of orthogonal mapping of traces of inclined planes with a surface, especially terrain," *International Yearbook of Cartography*, 3, 26–35.

Toth, T. G. (1973) "Terrain representation – past and present – at the National Geographic Society," *Proceedings*, American Congress on Surveying and Mapping, Fall Convention, 9–31.

Upton, William B. (1970) *Landforms and Topographic Maps*, New York, Wiley.

Way, Douglas S. (1973) *Terrain Analysis*, Stroudsburg, Pa., Dowden, Hutchinson & Ross.

Author Index

Subject Index

Absolute quantities, 31, 57
Accumulated symbols, 28–9; hints for drawing, 140–2
Accuracy of isolines, 18
Area symbols, for qualitative data, 9–12; for quantitative data, 33–40; hints for production, 142–6
Areal scaling of symbols, 20–5
Art work, camera-ready (single piece), 117–19; separations, 117–19; in production, 117–20; in reproduction, 109–11; size and proportions of, 73–4
Articulation in composition, 99
Automation, *see* Computer-aided production

Balance in layout, 75
Base maps, generalization, 88–90; projections, 78–85; sources of, 76–7
Bearings or azimuths, 79
Blockout film, 142
Blow-up maps, 97, 99

Camera-ready art work (single-piece), 117–18, 119–21
Cameras, 110–13
Captions, 36, 60, 61
Cartograms, as base for choropleth map, 50–2; hints for drawing, 152–4; value by area type, 33–6
Cartographic journals, 159
Cathode ray tubes, 125–6
Centrality in composition, 101
Choropleth maps, computer-aided, 128–9; defined, 36; execution of, 39, 144–6; grouping methods (classes), 36–9; shading principles, 36–40; two-variable type, 49–50
Circles, overlap of, 139, 140; scaling of, 20–7; segmented, 25–7
Closed forms in composition, 107
Coastlines, 78, 88–91
Compiling, 85, 88–91
Composition, 97–105
Computer-aided production, 121–32; hardware, 122–7; readings, 163–4; software, 127–32

Computer on microfilm, 126–7
Computer programs, 128–32
Continuous phenomena, 15
Continuous tones, 115
Contours, 15
Contrast, 98, 101–3, 105
Control points, 18
Copyright, 77–8
Corrections, 151–2
Correlation, cartographic, 47–52; coefficient of, 53; statistical, 52–7

Darkness, 9, 36–7, 101
Dasymetric maps, 40–1
Data mapped, 5–6
Decagraph, 46
Diazo copy, 110
Digitizing, 122–3
Discrete phenomena, 19
Drafting tools and equipment, 134–7
Dry-transfer materials, 142–9

Equidistance on projections, 79

Fidelity and map scale, 92–4
Figure-ground relations, 98–101
Flannery adjustment, 23–5
Flow lines, 43–4

Generalization, 85–91; readings, 161–2
Graphic design, 97–105; readings, 161–2
Graphic films, 142–6
Grouped data, 29–30

Halftones, 114–15
Harvard Laboratory for Computer Graphics, 128–30
History of mapping, 1; readings, 159
Homogeneity in composition, 98

Index maps, 97, 99
Interpolation, 16
Inset maps, 97
Isarithmic mapping, accuracy of, 18, 42; execution of, 16, 138; for data at points, 15–18; isopleths for area data, 41–3, 45

Isolines, *see above*
Isometric lines, 45
Isopleth maps, 41–3, 45

Kroy lettering machine, 150

Labels, 16, 146–9
Landform mapping, overview, 6; readings, 165–6
Land–water distinction, 98–9
Layout, 73–5
Latitude and longitude, 46, 67, 80–1, 95
Legends, arrangement, 69; for scaled circles, 23, 25–7, 29–30; headings for, 60–2; in layout, 74–5
Legibility of lettering, 64–5
Lettering, conventions, 63–4; execution of, 146–51; placement, 65–70; readings, 161; sizes, 65; styles, 63–5; variations, 63–5
Letterpress printing, 110–11
Line work, 137–8
Linear scaling of symbols, 20–1
Lithography, 111–14

Mechanical dot screens, 144–5

Negative art work, 120–1
Numerical methods, 52–7; readings, 161

Offset printing, 111–14
Orientation, 95–9

Patterns, dry transfer materials, 143–7; for qualitative and ranked data, 10, 11, 14; for quantitative data, 36–40
Peelcoats, 121
Phenomena represented, continuous versus discrete, 5, 15, 19, 45; in mapping process, 3
Photographic films, 114–15
Photostats, 109–10
Plate-maker, 112
Plotters, 124–5
Point symbols, *see* Spot symbols
Positive art work, 119, 121